Georges Mink, Iwona Reichardt (eds.)

THE END OF THE SOVIET WORLD?
ESSAYS ON POST-COMMUNIST POLITICAL AND SOCIAL CHANGE

Three Revolutions Volume IV

Bibliografische Information der Deutschen Nationalbibliothek

Die Deutsche Nationalbibliothek verzeichnet diese Publikation in der Deutschen Nationalbibliografie; detaillierte bibliografische Daten sind im Internet über http://dnb.d-nb.de abrufbar.

Bibliographic information published by the Deutsche Nationalbibliothek

The Deutsche Nationalbibliothek lists this publication in the Deutsche Nationalbibliografie; detailed bibliographic data are available on the Internet at http://dnb.d-nb.de.

Cover photo: "The Broken Altar", taken by Nina Lyashonok in 2024 after the Transfiguration Cathedral, which is located in the heart of Odesa's UNESCO-listed historic center, had been attacked by Russian missiles. © copyright 2024 by Nina Lyashonok. Used with kind permission.

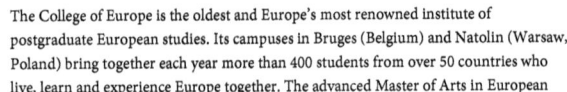

 The College of Europe is the oldest and Europe's most renowned institute of postgraduate European studies. Its campuses in Bruges (Belgium) and Natolin (Warsaw, Poland) bring together each year more than 400 students from over 50 countries who live, learn and experience Europe together. The advanced Master of Arts in European Interdisciplinary Studies offered at the College of Europe in Natolin provides students with the wider perspective on Europe and prepares them for fascinating international careers. The programme fosters excellence in research through the academic expertise of its faculty, as well as via two established Chairs: one in European History and Civilisation, another on the European Neighbourhood Policy and the EU's neighbours.

 This publication is conducted in the framework of the Three Ukrainian Revolutions (3R) Project of the European Civilisation Chair at the College of Europe in Natolin (Warsaw). The project is supported by funding from the European Commission. The production of this publication does not constitute an endorsement of the contents which reflect the views only of the authors, and the Commission cannot be held responsible for any use which may be made of the information contained therein.

ISBN (Print): 978-3-8382-1961-5
ISBN (E-Book [PDF]): 978-3-8382-7961-9
© *ibidem*-Verlag, Hannover • Stuttgart 2025

Leuschnerstraße 40
30457 Hannover
Germany / Deutschland
info@ibidem.eu

Alle Rechte vorbehalten

Das Werk einschließlich aller seiner Teile ist urheberrechtlich geschützt. Jede Verwertung außerhalb der engen Grenzen des Urheberrechtsgesetzes ist ohne Zustimmung des Verlages unzulässig und strafbar. Dies gilt insbesondere für Vervielfältigungen, Übersetzungen, Mikroverfilmungen und elektronische Speicherformen sowie die Einspeicherung und Verarbeitung in elektronischen Systemen.

All rights reserved. No part of this publication may be reproduced, stored in or introduced into a retrieval system, or transmitted, in any form, or by any means (electronic, mechanical, photocopying, recording or otherwise) without the prior written permission of the publisher. Any person who commits any unauthorized act in relation to this publication may be liable to criminal prosecution and civil claims for damages.

Printed in the EU

Contents

Acknowledgements 7

Georges Mink, Iwona Reichardt
Foreword: Reflections on the Long-Lasting Agony of the Soviet World 11

Part I: The Long-Term Transformation of the Post-soviet Space

Marek Cichocki
War in Ukraine and the Narrative About a New Cold War 33

Georges Mink
Geostrategic Phantasmagoria: The Geopolitical Discourse from Russian Imperialism to Post-soviet Memory: History Uses and Abuses as the Method of Putin's War Legitimacy 53

Wojciech Michnik
Nato's Enlargement, Not Expansion: The Ultimate Escape from the Soviet World? 73

Kinga Anna Gajda
Westernisation vs Easternisation 99

Part II: Ukraine and Its Departure from the Soviet World

Kataryna Wolczuk
Ukraine's Integration with the European Union 123

Andrew Wilson
The Future of Political Technology in Ukraine 147

Garry Kasparov
A Change Will Take Place in Russia Only When Ukraine Wins on the Battlefield 165

Part III: The Unfinished Transformation

Iwona Reichardt
Unfinished Transformation: From Gorbachev's Failed Reforms to an Aggressor State 175

Justyna Olędzka, Kacper Wańczyk
Belarus: New Society, Old State 187

Magdalena Lachowicz
Occupation in the Name of Destabilisation: Russia's Policies Towards Donetsk and Luhansk 209

Anton Saifullayeu
Is the Decolonisation of Eastern Europe Possible? The Cases of Ukraine and Belarus 239

Richard Butterwick
Afterword 267

Author Biographies 273

Acknowledgements

The "Three Revolutions" (3R) research project has been carried out since 2015 by the Chair of European Civilization at the College of Europe in Natolin. In the first phase of the project (2015-2019) we primarily focused on the process of social and political mobilisation in Ukraine since 1990. Specifically, our analysis was centred on the three revolutions: the 1990 Revolution on Granite, the 2004 Orange Revolution and the 2013-2014 Revolution of Dignity. During this stage we collected over 100 verbal testimonies from direct participants in all three revolutionary events in Ukraine. The interviews were completed by testimonies given during three historical workshops which were based on the Cold War Project model and organised in 2017 at the College of Europe campus in Natolin where the first international symposium on Three Ukrainian Revolutions was held. The findings from this workshop were verified again during the second and third symposia, which were held at the Natolin campus in 2018 and 2019 respectively.

    The outcomes of this stage of the project included a three-volume publication, with the first two volumes published in 2019. The first volume, titled *Three Revolutions: Mobilisation and Change in Contemporary Ukraine I: Theoretical Aspects and Analyses on Religion, Memory, and Identity*, was edited by Paweł Kowal, Georges Mink and Iwona Reichardt. It includes articles by international experts and scholars on topics related to the revolutionary events that have unfolded in Ukraine since 1990. The second volume, titled *Three Revolutions: Mobilization and Change in Contemporary Ukraine II: An Oral History of the Revolution on Granite, Orange Revolution, and Revolution of Dignity*, was edited by Paweł Kowal, Georges Mink, Iwona Reichardt and Adam Reichardt. It presents interviews with participants and eyewitnesses of the events in Ukraine and documents a series of workshop discussions conducted at the symposium held in 2017. The third volume, published in 2022, is titled *Three Revolutions: Mobilization and Change in Contemporary Ukraine III: Archival Records and Historical Sources*. Edited by Paweł Kowal,

Iwona Reichardt and Kateryna Pryshchepa, it includes original historical sources (primarily telegrams and KGB reports) from the time of the Revolution on Granite.

All three volumes were presented to the public during international conferences and academic conventions where they were discussed with scholars and subject specialists.

Since February 2022, with the start of Russia's full-scale invasion of Ukraine, the findings of the 3R project have provoked new research questions: Had there been no revolutions in Ukraine, would there have been a war? Had there been no revolutions in Ukraine, would there be a Ukraine at all?

To answer them, the 3R project entered into its second phase, which – because of the new context, both internal in Ukraine and internationally, required a new approach. Thus, this time the 3R research focused on analysing both the resistance of Ukrainian society to the Russian aggression, pointing to the connection between this experience and the earlier revolutions and the international response to Russia's aggression and breaches of international law. Reflecting on the earlier findings, a new research hypothesis was formulated of the long end of the Soviet world. This is observed to have been taking place in Ukraine and it will determine the future of the entire post-Soviet space. In this process, the experience of the three revolutions has and will continue to be of crucial importance.

The final outcomes of the project include the fourth international symposium "Ten Years of Russia's War against Ukraine: The Long End of the Post-Soviet Era", held on 26 March 2024 at the College of Europe campus in Natolin. During this gathering a workshop with direct participants of the events was again organised. Oral history testimonies of foreign diplomats who were in Kyiv at the time of the outbreak of the full-scale war were collected and confronted with expert analyses. These and other findings of the 3R project, are now presented to you in the last volume of the 3R publication series, titled *The End of the Soviet World? Essays on post-communist political and social change*.

As we are completing the project and presenting to you its final publication, we would like to express our special gratitude to the Vice Rector of the College of Europe Natolin Campus, Ewa

Ośniecka-Tamecka for offering us the opportunity to research Ukraine's transformation. We would also like to express our gratitude to Professor Richard Butterwick for believing in the academic value of this endeavour and supporting us at every stage of the project.

From the very beginning we were also supported by numerous institutions that pursue Ukrainian studies worldwide. They include: the Harvard Ukrainian Research Institute, the Canadian Institute of Ukrainian Studies at the University of Alberta, the School of Slavonic and East European Studies at the University College London, the National University of Kyiv-Mohyla Academy in Kyiv, the Institute of Political Studies at the Polish Academy of Sciences in Warsaw, the Centre for East European Studies at the Warsaw University, and Centre d'études des mondes russe, caucasien et centre européen (CNRS). Here we would like to express our deep appreciation to them for their continued support. We would also like to thank the experts who were part of our project since its first phase, providing us with their expertise and analyses. Among them were especially: Kateryna Wolczuk, Andrew Wilson, Olga Onuch, Alexandra Goujon, Alexandra Hnatiuk, Jan Tombiński, Marek Cichocki and Bogumiła Berdychowska.

In addition, we would like to express our gratitude to those who helped us implement all aspects of the project and the publication of this volume. A special thanks goes to our colleagues from the College of Europe in Natolin: Paweł Michalski, Anna Banach and Monika Bierwagen.

We would also like to thank Andreas Umland, who is the editor of the series "Soviet and Post-Soviet Politics and Society" published by Ibidem-Verlag but also a respected expert in Ukrainian history studies, for the opportunity to publish our books under his aegis. We would also like to express our gratitude to the whole team of *ibidem*-Verlag for their assistance during the whole editorial process.

We are also very grateful to the chairholder of the Chair of European Civilization, Professor Richard Butterwick, for his academic oversight and willingness to share academic advice.

Finally we would like to thank the reviewers of this volume Professor Marie-Claude Maurel and Professor Tomasz Stępniewski.

The Editors

Foreword
Reflections on the Long-Lasting Agony of the Soviet World

Georges Mink, Iwona Reichardt

We invite you to read this fourth and final volume of the publication which we have prepared in the framework of the Three Ukrainian Revolutions (3R) two-phased project carried out by the College of Europe in Natolin from 2015 until 2021 and from 2022 until 2024. Titled *The End of the Soviet World: Essays on Post-Communist Social and Political Change*, this collection is an outcome of the second phase of the project. It features academic analyses and essays exploring the transformations that have occurred in the countries that were once a part of the Soviet Union. The authors of the essays examine the ongoing, multifaceted transitions and the continued unravelling of Soviet legacy in modern Ukraine and in the region. However, in the selected chapters they also analyse the efforts to preserve the remnants of the Soviet world, which can be particularly observed in Russia and Belarus.

When in 2022 we started the second phase of the 3R project — "Three Revolutions and the War" — we hoped that with the publication of this book we would be able to announce the end of the Soviet, or even post-Soviet, world. However, as we continued to analyse the changes in the republics, as well as in the Russian Federation, together with the geopolitical shifts taking place in the region since the early 2000s, we concluded that this end may be more adequately called a slow agony. In other words, it is a long lasting process characterised by both complex and changing dynamics. As such, it requires new analytical approaches and a reconsideration of some established concepts. In parallel, as we can see in the analysis of the debate on the new Cold War theory explored by Marek Cichocki in his contribution, the ongoing decomposition of the Soviet reality still points to some features which are rooted in 20th century experiences and which have not ended with the formal dissolution of the USSR.

Admittedly, despite some desired changes, including the decline of the power of the communist elite, the Soviet legacy has remained a persistent element of the post-Soviet world. Depending on the state, this legacy has taken different forms and demonstrated different levels of intensity and scale. Consequently, while in Ukraine we can now talk about a decisive and conscious departure from anything Soviet, in Russia and Belarus we observe the reverse. Empirical evidence shows either cementing or reintroducing of old Soviet patterns and aesthetics in public spaces. The most extreme example of the latter are the monuments to Stalin which are being erected in today's Russia. In Belarus, the authoritarian system was set in motion almost right after the August 2020 protests. Justyna Olędzka and Kacper Wańczyk in their contribution argue that, despite the earlier hopes, the power system has not disintegrated nor has there been a complete de-legitimisation of Lukashenka's leadership. In other words, Belarus has managed to conserve its authoritarian system.

The tensions that the dynamics between the departure (ex. in Ukraine) vs. conservation (ex. in Russia) of Soviet legacy generate should neither be neglected nor underestimated. This is especially true when one of the parties involved in this dispute is the Russian Federation (former centre of the empire). In the most extreme case, as we can see in Ukraine, historical argumentation over shared legacy can be used in the rhetoric that is meant to justify a war.

The question thus remains: when will the Soviet world and its legacy finally come to an end? How long do we need to wait for this agony to be completed? As social scientists we avoid predictions about the future, but we can always draw some valuable conclusions from the past.

History thus shows that the Soviet system has already been painfully, although not fatally, injured for a few times. These injuries were the result of the work and determination of large social and political movements formed in different socialist states in the second half of the 20th century: in 1956 in Hungary, in 1968 in

Czechoslovakia, and in 1980-1981 in Poland. Yet, more than anything else, the changes that took place in 1989 across Central Europe and in 1991 on the territory of the former USSR marked the beginning of the long-lasting Soviet agony. This process, which was significantly different than the transformation in Central Europe and the Baltic states, took a special form in the former Soviet republics. Faced with numerous existential problems that came with the rapid transformation from a command economy to an uncontrolled free market, but also the collapse of an empire, these countries have in fact built what we now call the "post-Soviet world". The end of this geopolitical entity has also been announced already on at least a few occasions. In the first phase of our project we analysed the three Ukrainian revolutions (the 1990 Granite Revolution, the 2004 Orange Revolution and the 2013-2014 Revolution of Dignity) which catalysed the departure from the post-Soviet reality in Ukraine. The decision of the Ukrainian society to protest Viktor Yanukovych's decision not to sign the Association Agreement with the European Union can thus be interpreted as its determination to continue a path to liberate Ukraine from Moscow's control. In other words, it is a geopolitical choice, with all of its consequences.

Thus, to fully understand the agony of the Soviet world, we need to take into account not only all of the elements of the Soviet system but also recognise that what we are witnessing today is a global reshuffling of geopolitical cards. The strength of some actors, such as the United States and Western Europe, seem to be permanently tested, from inside and outside, while others (Russia and China especially) seem to have used the opportunity to advance their positions, even when it means breaching of international laws. The latter two countries have also taken advantage of the many crises in the West as well as some of its mistakes, especially when it comes to policies towards Eastern Europe (consider German *Ostpolitik* since 2014). Observing these new dynamics, we can thus say that when Vladimir Putin first called the collapse of the Soviet Union the greatest geopolitical catastrophe of the 20th century he, albeit indirectly, announced the completion of the Soviet period and proclaimed a return to the tradition of the eternal Russian empire.

For the reasons explained above, we propose a distinction between what we call *post-Soviet geopolitics*, which points to the role that Russia (now also backed by China and in co-operation with North Korea) has played in international affairs since the end of the Cold War from the *anthropological approach to Soviet legacy* which is expressed through the concepts of *Homo Sovieticus* and *Homo Post-Sovieticus*. Admittedly, these two categories, despite their name, do not allow us to depict region-specific transformations, which are necessary for the analysis of the Soviet decline. This limitation can be explained by a wide range of sociological research which shows that reactions similar to those assigned to *Homo Sovieticus* especially but also to *Homo Post-Sovieticus,* although to a smaller degree, are not necessarily limited to people who experienced Soviet authoritarianism or post-Soviet transformation. They are also observed in other non-democratic systems (from totalitarian to authoritarian). The opposite yet can be said about the geopolitical changes, which we are seeing now in some of the post-Soviet republics, and which clearly point to the process of the decomposition (accelerated in some cases, slower in others) of the Soviet world. The case of Ukraine, which we deeply researched in the first phase of the 3R project, serves here as the best example.

The argumentation presented above is not meant to suggest that the anthropological approach should be discredited, or entirely abandoned. Its framework allows us to notice, which Kinga Anna Gajda explores in the chapter on Westernisation vs. Easternisation, that the stimulus for the decline of what we call *Homo Sovieticus* or *Homo Post-Sovieticus* is the attraction of the Western model of modernity. This model is said to assign the highest value to two systems: liberal democracy and free market economy. However, the rapid pace of Westernisation, meaning an adoption of these two systems in a country which did not have them in place before, can also be painful and bring on some negative social consequences. We have seen this in Central Europe where rapid economic transformation contributed to vast inequalities, which, in turn, have created a fertile ground for discontent and populism. The consequences of this "imitation" of the ultra-liberal model have been well analysed by Ivan Krastev and Stephen Holmes in their book *The Light that Failed: Why the West is Losing the Fight for Democracy*.[1]

Similar tendencies have been recorded in the former Soviet republics, including the Russian Federation. In this region, however, the adoption of the Western model faces additional challenges: corruption and oligarchisation. The academic literature has long discussed the capture of control over strategic resources and its detrimental impact, particularly on democratic institutions. Today, especially in Russia, power is wielded by those who control energy and mineral resources, as well as by those with authority over the nation's nuclear arsenal.

Homo Sovieticus and Homo Post-Sovieticus

The concept of *Homo Sovieticus*, which describes a set of traits characteristic of a specific personality type, was popularised by the Soviet dissident writer and philosopher Alexander Zinoviev. Yet, as previously mentioned, the universality of these traits presents a limitation to this analytical category. Their presence across various political and social systems indicates that psychological responses to life under authoritarian regimes are similar, regardless of geography or historical period. This is why an observation made by Polish poet Antoni Słonimski, who traveled to Soviet Russia in 1932, continues to be relevant today—not only in regards to contemporary Russia but towards other contexts as well. Słonimski wrote: "*Russians live in fear of their own authorities. Despite the threat of the war, which is less strong on Russia's vast territory (...) than in crowded European cities, Russians live in a permanent state of alert. They are a bit like soldiers who live in trenches outside the frontline and who do not know what will the night bring for them nor whether it will take them to the first positions. (...) Every carelessly stated opinion can be the cause for an investigation.*"[2]

One of the defining traits of *Homo Sovieticus* is a strong dependence on the state. In the Soviet system, the state controlled

---

1 Holmes, S., Krastev, I., 2020, *The Light That Failed: Why the West Is Losing the Fight for Democracy*, New York: Pegasus Books.
2 Słonimski, A., 2007, *Moja podróż do Rosji (w 1932 roku)*, Łomianki: LTW, p. 111.

nearly every aspect of life, including education and health. This pervasive control fostered a sense of submissiveness and reliance, enabling individuals to shift personal responsibilities onto state decisions. Such systems promote conformity, pressuring people to conceal actions or beliefs that could result in punishment. Sociological research into axiological systems of the people living in the Soviet world thus pointed to such defence mechanisms as being double-faced and showing certain schizophrenia in expressing opinions. In other words, while in public people were repeating the official versions and interpretations of reality, they often criticised them in private.

Homo Sovieticus did not disappear with the dissolution of the Soviet Union. On the contrary, as a model of human behaviour it remained in many post-Soviet republics for a long time. The books by Svetlana Alexievich, Belarusian writer and Nobel Prize recipient in Literature, explore this topic from a micro perspective, bringing valuable insights into the experience of vast social groups. Her writings also show that people's mentality and habits, which resulted from decades of life in an authoritarian system, have survived the change of the political system. This was true especially for the representatives of the older generation. Numerous studies show that this group remains highly susceptible to Kremlin propaganda, even when living in the independent republics. The same applies to Soviet nostalgia, as idealizing the past has become a coping mechanism for many people facing the difficulties of post-Soviet life.

The term *Homo Post-Sovieticus* has often been used as a reference to people who struggle when adapting to the new political and economic systems. Frequently disappointed with the unfulfilled promises, these people have often had no choice but to survive in the often brutal capitalist world. To do so, some of them use familiar behaviour patterns which they have inherited from Soviet times. These include a high degree of cynicism towards the institution of the state and the lack of trust in official narratives and ideology. The popularity of non-institutional and non-official practices and projects which we have seen among post-Soviet societies since the beginning of the transformation are a perfect illustration of these psychological experiences in which a state or an institution is perceived as the enemy of a human being.

A discourse analysis of Putin's system points to two pillars of power: a recreation of the empire and military aggression. These two features are what today's Russia has in common with the Soviet Union. In addition, the ideological foundation of Putin's power derives from Russian/Orthodox imperialism, Russian/Orthodox conservatism, pan-Slavism and Eurasianism. Putin takes advantage of this ideological mishmash because the collective memory of the Russian people, which was formed in the Soviet system to be later only reinforced by the propaganda tubes during his own rule, allows him to do so. The education process of Soviet citizens included military trainings, while their lives were spent in numerous military and patriotic associations. The calendars of the Soviet people were filled with military holidays, while commemorations of the sacrifice of those who fought in the Great Patriotic War were perceived as a civic duty. That is why, Georges Mink in his chapter on the strategic phantasmagoria, points to a certain militarisation of collective memory in today's Russia.

Geopolitics and the promise of departure from the post-Soviet system

Taking into account the above we can formulate a hypothesis that the collapse of the Soviet world is dependent on the geopolitical situation. In strictly geopolitical terms, the end of the Soviet, or post-Soviet, world reflects radical transformation in international dynamics which prevailed in the post-Soviet republics after the collapse of the USSR. Namely, after decades of Russia's attempts to maintain control over the former republics, the events which have taken place in recent years may indicate the end of the period of Russian-led rebuilding of the empire. Instead a new path towards re-organisation of alliances and spheres of influence has been undertaken by the former republics. In Kataryna Wolczuk's and Wojciech Michnik's contributions, this topic is discussed in regards to Ukraine's integration with both the EU and NATO. These two processes, although far from completed, are now determining this country's development path and lead it towards the final abandonment of the Soviet world.

Despite the dissolution of the USSR in 1991 the Russian Federation has tried to maintain its influence over the former Soviet republics by establishing numerous alliances: economic, military or political. These attempts got circumvented in recent decades when the so-called "coloured revolutions" erupted throughout the former Soviet republics. Highly anti-Soviet, but also anti-Russian, these protest actions proved troublesome to the Russian authorities. The Kremlin has correctly recognised them as fatal blows to the post-Soviet world and started reorganising its own policies and decisions to counteract them. These conclusions were reached by our research team when we worked on the first phase of the 3R project. In our academic investigation we have used a whole series of enquiry methods, starting with historical workshops in which we confronted history witnesses and most important revolutionaries to hundreds of interviews which we conducted with the oral history method with participants of numerous revolutionary actors. The analysis which we carried out on this material allowed us to confirm our hypothesis and recognise the three Ukrainian revolutions as turning points in the process of building modern Ukraine.

In the second phase of the project, when we focused on the three revolutions and the war, we expand this hypothesis to argue that these revolutions should be also treated as milestones in the process of Ukraine's de-Sovietisation and correlate with the consolidation of national identity of the Ukrainian society and its sense of belonging to the European civilisational community. This analysis has, to some extent, attempted to answer the question asked at a 3R symposium in December 2022 by Ukraine's former Ambassador to Poland — Andrii Deshchytsia. As a former revolutionary taking part in all three Ukrainian revolutions but also as a member of Ukrainian government and its representative abroad Deshchytsia then asked: "Would there be a war, had there been no revolutions?" Andrew Wilson, while analysing the role of political technology in Ukraine and how it was used at the moments of protest, such as the Maidans, argues in his contribution that a true departure from the

Soviet world, in Ukraine's case, means that "there will be no more Maidans. Just normal protests; not existential struggles against a 'regime'".

While preparing this publication, we confirmed that Russia's decision to regain control over Ukraine, by means of a full-scale invasion in this country, was caused by Ukraine's confirmations of its true independence. Russia's desire to take over Ukraine through a full-scale invasion has led to a situation where the latter has now cut itself completely off from any relations with Moscow. The only interstate interactions that are now in place are those between their fighting armies. While the decisions made by the Ukrainian authorities point to advancement of the decolonisation process, the policies that the Russian Federation has been carrying out towards native Ukrainians in the four regions that are currently under its occupation resemble 19th century colonialism. Kidnapping of children and their forced Russification, Russification of education and rewriting of school textbooks, passportisation, as well as open repressions of grassroots national movements clearly resemble the colonial brutality of previous periods, just implemented with modern means of "persuasion". This topic is explored by Magdalena Lachowicz in her chapter on Russia's policies towards the Donetsk and Luhansk "people's republics". The topic of decolonisation of Eastern Europe is, in turn, analysed by Anton Saifullayeu. However, the postulate for greater inclusion of decolonisation theory into studies of post-Soviet transformation is also formulated by Iwona Reichardt in the chapter on the unfinished transformation in Russia and Belarus.

As a result of Russia's war, which in Ukraine started in 2014, the Ukrainian nation, which in its centuries' long history underwent different phases of development, became truly consolidated and — as a European nation — decided to opt for the EU and NATO path. This decision was not accepted by the Kremlin from the very beginning. We could observe Moscow's reactions in 2013, when it forced President Viktor Yanukovych not to sign the Association Agreement with the EU; and we could see it in 2014 when Russia annexed Crimea and started military operations in eastern parts of

Ukraine. Finally, we could see it in 2022 when the Russian Federation launched its full-scale invasion of Ukraine. As a result of all these activities initiated by Russia against Ukraine, this country once central for Russia's sphere of influence, has now turned into a battlefield, where the fate of the old Soviet order is being fought over. Although fought on Ukraine's territory, this war is not only to decide about the future of Ukraine. Its outcome will surely have an effect on the condition of the region, but also Europe as a whole.

In the article "La longue guerre d'Ukraine" ("The Long War in Ukraine"), published in December 2022 in the French journal *Le Grand Continent*, which specialises in geopolitics, a renowned French diplomat Jean-Marie Guéhenno argues that the decline of the Soviet Union has benefited European integration. He writes: "What does the war in Ukraine mean for Europe? On the face of it, it is accelerating a geopolitical awakening among Europeans, who—Germany included—are increasing their military budgets and managing to overcome their differences by voting for and then renewing an imposing package of sanctions against Russia and adopting measures to help Ukraine, mainly in the humanitarian field. A powerful wave of solidarity seems to have swept across Europe, where millions of Ukrainian refugees have been generously welcomed. The images of devastated Ukrainian cities and the faces of Ukrainians fleeing the bombs hold up a mirror to the citizens of Europe, lulled to sleep by decades of peace, which suddenly throws them into a world of war and destruction. Ukrainian cities and Ukrainian faces have the familiarity of old Europe, but the world of devastation and terror that they express is not the world to which Europeans have been accustomed for three quarters of a century of peace—with the exception of the war in Yugoslavia. This discrepancy is provoking a radical shock. Will this shock accelerate the political transformation of the European Union and bind it together in the face of a Russian adversary whose brutality and contempt for the law are the antithesis of the values on which Europe claims to be built? Is a European political identity emerging in the face of

Russia? Will Russia give rise to the kind of European patriotism that the terrorist attacks of the past few years have shown?"[3]

The world famous chess master and Russian oppositionist, Garry Kasparov, makes a poignant statement about the gravity of the situation and the significance of this war. In his chapter, Kasparov states that: "NATO was established in 1949 to save Europe from a Russian invasion. At that time, the threat was to be found east of the Rhine river. Today, it can be found east of the Dnieper river, but it's the same threat. Ukraine is the only country that has spilled its blood fulfilling NATO's purpose."

The war in Ukraine is yet only the beginning of the decline of Russia's influences in the post-Soviet space. Geopolitical changes have also been taking place in Central Asia. Experts on this region clearly suggests that its countries, traditionally under strong Russian influence, are now undergoing a strong re-orientation, turning towards China. Beijing has also been significantly investing in this region, especially through the New Silk Road project. Its beneficiaries include Kazakhstan, Uzbekistan and Turkmenistan which in parallel to establishing partnerships with China are now also testing other directions in their foreign policy choices. Namely, they are showing their openness to co-operation with Turkey but also the European Union.

Other non-Central Asian, post-Soviet republics have also been openly stating their preferences for Western integration. In addition to Ukraine, this group also includes Moldova, and to some degree also Georgia. Despite some challenges, including internal politics, both states have in recent years strengthened their official integration with the West in general, and the European Union in particular. While in the case of Georgia the steady pro-European path is now more of the unknown, given the results of its 2024 parliamentary elections, in the case of Moldova, there is more reason for cautious optimism. In both cases, however, we are dealing with countries whose societies are divided between those that are pro-West-

---

3   Guéhenno, J-M., 2022, "La longue guerre d'Ukraine", *Le Grand Continent*. https://legrandcontinent.eu/fr/2022/12/12/la-longue-guerre-dukraine/.

ern and those that remain under Russia's influence. The weak economic situation in both of these states makes them particularly vulnerable to Kremlin interference and manipulation. Evidence shows that to halt the pro-European direction in both of these states Russia uses a plethora of methods, ranging from bribes and cyberattacks to all kinds of provocations.

All in all, the war in Ukraine, which started in 2014 with the annexation of Crimea and took the form of the full-scale invasion in 2022, can be treated as a turning point in the process of the final agony of the post-Soviet world. It can be explained by the following factors.

First, as a result of the war, Russia's role as a protective superpower is no longer justified. By attempting to reassert control over Ukraine, Russia has triggered the opposite effect, undermining its traditional role, at least in the view of some states and organisations, as a security guarantor in the post-Soviet space. Second, as mentioned earlier, the conflict unfolding on the battlefield in Ukraine is not only about Ukraine itself. Several post-Soviet republics with histories of Russian dominance are now reassessing their relations with the Kremlin. These include Moldova, Kazakhstan, and, to some extent, Georgia and Belarus. Third, the war in Ukraine has revealed the growing distance some Central Asian and South Caucasus countries are placing between themselves and Russia. Kazakhstan, in particular, has been vocal, refusing to recognise Russia's annexation of Ukrainian territories. Fourth, Russia's full-scale invasion of Ukraine has intensified its diplomatic isolation, evident through international sanctions and the deterioration of relations with Western nations. In contrast, Ukraine's ties with NATO states have only strengthened, prompting Russia to seek military alliances with non-Western countries. Today, Russia's allies include Iran as well as North Korea, whose soldiers are now fighting alongside Russian forces in the war against Ukraine. These developments support the hypothesis of an ongoing fragmentation of the post-Soviet space, producing surprising outcomes beyond the region.

The post-Soviet era was marked by efforts to maintain cohesion among former Soviet republics under the influence of the Russian Federation. This was intended to be achieved through organisations such as the Commonwealth of Independent States (CIS), the Eurasian Economic Union (EAEU), and the Collective Security Treaty Organization (CSTO). However, this cohesion has significantly weakened as a result of the war in Ukraine. First, the Commonwealth of Independent States, established after the dissolution of the USSR, has largely lost its relevance and purpose. Several member states, such as Ukraine and Georgia, have either withdrawn completely or limited their participation, while others, particularly in Central Asia, are gradually distancing themselves from this organisation. The Eurasian Economic Union, initiated by Moscow as a counterweight to the European Union, has struggled to have a meaningful impact on the regional economy. Moreover, internal tensions, especially between Kazakhstan and Russia, are further undermining its effectiveness. Similarly, BRICS, intended as a rival to Western economic alliances, remains far from achieving its objectives.

A discussion on the geopolitical changes in the post-Soviet space should not ignore the changes that have taken place in parallel in the West and which have an effect also on this region, especially in the wartime reality. Some countries, such as Poland, Romania, and the Baltic states, have become frontline states, which makes them at high risk of the next stage of invasion, while others that were previously neutral, such as Finland and Sweden, have joined NATO, further isolating Russia from the Western world. All of these nations have significantly increased their military budgets as well as efforts aimed at countering Russian influence. They have also all been reporting acts of sabotage on their territories which includes interference in GPS systems, arsons, and cyber-attacks, including disruptions in banking systems.

In geopolitical terms, the incomplete end of the Soviet era has already led to a decline in Russian influence over the former Soviet republics and a redefinition of Russia's spheres of influence. The Russian Federation, which has long acted as a regional hegemon, has now lost its absolute power. It faces growing pressure from other significant players, such as China, Turkey, and the European

Union. In this context, the war in Ukraine represents a pivotal moment that has accelerated the fragmentation of the post-Soviet order and reinforced the tendency of neighbouring states to distance themselves from Moscow. This marks the end of an era in which Russia could present itself as the unquestioned centre of the Sovietised region. Ukraine's role in this process is unquestionable.

Russia's imperial traditions

From today's perspective, both the Soviet and post-Soviet periods appear as relatively brief chapters in Russia's long imperial history. Putin's Russia reveals a clear ambition to revive imperial aspirations, reminiscent in some ways of pre-Soviet Russia, particularly the final phase and legacy of the Russian Empire. As a result, the idea of Russia's deep and enduring authoritarian roots is compelling, especially in light of discussions surrounding the potential rapid collapse and fragmentation of the Russian Federation. This vision of Russia's future is sometimes expressed in both media and academic discourse. However, their validation remains distant, as there are currently too few indicators to suggest an imminent breakup of the federation.

Instead, what we see is a form of enduring imperial authoritarianism evident in many of Putin's speeches, military activities and Russia's broader geopolitical strategy. Under Putin, there has been a clear revival of the Russian Empire's legacy and a valorisation of tsarist periods as historical models. He frequently references figures such as Peter the Great, who expanded Russia's territory through conquest, and Catherine the Great, who solidified its imperial power. Putin often emphasises Russia's historical role as a great power, framing it as a continuing duty to protect and extend influence over "historic lands".

The concept of *Russkiy mir* (*Russian World*) serves as a modern extension of the idea of a cultural and spiritual space that Russia must defend and promote. This notion extends beyond Russia's current borders to encompass territories where imperial or Soviet Russia once held power, including Ukraine, Belarus, and other former Soviet republics, which the Kremlin perceives as integral parts of Russia's sphere of influence. In the post-Soviet era, Russia has cultivated a form of nationalism, which combines tsarist imperial grandeur with conservative values endorsed by the Orthodox Church. This church-state alliance reinforces the notion of an imperial "civilizing mission," a central theme of the former Russian Empire.

The war in Ukraine serves as evidence of Russia's revived imperial ambitions. The annexation of Crimea in 2014 and the full-scale invasion in 2022 should thus be treated as the continuation of the territorial expansion strategies employed by the Russian Empire, where geographic conquest was a key means of consolidating state power. Russia views Crimea not only as a strategically important peninsula which enables a strategic position on the Black Sea but also as a crucial part of its imperial heritage, having been annexed by the Russian Empire under Catherine the Great in 1783. Putin frames the re-acquisition of Crimea as a restoration of the natural order, correcting what he considers a historical mistake: the transfer of Crimea to Soviet Ukraine in 1954.

Putin has also justified the 2022 invasion of Ukraine by referencing Russia's imperial history, claiming that modern Ukraine owes its existence to the errors made by Soviet leaders, particularly Lenin. He depicts Kyiv as the "mother of all Russian cities", positioning it as an essential part of Russia's historical heartland. However, Russia's imperialist ambitions under Putin extend beyond Ukraine.

Russian interventions throughout the post-Soviet and broader Eurasian regions reveal a persistent desire to re-establish hegemonic influence. Russia has been asserting itself as the dominant power in the Caucasus, evident in its support for Armenia and its ambiguous role in the conflict between Armenia and Azerbaijan over Nagorno-Karabakh. In Georgia, Russia has employed a similar strategy, seizing entire regions in 2008 and bringing South Ossetia and Abkhazia under its control. Here, Russia presents itself as both an arbiter and a superpower intent on preserving its imperial influence over the republics of the Caucasus—a region the Russian Empire gradually annexed in the 19th century. In Central Asia, Russia seeks to position itself as a guarantor of security and stability, echoing its imperial policies of expansion in the region under the tsars. Despite China's growing influence in this region, Russia continues to assert its presence through military means (via the Collective Security Treaty Organization) and economic mechanisms (such as the Eurasian Economic Union).

Finally, we need to take into account the ideological shift driven by Putin and his advisors, who have turned Soviet "imperialism" into an expansionist nationalism. The Soviet Union, an imperial superpower in its own right, was characterised by the so-called Marxist proletarian international solidarity (internationalism) which meant using military conquests to promote communist ideology. Fuelled by this ideology, the Red Army sought to ignite a global revolution shortly after the Bolshevik Revolution. Its first major offensive, in 1920-1921, targeted Poland as a gateway to Western Europe, where revolutionary fervour was already spreading (notably in Bavaria and Budapest). This effort reflected Karl Marx's vision of a proletarian revolution in the developed capitalist states. Today, Russia's approach is markedly different. The Kremlin no longer seeks to export a universal ideology. Instead, Putin focuses on promoting a nationalist vision centred on Russian historical greatness. This vision emphasises the defence of "Russian civilisation" and the consolidation of territories viewed as historically Russian.

Unlike the Soviet Union which was trying to support communist movements worldwide, Putin's Russia concentrates its efforts on its near neighbours which it does by defending their Russian-speaking populations. This strategy seems closer to tsarist imperialism which also aimed more at protecting Orthodox and Russian minorities in areas that were under foreign domination than at a global expansion of the tsarist system. This does not mean that Russia limits its operations and is not active in the broader world. It remains engaged, especially economically, but not only, on the African continent where it uses private militia forces to extract natural resources.

The mechanisms of the authoritarian power, concentrated in Putin's and his elite's hands, are a mirror reflection of the imperial post-Soviet model. In this model, there is strong oligarchy which allows for a smooth transfer of goods and capital between the Russian president and the privileged political and military elite. The centralisation of power around a strong leader, application of repressions in order to maintain order and promotion of conservative nationalism are all elements that could be found in the tsarist system. Even the model of repressions against political opponents and strict control over media resembles practices of the Russian empire where tsars were using the secret police and censorship to silence any discontent. Murders by poisoning, infiltration of opposition groups abroad, diplomatic provocations all resemble the tsarist system of Okhrana, which was the popular name for the Department for the Protection of Public Safety and Order, but in today's context and with today's tools. Such authoritarian control allows Putin to rule by strengthening the idea of a strong Russia which, nonetheless is constantly threatened from within and abroad.

Disintegration of the Russian Federation?

Returning to the question as how far away we are from the end of the post-Soviet world, or — as some authors propose — the collapse of the Russian Federation; admittedly, while we may see many experts pose such a question, we also notice that the final answers are no to be obtained yet. For example, Paweł Kowal, one of the main researchers and the co-leader in the 3R project, in his well-known theory of the Five Rings of the Empire states the following:

> "The process of rebuilding the Russian imperial rings of influence may appear to some as a simple construction of a 'strong Russia'. Yet, the idea to build the Third Empire is not grounded in a sustainable economy or sound social policies. Moreover, the radical policies of the Kremlin today are not solely due to authorities trying to maintain power, but are to a large degree — and paradoxically — a symptom that the process of Russia's de-imperalisation has entered a decisive new phase."

In a similar vein, French specialist in Soviet and post-Soviet economics Georges Sokolof titled his extensive economic analysis of the post-Soviet Russia *La Puissance pauvre* (*The Poor Power*). Numerous think tanks focused on the developments in the region estimate that Russia has enough resources to wage war in Ukraine only until the end of 2024, which would prove Putin's weakness. However, such scenarios for the near future are purely probabilistic. Thus numerous speculations are built around the predictions of potential fracturing of the Russian Federation, ranging from minor fractures to definitive fragmentation and radical disintegration of the state.

At the moment this is only a dream. One which may be visualised, as it was attempted by Alexander Etkind his recent book *Russia Against Modernity*, but still a dream. Yet in order to take a break from the worrisome reality we came to witness in recent years, let us allow ourselves to dream, at least for a short moment, and read the vision of the future that Etkind offers: "The Federation's dismemberment threw up an enormous number of legal, strategic and economic questions. Settling borders, rebuilding trade and negotiating security arrangements took decades. Dealing with the legacy of the heinous war and creating new statehoods did not happen immediately. But the peoples of the former Federation learned how to make their own way. History continued, and the international community took note of the changes. A peace conference was held, modelled after the Paris Peace Conference of 1918-19. A new Eurasian Treaty completed the work begun at Versailles a century earlier. From Ukraine to Mongolia, the neighbours of the new countries mediated."[4] As we were finalizing the editorial work on this volume we were also observing the final stage of Donald Trump's campaign in America and his victory. As observers of political changes we ask ourselves: what will this choice of the American society bring to our region? One of the most pessimistic hypotheses is that a part of sovereign Ukraine will become a demilitarised zone, in line with the Korean model. An even worse model would be that of Transnistria, which is a breakaway territory under Russia's control. Such a development would significantly prolong the process of the empire's collapse, spreading pessimism in the post-Soviet republics and among its very many ethnic minorities that have chosen the path of escaping from the unwanted "guardian". To use the words of another American, this time writer, Mark

---

4   Etkind, A. ,2023, *Russia against modernity*, Cambridge, UK: Polity, p.143.

Twain, the reports of the empire's death are still greatly exaggerated.

***

As with this publication we are completing an almost decade-long project, we encourage today's and future scholars and researchers to refer to all of our four volumes of the 3R publication and use the findings we present in them in their explorations of the topic of social change and mobilisation in Ukraine and political changes in the post-Soviet republics. We envision that the discussion and analysis of these topics will continue beyond the scope of our project and that the research that we have conducted at the College of Europe in Natolin will serve as an inspiration for further academic investigation. We once again thank all who have contributed to the success of this endeavour.

Special words of gratitude go to the leadership of the College of Europe in Natolin and especially Vice Rector Ewa Ośniecka-Tamecka for the support she has offered us working on the project during each of its stages. We are also very grateful to the chairholder of the Chair of European Civilization, Professor Richard Butterwick, for his academic oversight and willingness to share academic advice. There is also no doubt that this project would not have taken place had there been no Professor Paweł Kowal, who was one of the initiators and main leaders of the 3R endeavour at the College of Europe in Natolin. He was also among the main researchers and one of the editors of the first three volumes of this publication. Since October 2023, Professor Kowal has taken on new political roles in Poland. He is now the Chairman of the Foreign Relations Committee at the Lower House of the Polish Parliament (Sejm). Most importantly, he is the chairman of the Council for Co-operation with Ukraine which is tasked to deal with bilateral Polish-Ukrainian relations and Poland's involvement in Ukraine's reconstruction. These obligations made it impossible for Professor Kowal to have the same role in the second phase of the 3R project as he had in it before. However, throughout the whole time he remained with us in spirit and many of his ideas discussed throughout the project are reflected in this volume.

Part I
The Long-Term Transformation of the Post-soviet Space

War in Ukraine and the Narrative About a New Cold War

Marek Cichocki

Over the past several years we have seen such notions as a "New Cold War" or a "Second Cold War" often used in the interpretation of the current conflict between Russia and the West. These two terms have also been applied to describe a variety of phenomena that contributed to the deepening crisis of the post-Cold War liberal world order and to the conflict between the United States and China. However, it is worth noticing that the term "Second Cold War" was originally used as a reference to the period which followed the détente policy that characterised US-Soviet relations in the 1970s. Namely, in 1979, in response to the Soviet deployment of SS-20 missiles in Eastern Europe, NATO reached what it called a "double-decision". It offered disarmament talks to Moscow and, had they failed, threatened to deploy modern medium-range nuclear missiles in Western Europe by 1983. Only a few days after NATO had announced this policy, the Kremlin decided to send military troops to Afghanistan. Thereby, a new spiral of armament and ideological hostility between the East and the West had started. It included the boycott of the 1980 Summer Olympics in Moscow and the introduction of martial law in Poland in 1981. These events eventually led to the disarmament policy of the mid-1980s. During the latter period the world witnessed the largest psychological breakthrough in US-Soviet relations. It took the form of the 1986 Reykjavik Summit[1], a meeting between the US President Ronald Reagan and the Soviet leader, Mikhail Gorbachev, which ultimately brought the end of the Cold War after 1989.

---

1   Adelman, K., 2014, *Reagan at Reykjavik: Forty-Eight Hours That Ended the Cold War*, New York: Harper Collins Publishers.

US, Russia and China: Return of the Cold War as an explanatory model

The Russian invasion of Ukraine in 2022 has significantly changed the earlier interpretation of the Cold War, meaning the era which started after the Second World War and ended in 1989-1991. It has also renewed interest and reflection into the influence and legacy of the events which took place during the Cold War as well as the impact that the end of the Cold War has had on the current situation in international affairs. The recent changes in security policy, which are also a result of Russia's aggression against Ukraine, have led to a revision of such concepts as: the post-Cold War era, the post-Cold War order, and finally the very concept of the Cold War. Consequently, we can now argue that the war in Ukraine has increased the popularity of such notions as the New Cold War or the Second Cold War, which are widely used in political commentaries, media and academic discourse.[2]

Despite some reservations, articulated mainly by historians and political scientists[3], the above concepts are starting to function as keys in explanations of the current crisis in the system of international security. As such, they are used in public debates and the media where the war in Ukraine is often presented as the starting moment of a new global Cold War. Its outbreak has led to the open questioning of the main principles of the post-Cold War international order and triggered a re-crystallisation of the division of the world into opposing and competing blocs: the West on the one side, and revisionist, anti-Western powers, such as Russia and China, and their allies on the other.[4]

Ukrainian historian Serhii Plokhy has correctly recognised that for many observers of international affairs "Russia's aggression against Ukraine and the mobilisation of the West and its allies

---

2 Ellison, J., Cox, M., Hanhimäki, J.M., Harrison, H.M., Ludlow, N.P., Romano, A., Spohr, K. & Zubok, V., 2023, "The war in Ukraine", *Cold War History*, 23 (1), pp. 121-206.
3 Monaghan, A., 2015, *"New Cold War"? Abusing History, Misunderstanding Russia*, Chatham House.
4 Greenway, H.D.S., 2022, "Welcome to Cold War II", *The Boston Globe*, 25 February.

to fight that aggression brought back images of the Cold War. Indeed, the new war revived old animosities, restored flagging alliances, and established old fault lines. The Cold War also provided a language and explanatory frame to describe and understand the new global conflict. There is little doubt, however, that despite numerous parallels with the past, today the world is entering a new era. The peace dividend which came with the end of the Cold War has been fully spent, if not squandered, over the last thirty years. The world is returning to the era of great-power rivalries on a scale unseen since the fall of the Berlin Wall in 1989. The Russo-Ukrainian war, like nothing else, undermined the foundations of the post-Cold War order, triggering processes that would lead to the formation of a new international order."[5]

This perspective presents the war in Ukraine as the key event in a broader conflict, which fits the category of Cold War but is not limited to it. The notions of a New or Second Cold War inspire comparisons with the 20th century conflict between the West/NATO and the Soviet Union and today's rivalry between Russia and the West. From the American standpoint, however, the current world division and strategic rivalry is more set along the line of US-China relations, while the conflict with Russia is more of a "proxy war". In 2021, a few months before the Russian invasion in Ukraine, two political scientists, Hal Brands and John Lewis Gaddis, published an article in *Foreign Affairs* titled "The New Cold War. America, China, and the Echoes of History". In it, they argued that even though today's international context is different than that of the Cold War, the United States and China are nonetheless 'entering into the phase of their own Cold War'".[6]

Similarly, historian Niall Ferguson in an article for the *National Review*, which was published in 2020, wrote that: "There was a First World War. Then there was a Second. They were not identical. But they were sufficiently similar for no one to argue about the nomenclature. Similarly, there was Cold War I. And now we are in Cold

---

5 Plokhy, S., 2023, *The Russo-Ukrainian War*, London: Allen Lane, p. 295.
6 Brands, H. and Gaddis, J.L., 2021, "The New Cold War: America, China, and the Echoes of History", *Foreign Affairs*, 100 (6) November/December.

War II", adding that "this time, it's with China"[7]. For a few years now Ferguson has been consistently arguing about the coming of the New Cold War and presenting it in the context of the Russian invasion in Ukraine. The latter he describes as the first hot war at the time of the new global Cold War, thereby pointing to a striking comparison between the two periods. Additionally, just like after the Second World War, public opinion and the political establishment in the West (and especially the US) needed at least five years and the Korean War to understand that their political community was in the state of a Cold War with Stalinist Russia, today, after years of self-deception and with the war in Ukraine, the West has finally recognised that Putinist Russia, together with China as its ally, has declared another Cold War against it.[8]

Regardless of the question of what actually constitutes the epicentre of the events which triggered the process of questioning the post-Cold War world order and the process of shaping a new type of order — be it the rivalry and conflict between the United States and China, the Russian-Ukrainian war, or both conflicts together — what draws attention is that the concept of a Cold War, Second or New, has started to dominate the terminology used to describe these phenomena. As a result, we are now faced with some fundamental questions that still await serious answers.

These questions touch upon the relationship between the old and new Cold War and how in today's context we should assess the period of three decades of the post-Cold War order in Europe and the world. Was this order, initially envisioned as transformative, which means it was to be based on fundamentally different principles than before (for example geopolitics were to be abandoned in favour of geoeconomics[9], ideological and material contradictions were to be abandoned in favour of multilateral, global cooperation, and finally the history of hierarchical state identity was to be re-

---

7   Ferguson, N., 2020, "Cold War II", *National Review*, 17 December.
8   Ferguson, N., 2023, "Cold War II: Niall Ferguson On The Emerging Conflict With China", interview by P. Robinson, Hoover Institution, 1 May.
9   Luttwek, E., 1990, "From Geopolitics to Geo-Economics: Logic of Conflict, Grammar of Commerce", *The National Interest*, Summer, pp. 17-23.

placed by a fluid, networked post-modernity in international politics[10]), only a short and transient episode? Was it a brief break, a state of cold peace after the collapse of the bipolar division of the world? Or maybe there is some coherent continuity between the old Cold War and the new Cold War? Maybe it is the emerging post-Cold War order and the current new Cold War that together create a fundamentally new, yet unrecognised international situation? We describe it imprecisely using historical analogies and references to the old Cold War which is the closest geopolitical experience we have, thereby constructing a sense of continuity and understanding. As stated above, these questions still await serious answers.

Identifying the new Cold War turn in Putin's Russia

In Europe overall, but especially in Central and Eastern Europe, the application of the old concept of the Cold War in descriptions of the new geostrategic division of the world brings back old experiences from the confrontation between the Soviet Union and the West. British journalist and international commentator, Edward Lucas, with his 2008 book on Putin's Russia has significantly contributed to the revival of the discourse about the relationship between the West and Russia which is based on references to the Cold War. The title of his book, which has had many editions already, *The New Cold War. Putin's Russia and the Threat to the West*[11,] has provoked scholarly questions as how justified it is to bring back the old Cold War concepts into today's discourse. At the time of the first publication of Lucas's book politicians and public opinion in the West were still focused on the global fight with terrorism and the consequences of the US-led intervention in Afghanistan and Iraq. These two topics were seen as examples of a clear demarcation line in the security policy, which separated previous Cold War conventional conflicts and rivalry between two enemy blocs from today's global security architecture, assumedly based on a completely different logic. The

---

10 Cooper, R., 2003, *The Breaking of Nations: Order and Chaos in the Twenty-First Century*, London: Atlantic Books.
11 Lucas, E., 2008, *The New Cold War*, London: Palgrave Macmillan.

latter was meant to represent new types of wars and conflicts which were less defined by actual borders. In essence they were to be more shaped by networks and hybrid in nature. As such they are a characteristic of non-traditional, post-modern politics which relies less on conventional means, both in terms of intensity and scale.[12]

Lucas argued otherwise, stressing the need to bring back Cold War experiences into today's analysis of Putin's policies towards the West. In this regard, he pointed to the internal changes which took place in Russia during Putin's second term. They included politically-motivated repressions and murders of such figures as Anna Politkovskaya, an independent journalist who had reported on Russian crimes committed during the Chechen wars, and Alexander Litvinenko, Putin's critic and former KGB agent who had found refuge in Great Britain where he was eventually poisoned. These two murders marked a complete cutting off from the process of Russia's democratisation that was started two decades prior by Mikhail Gorbachev and accompanied by a hope for a different future for the Russian people. This internal turn towards authoritarian rule which Putin had taken also meant a return of the Kremlin's confrontational policy towards the West. As Lucas notes: "In the aftermath of victory in the Cold War, the West's moral stock was high, while the Soviet Union's anti-Westernism seemed a laughable historical relic. But as that period has passed, Russia's public rhetoric has become increasingly caustic. In 2007 Putin denounced America as a 'pernicious force in world politics'".[13]

According to Lucas, Russia's turn toward the New Cold War was a consequence of the internal repressions the Kremlin imposed on its opponents which were accompanied by the more noticeably pronounced anti-Western rhetoric. The confrontational nature of Putin's speech at the Munich Security Forum in 2007, but above all Russia's invasion into Georgia in 2008, verified Lucas's thesis that Russia's relations with the West saw a return to the logic of rivalry and confrontation, one that resembled the time of the Cold War.

---

12 See: Kaldor, M., 2012, *New and Old Wars: Organized Violence in a Global Era*, Stanford University Press; Münkler, H., 2004, *The New Wars*, Cambridge: Polity Press; Kaldor, M., 2013, "In Defense of New Wars", *Stability*, 2 (1), pp. 1-16.
13 Lucas, E., *op. cit.*, p. 3.

Soviet and Post-Soviet Politics and Society (SPPS) Vol. 280
ISSN 1614-3515

General Editor: Andreas Umland,
Stockholm Centre for Eastern European Studies, andreas.umland@ui.se

Commissioning Editor: Max Jakob Horstmann,
London, mjh@ibidem.eu

EDITORIAL COMMITTEE*

DOMESTIC & COMPARATIVE POLITICS
Prof. **Ellen Bos**, *Andrássy University of Budapest*
Dr. **Gergana Dimova**, *Florida State University*
Prof. **Heiko Pleines**, *University of Bremen*
Dr. **Sarah Whitmore**, *Oxford Brookes University*
Dr. **Harald Wydra**, *University of Cambridge*

SOCIETY, CLASS & ETHNICITY
Col. **David Glantz**, *"Journal of Slavic Military Studies"*
Dr. **Marlène Laruelle**, *George Washington University*
Dr. **Stephen Shulman**, *Southern Illinois University*
Prof. **Stefan Troebst**, *University of Leipzig*

POLITICAL ECONOMY & PUBLIC POLICY
Prof. **Andreas Goldthau**, *University of Erfurt*
Dr. **Robert Kravchuk**, *University of North Carolina*
Dr. **David Lane**, *University of Cambridge*
Dr. **Carol Leonard**, *University of Oxford*
Dr. **Maria Popova**, *McGill University, Montreal*

FOREIGN POLICY & INTERNATIONAL AFFAIRS
Dr. **Peter Duncan**, *University College London*
Prof. **Andreas Heinemann-Grüder**, *University of Bonn*
Prof. **Gerhard Mangott**, *University of Innsbruck*
Dr. **Diana Schmidt-Pfister**, *University of Konstanz*
Dr. **Lisbeth Tarlow**, *Harvard University, Cambridge*
Dr. **Christian Wipperfürth**, *N-Ost Network, Berlin*
Dr. **William Zimmerman**, *University of Michigan*

HISTORY, CULTURE & THOUGHT
Dr. **Catherine Andreyev**, *University of Oxford*
Prof. **Mark Bassin**, *Södertörn University*
Prof. **Karsten Brüggemann**, *Tallinn University*
Prof. **Alexander Etkind**, *Central European University*
Prof. **Gasan Gusejnov**, *Free University of Berlin*
Prof. **Leonid Luks**, *Catholic University of Eichstaett*
Dr. **Olga Malinova**, *Russian Academy of Sciences*
Dr. **Richard Mole**, *University College London*
Prof. **Andrei Rogatchevski**, *University of Tromsø*
Dr. **Mark Tauger**, *West Virginia University*

ADVISORY BOARD*

Prof. **Dominique Arel**, *University of Ottawa*
Prof. **Jörg Baberowski**, *Humboldt University of Berlin*
Prof. **Margarita Balmaceda**, *Seton Hall University*
Dr. **John Barber**, *University of Cambridge*
Prof. **Timm Beichelt**, *European University Viadrina*
Dr. **Katrin Boeckh**, *University of Munich*
Prof. em. **Archie Brown**, *University of Oxford*
Dr. **Vyacheslav Bryukhovetsky**, *Kyiv-Mohyla Academy*
Prof. **Timothy Colton**, *Harvard University, Cambridge*
Prof. **Paul D'Anieri**, *University of California*
Dr. **Heike Dörrenbächer**, *Friedrich Naumann Foundation*
Dr. **John Dunlop**, *Hoover Institution, Stanford, California*
Dr. **Sabine Fischer**, *SWP, Berlin*
Dr. **Geir Flikke**, *NUPI, Oslo*
Prof. **David Galbreath**, *University of Aberdeen*
Prof. **Frank Golczewski**, *University of Hamburg*
Dr. **Nikolas Gvosdev**, *Naval War College, Newport, RI*
Prof. **Mark von Hagen**, *Arizona State University*
Prof. **Guido Hausmann**, *University of Regensburg*
Prof. **Dale Herspring**, *Kansas State University*
Dr. **Stefani Hoffman**, *Hebrew University of Jerusalem*
Prof. em. **Andrzej Korbonski**, *University of California*
Dr. **Iris Kempe**, *"Caucasus Analytical Digest"*
Prof. **Herbert Küpper**, *Institut für Ostrecht Regensburg*
Prof. **Rainer Lindner**, *University of Konstanz*

Dr. **Luke March**, *University of Edinburgh*
Prof. **Michael McFaul**, *Stanford University, Palo Alto*
Prof. **Birgit Menzel**, *University of Mainz-Germersheim*
Dr. **Alex Pravda**, *University of Oxford*
Dr. **Erik van Ree**, *University of Amsterdam*
Dr. **Joachim Rogall**, *Robert Bosch Foundation Stuttgart*
Prof. **Peter Rutland**, *Wesleyan University, Middletown*
Prof. **Gwendolyn Sasse**, *University of Oxford*
Prof. **Jutta Scherrer**, *EHESS, Paris*
Prof. **Robert Service**, *University of Oxford*
Mr. **James Sherr**, *RIIA Chatham House London*
Dr. **Oxana Shevel**, *Tufts University, Medford*
Prof. **Eberhard Schneider**, *University of Siegen*
Prof. **Olexander Shnyrkov**, *Shevchenko University, Kyiv*
Prof. **Hans-Henning Schröder**, *SWP, Berlin*
Prof. **Yuri Shapoval**, *Ukrainian Academy of Sciences*
Dr. **Lisa Sundstrom**, *University of British Columbia*
Dr. **Philip Walters**, *"Religion, State and Society"*, Oxford
Prof. **Zenon Wasyliw**, *Ithaca College, New York State*
Dr. **Lucan Way**, *University of Toronto*
Dr. **Markus Wehner**, *"Frankfurter Allgemeine Zeitung"*
Dr. **Andrew Wilson**, *University College London*
Prof. **Jan Zielonka**, *University of Oxford*
Prof. **Andrei Zorin**, *University of Oxford*

* While the Editorial Committee and Advisory Board support the General Editor in the choice and improvement of manuscripts for publication, responsibility for remaining errors and misinterpretations in the series' volumes lies with the books' authors.

Soviet and Post-Soviet Politics and Society (SPPS)
ISSN 1614-3515

Founded in 2004 and refereed since 2007, SPPS makes available affordable English-, German-, and Russian-language studies on the history of the countries of the former Soviet bloc from the late Tsarist period to today. It publishes between 5 and 20 volumes per year and focuses on issues in transitions to and from democracy such as economic crisis, identity formation, civil society development, and constitutional reform in CEE and the NIS. SPPS also aims to highlight so far understudied themes in East European studies such as right-wing radicalism, religious life, higher education, or human rights protection. The authors and titles of all previously published volumes are listed at the end of this book. For a full description of the series and reviews of its books, see www.ibidem-verlag.de/red/spps.

Editorial correspondence & manuscripts should be sent to: Dr. Andreas Umland, Department of Political Science, Kyiv-Mohyla Academy, vul. Voloska 8/5, UA-04070 Kyiv, UKRAINE; andreas.umland@cantab.net

Business correspondence & review copy requests should be sent to: *ibidem* Press, Leuschnerstr. 40, 30457 Hannover, Germany; tel.: +49 511 2622200; fax: +49 511 2622201; spps@ibidem.eu.

Authors, reviewers, referees, and editors for (as well as all other persons sympathetic to) SPPS are invited to join its networks at www.facebook.com/group.php?gid=52638198614 www.linkedin.com/groups?about=&gid=103012 www.xing.com/net/spps-ibidem-verlag/

Recent Volumes

271 *Anton Shekhovtsov*
Russian Political Warfare
Essays on Kremlin Propaganda in Europe and the Neighbourhood, 2020–2023
With a foreword by Nathalie Loiseau
ISBN 978-3-8382-1821-2

272 *Андреа Пето*
Насилие и Молчание
Красная армия в Венгрии во Второй Мировой войне
ISBN 978-3-8382-1636-2

273 *Winfried Schneider-Deters*
Russia's War in Ukraine
Debates on Peace, Fascism, and War Crimes, 2022–2023
With a foreword by Klaus Gestwa
ISBN 978-3-8382-1876-2

274 *Rasmus Nilsson*
Uncanny Allies
Russia and Belarus on the Edge, 2012-2024
ISBN 978-3-8382-1288-3

275 *Anton Grushetskyi, Volodymyr Paniotto*
War and the Transformation of Ukrainian Society (2022–23)
Empirical Evidence
ISBN 978-3-8382-1944-8

276 *Christian Kaunert, Alex MacKenzie, Adrien Nonjon (Eds.)*
In the Eye of the Storm
Origins, Ideology, and Controversies of the Azov Brigade, 2014–23
ISBN 978-3-8382-1750-5

277 *Gian Marco Moisé*
The House Always Wins
The Corrupt Strategies that Shaped Kazakh Oil Politics and Business in the Nazarbayev Era
With a foreword by Alena Ledeneva
ISBN 978-3-8382-1917-2

278 *Mikhail Minakov*
The Post-Soviet Human
Philosophical Reflections on Social History after the End of Communism
ISBN 978-3-8382-1943-1

279 *Natalia Kudriavtseva, Debra A. Friedman (Eds.)*
Language and Power in Ukraine and Kazakhstan
Essays on Education, Ideology, Literature, Practice, and the Media
With a foreword by Laada Bilaniuk
ISBN 978-3-8382-1949-3

The war in Georgia especially sent such a signal. Regardless of the criticism that was directed at the then Georgian President Mikhail Saakashvili, who was regarded somewhat responsible for the conflict, the Russian attack on Georgia demonstrated that the Kremlin was ready to use force to rebuild its spheres of influence which it had lost after the collapse of the Soviet Union and which came at the price of its worsening of relations with the West[14].

Lucas's valid thesis about the beginning of a new Cold War between Russia and the West was mostly journalistic in style. It attracted a lot of attention, but—at the same time—created many interpretational challenges. Lucas did not provide a clear definition of what he understood as the new Cold War, nor did he theoretically justify the differences and similarities between the new Russia-West rivalry and the old Cold War. He only signalled certain conditions that should be taken into consideration when references to the new concept of the Cold War are made. First, the Cold War, in the old meaning of the term, belongs to history and will not come back. That is why any literal comparisons with this period are outdated and erroneous. Second, there are some clear differences: Putin's Russia is no longer a global enemy of the West; the clear ideological division between the two worlds—the communist world and the free democratic world—has also disappeared. Nonetheless, the relations between the West and Russia are entering a period of a difficult confrontation, which is something the political and economic elites in the West do not want to accept, for different reasons. In Lucas's view, the main mistake made by the West after 1991 was to believe that after the collapse of the Soviet Union, Russia was a "normal" state, one that other countries could engage with, economically and politically. This allowed Russia to return to its policy of rivalry with the West, also termed as a "sharp strategic conflict". Just like the old Cold War it takes place mainly in Europe.[15]

---

14 Asmus, R., 2010, *A Little War That Shook the World: Georgia, Russia, and the Future of the West*, London: Palgrave Macmillan.
15 Lucas, E., 2008, *op. cit.*, pp. 3, 8, 11.

Forgotten Balkan wars and the path for a new Cold War rivalry

Going beyond Lucas's interpretation, as he presented it in his 2008 book and which focused on the changes that had taken place in Russia's policies towards the West, and including today's perspective in it, which means over two years of Russia's full-scale invasion in Ukraine, we can agree with some general assumptions of the new Cold War theory. First it should be said that even though Russia's war against Ukraine actually started in 2014 and its historical context dates back to 19th century conflicts between Ukrainian nation- and state-building aspirations and traditional Russian imperialism, the true meaning of the 2022 invasion is that through this aggression, Russia openly declares it is in a conflict with the West, something that had been boiling in Russian political discourse for a while. In addition to the war in Ukraine, Russia's anti-Western strategy includes building an alliance with China and other powers which share revisionist positions towards the post-Cold War international order.

In this way the Kremlin has been attempting to make the conflict with Ukraine global. As a result, Europe is no longer its only area of rivalry, contrary to what Lucas could have argued in 2008. Yet, Europe is the main addressee of Russia's aggression. Russia wants to rebuild its spheres of influence not only in the former Soviet republics, now independent states, but also in the countries of Eastern and Central Europe as it was stated in the ultimatum issued by the Russian Minister of Foreign Affairs, Sergei Lavrov, on 17 December 2021 to the United States and NATO in regards to a new treaty guaranteeing security to Russia. Russia clearly wants more. Its goal is to question the essence of the world order which emerged as a result of the end of the Cold War and which, in the early 1990s, Moscow was, to some extent, co-creating with the West.

From the Russian perspective, the conflict with the West has been developing for some time. However, an analysis of the debate on the New Cold War requires to establish when this process actually started. The coming of Russia's open and declared confrontation with the West, which is multi-level and which we can see today, was a result of both the internal evolution of power structures in the Russian Federation after the collapse of the Soviet Union and the changes in the world order that took place in its aftermath. Nonetheless, the event which contributed the most to the perception that a competition between the West (especially the US and NATO) and Russia (and its allies) had never ceased to exist and continued in a new international context and areas, was the war in the former Yugoslavia. More precisely, these were the two conflicts: the 1992-1995 war in Bosnia and Herzegovina and the 1998-1999 war in Kosovo. The former proceeded NATO's Eastern enlargement, which is worth taking note. Overall, the war in the former Yugoslavia proved to be a decisive moment in the divergence of the shared security vision on both sides: Russia and the West. Thus, until 2022 the dominating Western perspective was based on the paradigm of a systemic transformation of international security policy in the post-Cold War order. However, Russia's perspective, which took the new international context after collapse of the Soviet Union into account, principally adhered to the continuation paradigm; to some kind of "overtime" in the old rivalry that was resolved in an inappropriate manner, and to the accompanying sense of a growing threat from the West.

The 2008 Russian aggression in Georgia and the recognition of the separatist republics, Abkhazia and South Ossetia, were also an integral part of this process and demonstrated how much the experience of the war in the former Yugoslavia determined the Kremlin's perception and security strategy. First and foremost, it reinforced the conviction that Russia's rivalry with the United States and NATO had not ended with the Cold War, but entered a new phase.

For historical, geopolitical and civilisational reasons, the 1990s Balkans turned into a new area of post-Cold War rivalry between Russia and the West, illustrating differences not only in interests but also perception. For the Western political elite and societies, the war in the former Yugoslavia first and foremost was a response to a humanitarian crisis, human rights' violations and a challenge of solving regional conflicts which erupted from ethnic and religious tensions as well as aggressive policies of the post-communist authoritarian and military regimes operating in the post-Soviet space. The causes of this war were rooted in traditional old world politics, while its end as it was orchestrated by the international community was meant to cement the new rules of the postmodern order, which inevitably came into being after the end of the Cold War. For Russia, on the other hand, the war in the former Yugoslavia was a proxy war between the East and West. It was waged based on the Cold War logic. This approach was a reflection of the Kremlin elite's thinking whose roots date back to the Cold War period but also include the historical understanding of the role that the Balkans played in European geopolitics. Historically speaking, this region was an area of a strong rivalry between the great powers: continental Europe, Russia and Turkey.

In the 1990s, Russia treated the war in Bosnia and Herzegovina as an opportunity to strengthen its international position after the collapse of the Soviet Union. At that time Moscow wanted to avoid isolation, even marginalisation, and return to the table as an equal and necessary partner of the West. Yet the war in the Balkans also started to serve the Kremlin as evidence of the still existing and insurmountable conflict of interests between Russia and the West.[16] Russia was also skilfully using the divisions between Western European states (mainly France and Great Britain) and the United States. They were caused by the embargo on weapons provision and the Western engagement in defence of the Bosniak population attacked by the Yugoslav Army, primarily in Sarajevo and UN-controlled security zones. Russia was also consistently building its position as an impartial arbitrator in regional conflicts and a key partner of the West in peace negotiations carried out in the frameworks of the United Nations Security Council, the Organisation for Security and Co-operation in Europe (OSCE), the Contact Group and UN peace missions on the territory of the former Yugoslavia. In this way Russian diplomats, under the leadership of Andrey Kozyrov, were trying to influence the security policy of the

---

16 Headley, J., 2003, "Sarajevo, February 1994: the First Russia-NATO conflict of the post-Cold War era", *Review of International Studies*, 29 (2), pp. 209-227.

West and stop NATO's intervention in the Balkans. They also wanted to create a situation in which the framework of international institutions would make it impossible to effectively resolve any conflict without Russia's participation.[17]

At the time of the Balkan wars, Moscow strengthened its alliance with Serbia's then president, Slobodan Milošević. This relationship was said to be based on historical, cultural and religious ties which connect Serbia with Russia as well as the identification of shared interests that existed between the authorities in Belgrade and Moscow, which both saw the West, and especially the US and NATO, as their enemy. This shared viewpoint was strengthened by the growing international position of the United States, especially after the First Gulf War in 1991 against Iraq, a Soviet ally during the Cold War. In Russia, especially among the nationalistic and communist groups, Serbia was seen as a "proxy" which after the collapse of Yugoslavia had to fight nationalistic separatism supported by the West.[18] That is why the Kremlin was willing to get involved militarily on Serbia's side. At first its involvement was indirect and included training and sending volunteers to Serbia as well as providing it with weapons. Yet, Russia also agreed to become Serbia's protectorate in its resistance to the West's attempts to turn the Balkans into its own spheres of influence. Arguably, the lack of a coherent strategy of the West together with the Kremlin's double game allowed for the war in Bosnia and Herzegovina to create conditions for a quick recreation of the old Cold War rivalry by means of proxy wars and fights over spheres of influence. In 1994, the earlier mentioned Kozyrev noted:

> "We are on the threshold of recreating in the Balkans, particularly in Bosnia, a type of patron-client relationship that used to characterise the Cold War period, when Moscow backed communist regimes [...] and Washington backed [...] the so-called free world forces. We are on the verge of entering the same kind of patron-client regime, but on a different basis. That is, Russian public opinion tends to believe that we have to be the protectors of the

---

17   Gallagher, T., 2003, *The Balkans After the Cold War: From Tyranny to Tragedy*, Routledge, pp. 141-143.
18   Lukic, R., Lynch, A., 1996, *Europe from the Balkans to the Urals: Disintegration of Yugoslavia and the Soviet Union*, Oxford: Oxford University Press, p. 332.

Serbs, and the United States there seems to be a kind of obsession with portraying the Muslim and Croat side as almost the innocent victim of the so-called Serbian aggression [...] That is the danger: that Washington starts to behave as patrons of the Muslim side and unilaterally lifts the arms embargo [...] So that leaves us with exactly a classic client-patron type of confrontation [...] That will be a total break with international legality."[19]

After the constitutional crisis in Russia in 1993 which led it towards a model of "imperial presidency" it became clear that Russia was also about to alter its foreign policy. Among other things, the Kremlin started departing from cooperation with the West for the sake of competition and stressing its separate interests. Russia was also more bravely and frequently signalling a return to the rivalry of the great powers. As a result, two events in 1995, the Deliberate Force operation, which meant using NATO forces against the Serbs and ending the war through the Dayton Peace Accords both took place in an atmosphere of worsening US-Russia relations and Russia's growing sense of being ignored by the West.[20]

The war in Bosnia may have created the conditions for the return of the logic of the old Cold War rivalry, but it did not lead to an open conflict. Until 1996 the Kremlin was not interested in entering into an open conflict with the West, mainly because it needed to maintain economic relations with it. Before 1996, the Clinton Administration was also consistently supporting Boris Yeltsin and his "reforms", treating Russia's democratisation as a security priority for the US. For this reason, the US had been avoiding any activities which would weaken Yeltsin's position.[21] Yet, the open conflict between the two states started during the Kosovo war, which proved to be a turning point in Russia's relations with the West after the Cold War. The culminating moment of this already open conflict between Russia and the West was NATO's Allied Force operation, which led to air strikes on Belgrade, and then a raid of Russian military units within the SFOR international forces on the territory of

---

19 *Ibidem*, p. 347.
20 Headley, J., 2003, "Sarajevo, February 1994: the First Russia-NATO conflict of the post-Cold War era", *Review of International Studies*, 29 (2), pp. 225-226.
21 Boys, J.D., 2015, *Clinton's grand strategy: US foreign policy in a post-Cold War world*, London, New York: Bloomsbury Academic, pp. 19-20, 124.

Kosovo and the takeover of Pristina airport which was needed to transfer new troops into Kosovo from Russia.

The Kremlin's reaction towards the Kosovo war was exceptionally rapid and did not match the scheme which was seen in the war in Bosnia. For instance, after having heard about the NATO bombing of Serbian targets in March 1999, Yevgeny Primakov, Kozyrev's successor foreign minister of Russia, who had just departed for a visit to Washington DC, decided to turn his plane back and return to Moscow. In the end, the American intervention against Serbia led to Russia's breaking of relations with NATO.

Attempts to rebuild them were undertaken in the following years, but these attempts took place in an atmosphere of rivalry, mutual accusations and hostility. "Over time, this became a metaphor for a dramatic turn of Russian foreign policy away from cooperation with the United States", Plokhy wrote assessing the new situation.[22] The 1999 crisis, deepened by the disagreement over Kosovo's sovereignty as it was pushed by the United States, was characterised by an open crisis between the Kremlin and the United States and the West. From the perspective of the evolution of NATO's strategy, the Kosovo war was the first activity of this type. It took place in the framework of a new model of operations which were carried outside the Alliance's territory. This change overlapped with the 1996 decision of the Clinton Administration to expand NATO and offer membership to the states that were once part of the Eastern bloc. The 1999 crisis was yet taking place when Russia's political context was quite different from what was known prior. At that time the Russian Federation was experiencing an increasingly more authoritarian rule of President Yeltsin; while the process of Vladimir Putin's rise to power and establishing new structures had already begun. The Russian state also felt the internal and international outcomes of the first Chechen war (1994-1996) and saw an overall turn in its foreign policy as it was started by Primakov after 1996. Last but not least, 1999 was also the beginning of the Second Chechen War.

---

22 Plokhy, S. *op. cit.*, p. 81.

A perfect illustration of the beginning of the new Cold War is an infamous conversation between presidents Boris Yeltsin and Bill Clinton at the OSCE summit in Istanbul in 1999. It comprehensively announced the coming of the new Putin era. Yeltsin then said: "I ask you one thing. Just give Europe to Russia. The US is not in Europe. Europe should be the business of Europeans. Russia is half European and half Asian". Clinton responded: "So you want Asia too?". Yeltsin: "Sure, sure, Bill. Eventually, we will have to agree on all of this". Clinton reacted: "I don't think the Europeans would like this very much". To that Yeltsin responded: "Not all […] you can take all the other states and provide security to them. I will take Europe and provide them security. Well, not I, Russia will […] Bill, I'm serious. Give Europe to Europe itself. Europe never felt as close to Russia as it does now".[23]

Pertinence and explanatory limits of the Cold War analogy

An analysis of sources on Russia's policy of the new Cold War confrontation with the West often includes references to the fall of the Berlin Wall and Germany's reunification. These two events are said to have had a deciding impact on Vladimir Putin, the future president of the Russian Federation but at that time a KGB officer in Dresden. Accordingly, for Putin both the reunification of Germany and the collapse of the Soviet Union proved to be, as he publically announced it in 2005, the greatest geopolitical catastrophe of the 20th century. As a witness of the takeover of Stasi buildings by German demonstrators in 1990 Putin was planning to prepare the defence of his own premises against an expected attack. However, his phone calls to the headquarters in Moscow remained unanswered.

This not only made Putin realise the scale of failure and humiliation of the former Soviet empire, which became visible at the

---

23 See: National Security Council and NSC Records Management System, 2024, *Declassified Documents Concerning Russian President Boris Yeltsin*. Clinton Digital Library. https://clinton.presidentiallibraries.us/items/show/57569 (Accessed: 20 July 2024); Thom, F., 2022, *Poutine ou l'obsession de la puissance*, Paris: Desclée de Brouwer.

end of the Cold War, but also became the source of his resentments, hatred and the need for revenge on the West, especially the United States.[24] However, as decisive as these events were for Russia's situation after the collapse of the USSR and the end of the Cold War, it was the war in the former Yugoslavia that was the key moment marking the beginning of the evolution of Russian foreign and security policy in opposition to the West. All said, this change, which started with the wars in Bosnia and Kosovo in the 1990s, has lasted until the current war in Ukraine. It has had a significant impact on the Russian perception of the US and the West. It reinforced the Kremlin in its conviction of the continuation of the Cold War reality and the belief that the West had being trying to destroy Russia. The Balkans were thus seen as an area of a new old conflict.[25]

In the middle of this process, which started with the war in Bosnia and has continued to the war in Ukraine, was the 2008 Russia's war against Georgia. Again, the interpretation of this event should not be reduced to Russia's attempt of rebuilding its former spheres of influence in the South Caucuses. The attack on Georgia and support to separatist territories, Abkhazia and South Ossetia, were for the Kremlin as a mirror reflection of what the West had done in the 1990s in the Balkans. For Russia, the status of the two separatist Georgian provinces was an analogy to the case of Kosovo's status and the relations it had with Serbia. In other words, it was an element of the new geopolitical rivalry between Russia and the West, which had become the leading theme of Russian politics, starting with the war in Bosnia. The sequence of events which took place after the war in Kosovo is also indicative. In 2003 and 2004 Georgia and Ukraine experienced large political protests, popularly known as coloured revolutions.

In February 2007 at the Munich Security Forum President Putin delivered his notoriously belligerent and anti-Western speech. In February 2008 Kosovo announced independence. Three weeks later, South Ossetia and Abkhazia, asked to be recognised by

---

24 Sarotte, M., 2015, *1989: The Struggle to Create Post-Cold War Europe*, Princeton: Princeton University Press, pp. 19, 86, 93-94.
25 Galeotti, M., 2018, "Do the Western Balkans Face a Coming Russian Storm?", ECFR Policy Brief.

Russia as independent. In August 2008 Russian troops entered Georgia. When analysing this series of events American diplomat and political analyst Ronald Asmus commented as follows: "For anyone familiar with the Kosovo conflict, the parallels between the Balkans in 1999 and what unfolded in Georgia starting in August were obvious". Asmus also noted that "it was almost as if the Russians had spent much of the subsequent decade carefully studying the West's political and military campaign in Kosovo and the Balkans and adapting it to their own ends. Moscow's terminology and rhetorical line of defense were almost a mirror image of the West's rationale on Kosovo a decade earlier. Russia justified its invasion of Georgia as a 'peacekeeping' operation to end the Tbilisi government's 'genocide' and 'ethnic cleansing' of South Ossetia".[26]

These striking similarities returned later in 2014, taking the form of the annexation of Crimea by the Russian Federation and the outbreak of the war in Donbas. In 2008, Moscow's goal was larger than Georgia's territory. Russia's play-off in South Caucuses for what had happened in the Balkans was meant to question the rules of the post-Cold War order, which did not allow to change state borders in Europe with the use of military force. The breaking of this rule meant that Russia's war against Georgia in 2008 was also a war aimed at the United States, NATO and the entire European security system which had emerged after the end of the Cold War and which was based on 1975 Helsinki Final Act and the 1990 Charter of Paris for a New Europe.[27]

The sequence of events which influenced Russia's foreign and security policy, starting with the war in Bosnia and Kosovo in the 1990s to the full-scale invasion in Ukraine in 2022, illustrates the actual continuity in Russia's perception of the West and Europe. This perception is characterised by a deep conviction that the conflict between the West and Russia did not end with the Cold War but has continued in new areas, with new methods, and in the context that has been changing to Russia's disadvantage. The fear of this

---

26 Asmus, R., 2010, *A Little War That Shook the World: Georgia, Russia, and the Future of the West*, London: Palgrave Macmillan, pp. 108-109.
27 *Ibidem*, p. 5.

approach in Russia's foreign policy has been loudly expressed in the last three decades by Russia's neighbours. Among them are the former Soviet republics as well as the satellite states of the former Eastern bloc: Poland, Czechia or Romania. Conversely, the Western states were — for a long time — adhering to their own convictions and assumptions about the irreversible nature of transformation changes in the global security policy in the post-Cold War era. This paradigm included Russia's integration with the new security system.

All said, the concept of a New or Second Cold War is justified to a certain degree, as long as it allows us to understand the dynamic of the continuity and when it points to specific historical sources of Russia's current conflict with the West. A similar evolution of power structures in Putin's Russia also shows continuity with the previous period. This process has its sources in the collapse of the Soviet Union and the loss of meaning and identity which came with it, but which earlier had been built on the conflict with the West and the communist ideology. The continuity thesis could also be justified with the argument of stability of the fundamental geopolitical factors. Namely, two geopolitical areas have been permanently colliding with each other in their fight over world domination. In the early 20th century, Halford MacKinder, a British scholar regarded as the father of geopolitics, identified them as the Transatlantic world and the Eurasian world. The conflict between these two worlds was often presented in geopolitical analyses and used for the explanation of both the Second World War and its aftermath — the Cold War. Contrary to the thinking of the supporters of the transformative nature of changes in the global security order after the Cold War, which was meant to lead to a departure from a traditional, geopolitical thinking about world politics, the conflict between the Transatlantic and Eurasian world has not disappeared and has now taken on a new form, which generates associations with the previous Cold War.[28] Finally, the thesis of the continuity between the old and new Cold War can be backed by the argument

---

28 Sempa, F., 2017, *Geopolitics: from the Cold War to the 21st Century*, Routledge, pp. 87-101.

that all of the leaders of today's world powers have experienced the Cold War and its end. This allows us to formulate a hypothesis that this experience has a strong influence on their own perception of today's world affairs and mutual relations.[29] In this sense, the logic of the old Cold War remains present in contemporary politics, and the statement formulated by Niall Ferguson "There was a First World War. Then there was a second... Similarly, there was a Cold War I. And now we are in Cold War II" remains justified, even though its aptness results just from common sense reasoning.

A question yet remains: to what extent the concept of the Second Cold War can be a source of erroneous assessments and calculations, or even harmful when it comes to the practical directives how the West should react to revisionist powers or design its strategy toward the war in Ukraine? On what basis we can presuppose that containment and deterrence strategies will work in the current conflict?[30] The activities of Russia, China or Iran in 2021-2024 indicate that we should remain sceptical towards the automatic effectiveness of these old strategies. Thus, possibly more correct are those who warn against the analogies with the Second Cold War in the foreseeing of the future and making strategic choices today, including the case of the war in Ukraine. They argue that simplifications, which are too far reaching and result from past examples, can lead to erroneous decisions with long-term consequences. The earlier mentioned alliance of revisionist anti-Western forces, the infiltration of today's societies and states by new technologies, the level of global interdependence and emergence of a new, post-modern type of power and ideology — all these, together, make the current conflict very different from the one that characterised the Cold War.[31]

---

29 Harrison, H.P., 2023, "Russia, the United States, Germany and the war in Ukraine: a new Cold War, but with a dangerous twist," in: Ellison, J., Cox, M., Hanhimäki, J.M., Harrison, H.M., Ludlow, N.P., Romano, A., Spohr, K. & Zubok, V., 2023, "The war in Ukraine", *Cold War History*, 23 (1), p. 154.

30 Herrmann, R., 2004, "Learning from the End of the Cold War", in: Herrmann, R., Lebow, R.N. (eds.), *Ending the Cold War: Interpretations, Causation, and the Study of International Relations*, London: Palgrave, p. 222.

31 Keane, J., 2020, *The New Despotism*, Cambridge, MA: Harvard University Press.

Conclusions

The debate about the New Cold War started long before Russia's invasion into Ukraine. It was a reaction to the authoritarian changes which were taking place internally in Russia in the first decade of the 21st century as well as Russia's war in Georgia in 2008. After 2016, under the administration of Donald Trump, the United States started to openly talk about the conflict between the United States and China, which has significantly changed the context of the debate on a New Cold War. Thus, some observers argue that the current global rivalry between powers has become centred on these two states. This picture has become even more complicated with Russia's war in Ukraine, which nonetheless confirms that the era of the New Cold War has already started. Russia's full-scale invasion into Ukraine, and its earlier annexation of Crimea, were to mark the outbreak of the first hot conflict in the New Cold War.

However, the historical roots of Russia's war with Ukraine go deep. They reach Russia's imperial expansion and Ukrainian nation- and state-building in the 19th century. More recently, they can be found in the Kremlin's actions and policies which, since 1991, have been aimed at halting the consequences of the collapse of the Soviet Union. Russia, thereby, aims at regaining control over the post-Soviet space and in long-term its spheres of influence in Europe. Nonetheless, the application of the Cold War paradigm to the current war in Ukraine allows us to see the meaning of this conflict in the context of a changing world order after the Cold War. This yet does not have an effect on the argument that as a model explaining a change of the world order the theory of the second, New Cold War raises some doubts which should be taken into consideration. The Russian perspective is based on the conviction of the continuity between today and the Cold War.

This thinking has been in place for over 25 years and was triggered by the wars in Bosnia and Herzegovina and Kosovo. It has also provided Putin with a basis for Russia's new policies and identity. This perception assumes that the Cold War has never ended, it only moved to new areas where it is being waged, with new methods. On the other hand, from the perspective of the political and ideological evolution of the West, the acceptance of the concept of the New Cold War leads, in a way, towards the abandonment of the earlier narratives about the transformative peace order and the end of history. Thus, the question remains: does this turn of perspective indeed present the power of the West, if in fact, it assumes an acceptance of the thinking about the Cold War, and its end, which is close to the Russian way of thinking?

Geostrategic Phantasmagoria[1]
The Geopolitical Discourse from Russian Imperialism to Post-soviet Memory: History Uses and Abuses as the Method of Putin's War Legitimacy

Georges Mink

Since 24 February 2022 Vladimir Putin's distortion of Ukrainian history to justify Russia's full-scale aggression against Ukraine has raised valid questions about the relationship that exists between Russian geopolitical permanence and historical justification; and thus, what international law and world order mean to the Kremlin today.

In the 1990s Zbigniew Brzeziński, who was always ahead of others in his analyses, coined the term "geostrategic phantasmagoria" while interpreting the changes in the states of the former Soviet Union after it had collapsed in early 1990s. The latter process took a very short time. As its result, the new Russian state lost, almost overnight, the traditional parameters which earlier had served as bases for its world vision and strategy. Indeed, no one had foreseen the quick pace of disintegration which put an end to the centuries-old rule that Russia had over many nations and which, in Brzeziński's view, resulted in a crisis of Russian national identity. While describing it he stressed: "During the last years of the previous century, Russians were frenetically searching for answers to the questions, what is Russia, what does it mean to be Russian, where does Russia begin and where does it end?"[2] Russian nationalists were first to offer answers to these very complex questions. Thus, when Vladimir Putin emerged as a key actor in Russian politics, he had been already provided with an elaborate, lofty and patriotic

---
1 Brzezinski, Z., 2023, *Le grand échiquier, l'Amérique et le reste du monde*, Paris: Fayard, Pluriel. Originally published as *The Grand Chessboard* in 1997, p. 131.
2 *Ibidem*.

historical narrative that he could later use when responding to the society's frustrations over its deficit of identity.

Yet to start a war against Ukraine, which Russia had already done twice: first in 2014 and later in 2022, Putin needed historical revisionism. To justify military aggression the Russian leader used historical arguments which quickly gave way to the discourse on military might and nuclear threat. As a result, the official Kremlin interpretation of history became known to the outside world, which inevitably became involved in the conflict, either because of the blocking of food exports, gas or fertiliser supplies, or because of the military support that Western allies offered to Ukraine. At the same time some autocratic states supported Russia. Ukraine's president, Volodymyr Zelenskyy, through his communication strategy, has also largely contributed to the Europeanisation and globalisation of his country's cause. One wonders what role and what effectiveness historical revisionism and historical memory games play in Putin's strategy since then. In Putin's own words, as he presented them in the essay published on the Kremlin's website on 12 July 2021 and titled *On the historical unification of Russians and Ukrainians*, the Russian president argues that the ninth-century Kyiv Rus' is the integral foundation of a people for whom the Ukrainian capital, this "mother of Russian cities" as he calls it, is the cradle. "Russians, Ukrainians and Belarusians are the heirs of the ancient Rus'", Putin wrote, "which was the largest country in Europe (...) History has decided that the centre of unification, continuing the tradition of the ancient Russian state, should become Moscow," he continues.[3] And further, Moscow is no longer the "third Rome", but the "new Kyiv", while the conversion of Kyiv's Grand Duke Vladimir (c. 955-1015) to Byzantine Christianity sealed Russia's spiritual destiny. We can thus formulate a hypothesis that 11 centuries later, Putin's reason for waging a war against Ukraine is motivated by an absurd dream: to restore the original empire.

---

3 Putin, V., 2021, "On the Historical Unity of Russians and Ukrainians", 12 July. http://en.kremlin.ru/events/president/news/66181 (Accessed: 24 August 2024).

Is this vision convincing enough to make Russians rally around the idea of a re-conquest? Is it not too abstract as a memory reference? Evidently, for his geopolitical strategy Putin needs a historical narrative that is not only based on collective cultural memory, but also on communicative memory.[4] It is about the memories of witnesses, which are still alive in the minds of the elders. This design must be subjected to an analysis that blends the concept of geopolitics with that of the uses of history and historical memory.

Dominant theories at the turn of the 21st century and Russian geopolitical thought

At its birth at the beginning of the 20th century, geopolitical thinking was based on a sort of Darwinian theory, pitting weaker states against stronger ones. It was dominated by the thought of Friedrich Ratzel, who believed that the driving force behind the formation of states was the struggle for "living space".

The person who inspired Germany's geopolitical strategies in the early 20th century the most was a geographer and senior officer named General Karl Haushofer, who was in close contact with Nazi party leaders.[5] His relations with Nazi dignitaries such as Rudolph Hess ultimately gave him access to Adolf Hitler. Haushofer's geopolitical concept of reconfiguring Germany's living space, claiming to be a victim of the Treaty of Versailles, became the inspiration for war.

At roughly the same time, the Soviet geopolitical strategy of territorial conquest was developed, sanctified by the messianic theory of the inevitable world revolution, notably by Lenin. It resulted in the Soviet defeat in the Polish-Soviet War in 1921, contrary to Bolshevik plans. Illustratively, it can be said that the meeting of these two geopolitical approaches resulted first in the 1922 Rapallo Treaty (with its secret clause of military collaboration) and then the

---

4   See for example: Assmann, A., 2019, "Between history and memory", in: Saryusz-Wolska, M. (ed.), *Anthology*. Warsaw: Wydawnictwo Uniwersytetu Warszawskiego.
5   Haushofer, K., 1986, *De la Géopolitique*. Paris: Fayard.

1939 Molotov-Ribbentrop Pact. After the victory over Nazi Germany in 1945, Stalin outlined his wish to surround the Soviet Union with a security belt. The Soviet leader was indeed obsessed by the memory of the threats posed to the young Bolshevik revolution by the Western countries supporting the White Russian armies. Thus, to justify the conquest of the USSR's neighbouring states Stalin used history, which he interpreted in his own way. In Stalinist rhetoric, the conquest was camouflaged by the notion of "friendly countries" or "friends" who were forced to refuse the Marshall Plan and accept the COMECON and the Warsaw Pact. All this shows that geopolitical concepts are indeed closely linked to the historical context and configuration of political geography, as well as strategic constructions produced by the actors of international relations.

While analysing Putin's thinking about geopolitics and history today, it is worth pointing to his dislike for Lenin, whom Putin blames for having supported centrifugal national liberation tendencies in Russia. Putin seems to deny the fact that Lenin's goal, through the declaration of the right of the peoples to self-determination, was to unleash the revolutionary energies of proletariats (or rather Bolshevik avant-garde) necessary to spread the idea of a global proletarian revolution in Europe, i.e. a new empire of world revolution. Already in 1992, as deputy mayor of the city of St Petersburg, Putin said that Lenin had planted a time bomb under Soviet Russia.[6] This rhetoric explains why in Putin's language the notion of imperial space is actually close to Stalin's understanding of the term, that is a violent and forceful takeover of other nations.[7]

However, Putin's semantics and rhetoric goes further. Thus, when Russia's current president claims to be defending Russia's "fellow citizens" or "compatriots" oppressed in Ukraine, it is necessary to decipher what these words stand for. The assumption that ethnicity is superior to citizenship is a political concept deriving from pseudo-naturalism. In Russia's case this means an assumption

---

6   Smoleński, P., 2022, Interview with Gajos, B. "Rosja to nie imperium, lecz szowinistyczne państwo narodowe", *Gazeta Wyborcza, Ale Historia*, 17-18 September.
7   Potulski, J., 2021, *The formation of spatial imaginaries in Russian political thought and practice*, Poznań: FNCE, pp. 42-44.

that all Russian speakers, regardless of citizenship, are bound together by one common ethnic denominator (blood) and are indebted to the Russian state for their very existence.[8] From this perspective, we may thus ask whether Latvia, an EU member state which has a large Russian-speaking minority, will be the next target in the process of the reconstruction of the Soviet empire? Is fragile Moldova, which is almost bilingual, also not at risk?

The evolution of memory games in the post-war period a reflection of the bloc division

Geopolitical concepts are closely related to historical context, political geography configuration and strategic constructs generated by actors involved in international relations. In the immediate aftermath of the Second World War, efforts were made to erase painful memories of the war-time atrocities by aligning historical and memory narratives with the idea that traumas must be forgotten. This assumption was in line with the thinking of Paul Ricoeur, a French philosopher who devoted much of his work to the relationship between history and memory as well as fluctuations between the overestimation of memory and its obliteration.[9]

The political dictate of the latter is best illustrated in the 1946 words of Sir Winston Churchill, which are now emblematically underscored in the guidebook to the House of European History in Brussels[10] where we can read: "We must all turn our backs upon the horror of the past. We must look to the future." Following the failure of Hitler's project, the world order became frozen by the Cold War from 1948 to 1989. This period can be described by means of a paradox that was formulated by a well-known French sociologist and specialist in international relations, Raymond Aron, who

---

8   See Mink, G., 2025, "'Polishness' in a European context" in: *Almanach*, Warszawa: Collegium Civitas, pp. 263-274.
9   Ricoeur, P., 2000, *La mémoire, l'histoire, l'oubli*, especially chapter: *Le niveau pathologique-thérapeutique : la mémoire empêchée*, Points: Seuil, p. 83.
10   House of European History, 2022, *Guidebook, Permanent Exhibition*. Bruxelles.

described it by the phrase "peace is impossible, war is improbable".[11] During that period, wars were, from a European perspective, very far away, located in former colonies. Western and Eastern Europe continued to live in the Aronian paradox during the period of nuclear deterrence. History was taking place on the periphery of the Western world and the memory of the history of the Second World War was repressed and pushed into the unconscious among its victims. The time horizon had consumed the fruits of post-war reconstruction and growing prosperity. The essence of the "Cold War" meant that armed and conventional confrontations often occurred in distant battlegrounds.

These conflicts served as testing grounds for the combat capabilities of superpowers like the Soviet Union, the United States and, to a lesser extent, Great Britain and France. The main and immediate training ground was separated by the threat of nuclear weapons of mass destruction. The last decades of the Cold War — between the 1970s and the 1980s — saw the emergence of polymorphous manifestations of memory. Paradigmatic studies were multiplying. These processes were just beginning to have an impact on geopolitics and the state of international relations. In these years, it was above all in the spaces of the nation states that national memory undertakings were concentrated. In the West, the ongoing construction of Europe required a reconciliation of memories between the driving countries of this process, France and Germany. The key moment of this development took place during the 1984 meeting of Helmut Kohl and François Mitterrand, who stood hand-in-hand in front of the tombs of the fallen soldiers from both nations who lost their lives at the Battle of Verdun.[12]

---

11   Aron, R., 1962, *Paix et Guerre entre les nations*, Paris: Calmann-Lévy.
12   The first signs of Polish-German reconciliation (between East and West) came with the letter from the Polish bishops to the German bishops in 1965 and the beginning of the diplomacy of forgiveness with Willy Brandt kneeling in front of the Warsaw Ghetto memorial in 1970.

Exploring the hidden history and painful memory of Stalinist and Nazi crimes

In the West, as if driven by a dissonance of memory, the young Germans of the 1968 generation demanded accountability for the crimes their forgetful grandparents had committed. This, in turn, was met by the revival of "historical negationism" in Western Europe, which focused on challenging the universally accepted narrative of the Holocaust, with the denial of the existence of the gas chambers. In France, the academic world was shaken notably by the activism of the negationist academic, Robert Faurisson, as well as, in a different way, by the controversy provoked by Hannah Arendt around the trial of Adolf Eichmann. Soon Germany also became confronted with a historians' quarrel (*Historikerstreit*) regarding the relativisation of the origins of Nazism with the work of Ernest Nolte[13] on the one hand, and, on the other, demands to denounce the Nazi criminals who found refuge in the post-war Germany with the blessing of the Allies. The movement to reactivate memory is symbolised by the slap in the face that was given to Chancellor Kurt Kissinger by Beate Klarsfeld, or by the exposure of the past of Kurt Waldheim, the Wehrmacht officer responsible for crimes in Yugoslavia and former secretary-general of the United Nations.

In the case of France, the ambiguities of the Gaullist narrative regarding the Resistance and the related responsibility of the Vichy government were tentatively put on the public agenda.[14] The French case is also interesting because of the intensification of the

---

13 Furet, F., Nolte, E. (eds.), 1998, *Fascisme et Communisme*, Paris: Plon, Commentaire.

14 The most heated debate centred on the narrative imposed by the victors of the Second World War concerning the period of the Vichy regime, which was characterised by servitude and criminality. This narrative was championed by General de Gaulle and the Communist Party. The shameful actions of the authorities under the occupying power were suppressed for decades, overshadowed by a heroic portrayal of "all-out resistance." The aim was to mend the divisions among the French by distorting history and overlooking its painful memories. See: Paxton, R., 1973, *La France de Vichy 1940-1944*, Paris: Seuil; Conan, E., Rousso, H., 1980, *Vichy, un passé qui ne passe pas,* Paris: Fayard.

work on memory politics. Several facts have shaken the foundations of French memory, destabilising the balance of identity. This was fertile soil for the birth of Pierre Nora's paradigm of "sites of memory". At that time, France was still digesting the effects of its 1968 Cultural Revolution and experiencing the oil crisis of the 1970s, which made it clear to the French that 30 years of post-war prosperity and carefree consumption had come to an end. It was also the end of an empire, with the breakaway of Algeria, the giving up of Vietnam for the sake of the Americans, followed by the victory of the Viet Cong and a somewhat chaotic withdrawal of France from its colonies in North Africa.

Nora and his team saw the need to appeal to a memory identity, to renew the glories of the past and the roots. The outcome of their work included a monumental list of sites of memory. The model spread to many countries, including Russia (under the direction of Georges Nivat). The paradigm was implemented wherever there was a social need driven by reconciliation efforts to repair bilateral relations. Hagen Schultz and Etienne François created an equally monumental inventory of Franco-German memorials. Hans Henning Hanf and Robert Traba compiled a large, four-volume, work on Polish-German memory sites (*lieux de memoire*). However, at the time of their work the wave of commemorations was not yet linked to international relations beyond the attempts to mitigate past conflicts in bilateral relations.[15]

Soviet Russia, on the other hand, is full of various memory claims from within. This process began during the so-called thaw of 1956, then developed widely in dissident literature, culminating in the Gulag phenomenon, under the major impact of Aleksandr Solzhenitsyn's *The Gulag Archipelago* or the songs of such bards as Alexander Galich, Vladimir Vysotsky and Bulat Okudzhava. In Russia, memory evidently served the civil society to reveal the historical truth about Stalinist Soviet crimes. After the brief thaw and Nikita Khrushchev's rise to power, despite or rather because of the

---

15 Mink, G., 2008, "Between reconciliation and the reactivation of past conflicts in Europe: rethinking social memory paradigms", *Czech Sociological Review*, (3), Prague.

dominance of Marxist-Leninist ideology, Soviet propaganda sought to consolidate the militarist model in collective memory.[16] Putin's discourse has been building up on this legacy. In fact, the discursive sources of Putinism, despite their diversity, clearly show to have two goals: the promotion of the idea of empire and the defence of the war. This is the common background of Sovietism, "orthodox" imperialism, Russian conservatism, pan-Slavism and Eurasianism. Putin can navigate this ideological mishmash because the collective memory of his supporters was shaped in the USSR and later reinforced by the Kremlin's propaganda outlets. The education of a Soviet citizen included military preparations, while their life was spent in various military-patriotic associations. The calendar was filled with military holidays, while commemorating those who fought in the Great Patriotic War was a civic duty. This contributed to the militarisation of collective Russian memory.

Memory, history and politics in the 1990s

Following the collapse of communism and the break-up of the two ideological blocs, commemorative events started to mushroom in Russia, opening up a wide repertoire of activities and large space for competing interpretations of the painful past of the 20th century. At that time, memory paradigms were linked to geopolitics, which did not get fundamentally changed in the analysis of the causes and consequences of the "Cold War". The geopolitical axis of the Cold War was that of East and West. This division partly persisted into the next period, as demands for historical memory shook the European institutions, including the European Parliament and other executive bodies of the European Union, but also the Parliamentary Assembly of the Council of Europe.

The 1990s and the first years of the 21st century saw an intensification of the exchange of blows between the actors representing the interests of national or state groups that considered themselves to have been robbed by the Second World War. The battle for

---

16 Mickiewicz, P., 2018, *Rosyjska myśl strategiczna i potencjał militarny w XXI wieku*, Warszawa: Wydawnictwo Naukowe PWN, pp. 27-28.

memory between Russia and the countries liberated from the communist bloc played out in discussions over the EU's asymmetric approach to memorialisation. This debate highlighted the need to reclassify communism as a totalitarian regime, on par with Hitler's regime. This battle resulted in an attempt to move from singular histories in a single museum narrative towards a transnational vision in a European House of History. Several transnational initiatives attacked the general design of the permanent exhibition in Brussels as ideological, Hegelian and neo-Marxist.[17] These initiatives highlighted the intentionality of the gaps in the museum's narrative.

Following a 2017 study visit to the exhibition dedicated to the history of communist crimes, or crimes of two totalitarianisms, an international group of historians and museum officials with the Platform of European Memory and Conscience published a comprehensive yet critical report.[18] These entrepreneurs of memory achieved real legislative success in the EU parliament. In 2009, the European Parliament established August 23rd as a day dedicated to commemorating the victims of the two totalitarian regimes. In line with this new approach, several EU member states banned elements of communist propaganda along with Nazi symbols. August 23rd has indeed a strong symbolic meaning; it was the date of the signing in 1939 of the Molotov-Ribbentrop Pact whose secret protocol postulated the invasion of Poland by the two totalitarian countries. This episode of European history remains to this day the most mobilising point in international memory relations between Russia and western historians, especially in declaring when the war began for the Russians.

In May 2009, Dmitry Medvedev, then Russian president, brought history to the level of an attribute of national "sovereignty" in reaction to the earlier mentioned symbolic initiatives undertaken by the EU and the Council of Europe to equate Stalinism (or even communism) with Nazism. On the 70th anniversary of the onset of

---

17 Ukielski, P., 2020, *"Memory of Poland, memory of neighbours, memory of Europe"*, *Political Theology*, p. 228.
18 *Ibidem*.

the Second World War and the signing of the German-Soviet pact, which Europe was preparing to commemorate then, Medvedev said: "One should not call black what is white, call one who was defending himself the aggressor." These words were accompanied by the creation of the Presidential Commission to Prevent Falsification of History Harmful to Russia's Interests to fight against the "falsification" of history.[19] In a style characteristic of police regimes built by autocrats, the Commission has been tasked with verifying any version of historical memory and historical narratives that would be incompatible with the official Kremlin interpretation. Its officials scrutinise the content of documents, media programmes and history-focused speeches, looking for alleged falsifications of facts and interpretations of "Russian history". The commission's prerogatives include preparing arguments to strengthen Russia's position in historical debates outside Russia. In 2012, Sergey Narishkin, the former head of the commission, became the head of the Russian Historical Society with a specific task of combating the so-called revisionism of Second World War history and proposing a unified version of school history textbooks. Many Russian historians protested at the time against the likely pressure from this supervisory body, which would legitimise arbitrary political censorship under the pretext of "tracking and combating misinterpretations of history abroad".

In the aftermath of the Cold War different interpretations of historical memory became possible. During this period Russia also saw the establishment of bilateral commissions of historians who worked on difficult matters and most painful aspects in bilateral histories. Such bodies included the Polish-Russian Group for Difficult Matters, which was chaired by Anatoly Torkunov on the Russian side and Adam Rotfeld on the Polish side. The goal of the group was to promote a positive message of neutralising contentious points in Polish-Russian history, which included the recogni-

---

19 Sieca-Kozlowski, E., 2024, *Poutine dans le texte*, CNRS Editions, p. 53.

tion of the 1940 massacre of the Polish elite. This war atrocity ordered by Stalin was carried out by the NKVD forces in the Katyn forest, near the city of Smolensk[20].

The existence of Memorial, a community organisation researching Stalinist crimes, was tolerated for three decades, from Yeltsin to Putin. However, the work of Memorial, beyond its actual task of uncovering painful history and reasserting the difficult memory of the Soviet violence, has also proved useful to Russian authorities. It created an illusion that Russia was open to critical historical analysis, and a democratic state. The moment the organisation was no longer needed (and even began to be defined as harmful), Memorial became labelled as a "foreign agent of influence". Its offices throughout Russia were first demolished, then closed. Many of Memorial's employees were persecuted or judicially harassed. Yet, Memorial did not cease to operate. It had to move its operations abroad and is based in democratic countries, outside Russia. However, even there it remains under hostile surveillance by Russian services.

Putin as an epigone and continuator of expansionist geopolitical ideas

Today, Putin seems to be an epigone and continuator of the vision put forward by Ratzel and Haushofer, but above all Stalin. Indeed, his views are basically the same as theirs, but he needs a different justification for his actions. For example, in June 2022 when he mentioned Peter the Great and his war against the Swedes, which lasted from 1700 to 1721, Putin said: "One can get the impression that he (Peter the Great—editor's note) was taking something away. He wasn't taking anything away, he was taking back what belonged to Russia." Putin then concluded with a smile: "Apparently it is now up to us to take back what belongs to Russia." A bit earlier, Putin added that: "Peter the Great went West, to Narva. Narva, in Estonia." It sounded as though Peter the Great was a personal role

---

[20] Rotfeld, A.D., Torkunov, A.V., 2010, *Białe plamy, czarne plamy: Sprawy trudne w relacjach polsko-rosyjskich (1918-2008)*, Warszawa: PISM, p. 907.

model for Putin. This also demonstrates the memory masquerade and reversal of symbolic meanings: Nazism, racism, antisemitism as well as references to the origins of Russia's greatness. With these symbols, Putin burdens not only Ukraine, but also the Baltic states.

Putin's portfolio of history and memory references does not yet end with European history. Since his speech delivered on 30 September 2022 to a gathering of Kremlin beneficiaries after the counting of the votes of the so-called democratic referenda, which allowed Putin to announce the annexation of four regions in Ukraine, the Russian president has been stressing the Huntingtonian-style conflict of civilisations. In so doing he has brought back to the generation of Russians who lived under Soviet rule an ideology which aims at making accusations against the colonial West, the American devil, and all perversions. The core of Putin's revisionist mobilisation discourse is not Russia's centuries-long history, as I quoted from Putin's 2021 essay in the introduction to this text, nor is it the conflict of civilisations. At the centre of his memory policy is the "Great Patriotic War".

Centrality of memory deposit – the "Great Patriotic War"

In the early 2000s, and even more since the 2014 illegal annexation of Crimea, a memory offensive has taken place, exploiting the topic of the 1941-45 Great Patriotic War against the Nazi regime, to the point that it has become a form of a mystical cult. In fact, in order to justify the reconstitution of the Russian empire by military means, Putin must not only have his army and generals behind him but also the population as a whole. It is a question of building legitimacy by resorting to the historical vision. Polish historian and expert on Russia, Bartłomiej Gajos, summed it up perfectly: "If Russia's leaders and the majority of the population had recognised that the war of 1941-1945 was not, after all, a war of liberation for the countries of Central and Eastern Europe, Tigran Keosajan, the husband of Margarita Simononian, the head of the former Russia Today, would not have been able to mobilise the viewers of his TV show to support the aggression against Ukraine by stating that those Russians who hold the 'No to war' slogans are at the same time saying 'no' to the Great Patriotic War."[21]

Putin's geopolitics of Russian conquest has nothing to do with historical truth verified by the academic approach. What counts is the mobilising effectiveness of the narrative. In order to achieve this effect, a certain type of memory must be used — a "reactive memory of the Russians". This is the memory of the Second World War. The Great Patriotic War is not a site of memory (*lieu de mémoire* in Pierre Nora's meaning of the term), even if it has several locations, such as the Battle of Stalingrad or the Soviet flag planted on the Reichstag in Berlin. It is rather, as I used to say, a "memory deposit".[22] Through its metaphorical connotations, this concept is more than *lieux de mémoire*. It is in fact a stock of resources that can be recycled in the present political or geopolitical contexts. Various actors draw on these "deposits of territorial or imagined events" as the symbolic material needed to sustain rivalries.

In the case of the Great Patriotic War, this is the living memory. This material is based, as Polish intellectual, Adam Michnik, metaphorically put it, on the "egoism of pain" connected to the human costs suffered by the Soviets, and on the exaltation of pride in victorious sacrifice. Although there remains an obstacle to these uses by Putin, namely the controversy over when the Great Patriotic War actually began and what actually happened between 1939 and 1941. Yet, the Kremlin narrative does not need to explain itself to the Russian population. Exploiting this *deposit of memory* is enough to gain the support of around 80 per cent of the population for Putin's strategy of including Ukraine in the empire. In fact, Russia's contemporary historical policy does not differ much from the historical policy of the Soviet Union. From this *deposit of history and historical memory*, selected are those periods and historical figures that suit the Kremlin's policy, satisfying its superpower interests. History is subject not only to selection, but also manipulation and

---

21 Smoleński, P, *op. cit.*, p. 41.
22 See: Mink, G., 2010, "Géopolitique, histoire et jeux de mémoire: pour une reconfiguration conceptuelle" in: Mink, G., Bonnard, P. (eds.), *Le Passé au Présent: Gisements mémoriels et actions historicisantes en Europe centrale et orientale*, Nanterre : Michel Houdiard Éditeur.

falsification. It is true that the circle of ideologues surrounding Putin has created a twisted hybrid in which there is room for celebrating the recapture of Moscow from the Poles, recognising the Tsar's family as martyrs, erecting a monument to the victims of Stalinism, but also red banners with a hammer and sickle, and complaints about the collapse of the Eastern Bloc. More than anything else the focus is on the topics that connect Russia with Eastern Europe during the Second World War.

In fact, it was already during the Second World War that the myth of the invincible and self-sacrificing Red Army, which dismissed certain inconvenient facts, was first created. The seizure of the Baltic republics or eastern parts of Poland, and especially the creation of the satellite socialist bloc after the war, pushed the experiences of the beginning of the war to the margins. These issues were only raised by the post-war émigrés from these states, often to the irritation of the societies of the free world in which they had found refuge. The great victory parade in the Red Square was among the iconic images of the victory in the war. So were the photographs of the Red Army liberating the Auschwitz extermination camp. It was supposedly the Soviet Union which destroyed the Third Reich in the first place; the involvement of the Western powers was in the background. The myth of Moscow as the conqueror of Hitler's regime and the recipient of Europe's eternal gratitude was developed in the following decades. It became the closing argument of all discussions, especially in Western European intellectual circles.[23] Many Westerners just could not see that the USSR was an aggressor, nor capable of exerting military pressure. Thus, Russian leaders after 1945 were able to gain semantic monopoly of the stigmatising vocabulary. Only they—and now, solely Vladimir Putin—had the authority to label someone a Nazi, a revisionist, or nostalgic for Hitler's regime. In Putin's view, everyone, except the USSR, was to blame for the outbreak of the Second World War.

Unquestionably, the Soviet Union, as a member of the anti-Hitler coalition, played a large role in the victory over Nazism. As

---

23 Thom, F., 2018, *Poutine ou l'obsession de la puissance*, Paris: Desclée de Brouwer.

a result, it suffered millions in losses of human life and terrible material losses. But this is not the whole truth. While the victory and its price was credited to the USSR, and later Russia, the nations that were most affected by the tragedy of this war were in fact Belarusians and Ukrainians. It may sound like a bit of an oversimplification, but we can daresay that while Moscow took the full credit of the victory over Nazism, it also put the blame for the wartime atrocities, which included collaboration with the Germans and complicity in the Holocaust, on the Baltic nations, Ukrainians and Belarusians. In other words, while victims and merits were presented as Soviet, guilt was linked to nationalists and fascists.[24] In addition, the repressions that befell the countries captured by the Red Army turned into a taboo.

Putin is all the more convinced of the effectiveness of his historical narrative the more he bolsters its arguments with his own family history. In so doing, he applies "communicative memory". We could see it well in his well-known text titled "75 years since the Great Victory. On a shared responsibility to history and the future", which was published in English.[25] In it Putin wrote:

> "They usually say that the war has left a deep imprint on every family's history. (...) For my parents, the war meant the terrible ordeals of the Siege of Leningrad where my two-year old brother Vitya died. It was the place where my mother miraculously managed to survive. My father, despite being exempt from active duty, volunteered to defend his hometown. He made the same decision as millions of Soviet citizens (...) and was severely wounded".[26]

This quote alone would suffice to establish a link with current events. Indicatively, Putin's text is addressed to Western readers, as if to convince them of the intergenerational basis that legitimises the "special operation" against Ukraine.

---

24 Ruchniewicz, K., 2022, "Putin nowym Hitlerem? Upadek mitu Moskwy jako pogromcy nazizmu", *Gazeta Wyborcza*, 9 March.
25 Putin, V., 2000, "75th Anniversary of the Great Victory: Shared Responsibility to History and our Future", 19 June. http://kremlin.ru/events/president/news/63527 (Accessed: 19 August 2024).
26 *Ibidem*.

"Such values as selflessness, patriotism, love for their home, their family and Motherland remain fundamental and integral to the Russian society to this day."[27] In his narrative, Putin creates a picture of a nation that is united by historical experience and ready to make the greatest sacrifices: "People of my age and I believe it is important that our children, grandchildren and great-grandchildren understand the torment and hardships their ancestors had to endure (...) Yes, they were defending their homes, children, loved ones and families, but more importantly, they shared the love for their homeland, their Motherland."[28] Putin emphasises social creativity which he deems necessary for the constant renewal of the Great Patriotic War "memory deposit". In the same article, he points to innovative grassroots initiatives such as the "Immortal Regiment", writing "This is the memory march that symbolised our gratitude, as well as the living connection and the blood ties between generations. Millions of people come out to the streets carrying the photographs of their relatives who defended their Motherland and defeated the Nazis. This means that their lives, the ordeals and sacrifices they endured, as well as the Victory that they passed to us will never be forgotten."[29]

Naturally, much has changed in recent decades. Central and Eastern European states have regained independence and are now a voice in historical debates. Yet, Moscow still sees the defeat of Hitler's regime as its primary right to hold a unique position in the system of international affairs. The Kremlin also appears to have an allergic reaction to anything that challenges the belief in Russia's inherent merits and its self-granted right to eternal gratitude.

How to prevent the erosion of living memory and not lose the historical legitimacy of the war?

Putin is aware that the passing of the Second World War generation means the weakening of living memory, whose instrumentalisation

---

27   Ibidem.
28   Ibidem.
29   Ibidem.

has allowed him to legitimise his international strategy and maintain the cohesion of the Russian nation. Thus to maintain it, Putin is now trying to replace "communicative memory" with "institutional memory". He explains his convictions as follows: "Neglecting the lessons of history inevitably leads to a harsh payback. We will firmly uphold the truth based on documented historical facts. We will continue to be honest and impartial about the events of the Second World War. This includes a large-scale project to establish Russia's largest collection of archival records, film and photo materials about the history of World War II and the pre-war period.[30]

As if that were not enough, the version of history presented in the official school textbook, which was distributed with wide and orchestrated efforts, is fully faithful to Putin's writings which he used to justify Russia's aggression against Ukraine and other imperialist attempts. The textbook was presented in Moscow in August 2022. It is authored by Vladimir Medinsky, chairman of the Interdepartmental Commission on History Education, Anatoly Torkunov, rector of the Moscow State Institute of International Relations, and Aleksandr Chubarian, long-time director of the Institute of General History. The preparatory works did not include any discussions about the content of the book neither with representatives of the academia or teaching organisations. There was also no information about who was behind this publication. In fact, those who should have been in the know were not even aware that such a textbook was being prepared. When we look at this textbook, we see that each of the chapters ends with "conclusions". There, pupils can read what they have learnt in the chapter they had worked on. For example, the "conclusions" in the chapter on the Great Patriotic War read as follows: "More than 4,000 monuments and commemorative plaques have been erected in Europe as a mark of respect for the fallen soldiers of the Red Army (...) But today's generation of Europeans does not remember or know the horrors of war (...)

---

30 For Russian historians this means an obligation to treat historical sources exclusively according to Putin's doxa.

This fact is being exploited by politicians. In Eastern European states, nationalists refer to the monuments commemorating the Soviet liberators as "symbols of the Soviet occupation" and demand their demolition (...) The violation and destruction of Soviet monuments is a betrayal of their own ancestors who, in 1945, welcomed Soviet soldiers with tears in their eyes as saviours from fascist barbarism."[31] This instrumentalisation of the last global conflict played a key role in the Russian society's acceptance of their country's military aggression against Ukraine. A journalist with the French daily *Le Monde*, and a former correspondent in Moscow, described this sentiment as follows: "Around the year 2012, a new slogan had emerged and became widely accepted by the population: no longer the traditional 'Never again', only 'We can do it again'. Thousands of Russians then wrote 'To Berlin', 'To Washington', 'To Lisbon' on their cars or children's prams transformed into cardboard tanks. Apparently, the cult of the 1945 victory, which was coined during the Soviet era, has been transformed into a cult of a war."[32]

Conclusions

Since Vladimir Putin became president of the Russian Federation for the third time in 2012, the memory of the Red Army's achievements has become the cornerstone of the official interpretation of Russian history. Its goal is to establish a permanent and mythical identity for the Russian Federation as that of a nation that can only be a victim to aggressors who, in turn, can only be Nazis. Can we say that since 2014, that is, when Russia openly started aggression against a democratic and sovereign country, brutally undermining international law and ridiculing the opinion of the vast majority of the international community, the myth of the USSR/Russia as the

---

31 Radziwon, M., 2023, "Specjalna operacja podręcznikowa: Zgniły Zachód i nasz wspaniały kraj", *Gazeta Wyborcza*, 29 September.
32 Vitkine, B., 2023, "En Russie, derrière le mythe de la victoire de 1945, le culte de la guerre sans fin". *Le Monde*. Available at: https://www.lemonde.fr/idees/article/2023/05/09/en-russie-derriere-le-mythe-de-la-victoire-de-1945-le-culte-de-la-guerre-sans-fin_6172574_3232.html (Accessed: 19 August 2024).

liberator from Hitler's regime, the defender of peace, saviour of Europe, has finally been coming to an end? This question is now being increasingly asked. The confronting versions of history and references to human memory have also increasingly been used to undermine the falsified narratives of Russian ideologues.

Increasingly, we are also seeing an interpretation of the course and consequences of the Second World War that is not so much presented as a joint defence of civilisation by Western allies and the USSR, but as a struggle between two of the worst regimes in human history, where one used cooperation with democracies as an asset in its subsequent expansion. In this context, Putin's pseudo-historical quibbles and his sense of entitlement to judge today's Ukraine and Ukrainians (and probably all other nations of the post-Soviet states) and the totality of Ukraine's thousand-year history, seem insane. Yet, it is a part of the wider and aggressive war campaign. Admittedly, the West is also not homogeneous when it comes to historical narratives and therefore has been finding it difficult to resist the pro-Russian propaganda.

Russia must be judged not by the war which ended almost 80 years ago, but by the one it started in February 2022. In it, it has been using methods which put it in line with such aggressors as the Third Reich. Russia had already practised these methods in Chechnya, against Georgia and in Moldova where it supported the Transnistrian separatists. It also tested them in Syria and has now been applying them in Ukraine. It is telling that in various caricatures published around the world, Putin's face often resembles that of Hitler. This makes the message about the nature of his regime more universal and better understood by different audiences. It can also be argued that Putin needed historical excuses to justify launching a geopolitical row. However, once the cannons started to fire, his historical discourse became blurred and incoherent. Perhaps this is because the memory of the sacrifice that was paid by Soviet Russia and its dependent Ukrainian population from 1941 to 1945 has now revitalised the reflection on the meaning of lives that are being lost, on both sides, also as a result of the war in Ukraine. Will this lead to a change in the Russian perception of conquest and its historical background? Unfortunately, as of today, such a hypothesis seems very unlikely.

Nato's Enlargement, Not Expansion
The Ultimate Escape from the Soviet World?

Wojciech Michnik

Russia's war against Ukraine has reignited the debate on the role and effectiveness of the North Atlantic Treaty Organization (NATO) in ensuring security in Central and Eastern Europe. For many countries in the region, which were former Soviet republics or members of the Warsaw Pact, joining NATO was not only seen as a validation of their security interests in a new strategic landscape but also a symbolic return to the Western world and an escape from the Soviet sphere of influence.[1] However, NATO's enlargement following the end of the Cold War faced strong opposition from Russia and criticism from certain Western academics who believed it could overextend the Alliance and provoke Russia.[2] Nevertheless, the newly admitted NATO member states in Central and Eastern Europe were determined to fully integrate into the Alliance's defence and military structures, demonstrating their commitment to enhancing their security and proving the sceptics wrong. As these states also joined the European Union (EU), it appeared that they were successfully moving away from their post-Soviet past. However, not all countries in the region experienced the same favourable circumstances, as seen in the cases of Georgia, Moldova, and particularly Ukraine. The war in Ukraine, starting with the annexation of Crimea in 2014 and culminating in Russia's full-scale invasion in 2022, revealed the ruthlessness of Russia as the direct successor to the Soviet Union and the heavy price that the Ukrainian society had to pay for seeking independence from the "old sphere of influence".

---

1   Kupiecki, R., 2016, *Organizacja Traktatu Północnoatlantyckiego*, Warszawa: Ministerstwo Spraw Zagranicznych.
2   Brown M., 1995, "The Flawed Logic of NATO Expansion", *Survival*, (37) 1, pp. 35–36; Kennan, G. F., 1997," A Fateful Error", *New York Times*, 5 February; Waltz, K. N., 2000, "NATO expansion: A realist's view", *Contemporary Security Policy*, 21 (2), pp. 23-38.

This chapter aims to revive the discussion on NATO's enlargement in the new context of Russia's war in Ukraine, while also highlighting the different narratives put forth by scholars and policymakers regarding NATO's eastward enlargement.[3] Some of the questions addressed below include: 1) What has been the impact of the post-Cold War NATO enlargement for the states of the Central and Eastern Europe; 2) How has Russia's War in Ukraine (2014-2024) changed the debate over NATO enlargement (especially in the context of future accession of Ukraine and other states in the region); and 3) Why in the context of the war, enlargement could be seen as an ultimate validation for escaping the colonial sphere of influence, symbolised first by the Soviet Union and then by Putin's Russia?

From these vantage points, the end of the Soviet world is not only seen as the definitive failure of attempts by the Kremlin to recreate it in any form but also as an independent decision by states (former Soviet republics and satellite countries) to seek protection under the NATO umbrella while distancing themselves from the aftermath of the post-Soviet era. Additionally, I argue in this chapter that the term "enlargement" is more precise and less politically charged than "expansion" when referring to NATO's inclusion of new member states. "Enlargement" implies the growth of a community of like-minded states, while "expansion" may carry connotations of aggressive behaviour. Although these terms are often used interchangeably, I delve into recent scholarly and policy debates to explore why this issue goes beyond mere semantics.

---

3   Goldgeier, J., Shifrinson J., 2023, "Evaluating NATO Enlargement: Scholarly Debates, Policy Implications, and Roads not Taken" in: Goldgeier J., Shifrinson, J. (eds.), *Evaluating NATO Enlargement: From Cold War Victory To The Russia-Ukraine War*, London: Palgrave Macmillan, pp. 1-42.

The end of the "sphere of influence"?

In 1989, then US president, George H. W. Bush, envisioned Europe as "whole, free and at peace", an idea embraced deeply by generations of Euro-Atlanticists.[4] More than three decades after the fall of the Soviet Union, Europe and its Transatlantic allies in Canada and the United States still face the European continent as a "liberal work in progress" or even rather an unfulfilled promise' than "mission accomplished".[5] In short, an idea of "Europe whole and free" turned not only to be part of a liberal internationalists agenda but also a tangible plan for securing the continent that brought totalitarian regimes; global conflicts and genocides upon the world. Therefore, by broadening the sphere of liberal democracies and providing new ones with security guarantees and economic stability, the European continent was meant to become more peaceful and stable.

By extension, the same purpose and principles for the Central and Eastern European states—those which suffered from the protracted Soviet occupations and interferences—would allow countries of the region to fully regain its political independence and escape shadows of the colonial and imperial Soviet World, that had dominated over this part of Europe for more than 70 years. For Estonians, Poles or Ukrainians, among others, even though the enlargement was not seen as an anti-Soviet or anti-Russian project, indirect implications of alignment with the free world in the West seemed rather straightforward. Consequently, enlarging NATO (and the European Union) into once Soviet-captive states of Central and Eastern Europe would not only depart from the Cold War divisions but simultaneously create a new security and political order in Europe.

There is no denying that this vision did not fully materialise, partly because of the lack of the coherent European strategy (both

---

4   Bush, G. H.W., 2019, "A Europe Whole and Free", Mainz, May. https://usa.usembassy.de/etexts/ga6-890531.htm (Accessed: 4 May 2024).
5   Kupiecki, R., 2019, "Europe Whole and Free: Mission Accomplished or an Unfulfilled Promise?" in: Dębski, S., Hamilton, D. S. (eds.), *Europe Whole and Free: Vision and Reality*, Warszawa: PISM.

within the EU and NATO) to implement it, but predominantly due to an aggressive and reversionistic polices of the Russian Federation. As early as in 2008 (and later in 2014) the Kremlin made it quite evident that it rejects the European security architecture and pursues a neo-imperialistic policy to recreate some kind of Soviet-style sphere of influence in Central and Eastern Europe. Hence, Russia's war in Georgia and annexation of Crimea "jolted many –although not all — Europeans out of their dream that the future belonged to 'civilian' powers." As Daniel Hamilton indicated, Russia sent a clear three-fold message: hard power remains important; borders can indeed be changed by force; and Russia is not somehow 'lost in transition,' as it is going its own way."[6] Yet, with Russia's invasion of Ukraine in 2022 and subsequent full-scale war, many countries in the region, that were once Soviet republics or members of the Warsaw Pact, saw NATO's enlargement eastward not only as a validation of their security interests in a new strategic landscape and a symbolic return to the Western world[7] but also, and most importantly, as an ultimate escape from Russia's "sphere of influence".

It is this old-fashioned geopolitical perspective of "spheres of influence" created, and recreated by tsars, communist secretary generals or the "new Russian dictator", which brings the contemporary Russian Federation so close to the Soviet world. And with the ongoing war in Ukraine as a grim reminder, there is little doubt for the societies in Georgia, Moldova or Ukraine what would be more beneficial for them: to be a part of an enlarged NATO (and European Union) or stay outside.

Enlarging rather than expanding NATO

From the early 1990s the issue of enlarging NATO eastward and including former members of the Warsaw Pact into the Alliance brought intense debates and controversies. Some of them were based on the policy-oriented calculus of NATO member states and

---

6   Hamilton, D. S., 2019, "Europe: Whole and Free or Fractured and Anxious?" in: Dębski, S., Hamilton D. S. (eds.), *op.cit.*, p. 342.
7   Kupiecki, R., 2016, *op.cit.*

their prospective allies (Brzezinski, 1994), while others reflected rather the attitudes of the academic circles in the area of international relations. James Goldgeier and Joshua Shifrinson, who are the scholarly editors of perhaps the most definite volume on NATO enlargement up to date—with their 2023 volume titled *Evaluating NATO Enlargement*—noted that the enlargement of NATO into Central and Eastern Europe has been one of the key aspects of the post-Cold War US foreign policy and European security. In the 1990s, when the idea of NATO enlargement was initially discussed, its proponents put forth several interconnected arguments, suggesting that enlargement would contribute to stabilizing Europe beyond Germany and promote the process of spreading democracy and free-market principles. At the same time, enlargement critics argued that it would oblige NATO's current members to defend several Central and Eastern European countries with uncertain strategic significance, potentially provoking tensions with Russia.[8] The neorealist scholars also criticised NATO's enlargement to the East, viewing it as a significant mistake in consolidating Western power against Moscow and a primary source of tension between NATO and Russia.[9] According to their perspective, enlargement would potentially generate the very threat that NATO was aimed to defend its members against. For instance, following Russia's annexation of Crimea in 2014, John Mearsheimer depicted NATO's efforts to strengthen relations with Ukraine and the possibility of Ukrainian membership in the Alliance as the root cause of the Russian-Ukrainian conflict.[10] From the neorealist viewpoint, Russia's invasion of Ukraine largely stemmed from NATO's "expansion", prompting Moscow to act.

In the 1990s, critics expressed concerns that the NATO's eastern enlargement, which took place in 1999 and 2004, would not only provoke Russia, spark a new Cold War but also fail to support democratic consolidation in Central Europe. However, subsequent

---

8   Goldgeier, J., Shifrinson J., *op.cit.*, pp. 1-2.
9   Ratti, L., 2023, "Realism" in: *In Research Handbook on NATO*, Cheltenham, UK: Edward Elgar Publishing, p. 28.
10 Mearsheimer, J., 2014, "Why the Ukraine Crisis Is the West's Fault: The Liberal Delusions That Provoked Putin", *Foreign Affairs*, 93 (5), pp. 77-89.

events have contradicted these predictions, including the democracy-hampering argument in the region. For instance, in Poland, NATO not only fostered a civilian consensus endorsing democratic oversight of the armed forces in line with NATO standards but also undermined arguments for defence self-sufficiency rooted in Poland's historical vulnerability and foreign influence. According to Rachel Epstein, these trends of democratisation and de-nationalisation have played a role in stabilizing post-communist Europe. Moreover, an evaluation of the seven nations that joined NATO in 2004 similarly suggests NATO's influence has been significant in various ways across these countries.[11] Unsurprisingly, the majority of those states which preferred NATO and the backing of the US military to serve as their primary security option are found in the region of Central and Eastern Europe. Nations neighbouring Ukraine, like Poland, Romania, and Slovakia, as well as those with significant Russian-speaking populations or borders with Russia, such as Latvia, Lithuania, and Estonia, have collectively urged the European Union and NATO for heightened security measures, placing greater emphasis on their NATO membership."[12]

This does not indicate that the critics of NATO eastern enlargement did not ask valid questions or raised important policy implications of admitting new states to the Alliance. Charles Kupchan, for instance, while quite sceptical about whether NATO's enlargement's added value for the United States addressed significant questions from both policy and academic perspectives, including what course of action "should NATO pursue now that its formal enlargement is proceeding? Should the eastward spread of NATO stop with the admission of Poland, Hungary and the Czech Republic? Or should it continue? If so, how, when and where should successive waves of enlargement take place? As NATO evolves, what

---

11   Epstein, R. A., 2005, "NATO Enlargement and the Spread of Democracy: Evidence and Expectations", *Security Studies*, 14 (1), pp. 63–105.
12   Johns, M., 2016, "Caught between Russia and NATO. The EU during and after the Ukrainian Crisis" in: Black, J.L., Johns, M. (eds.), *The Return of the Cold War: Ukraine, The West and Russia*, Routledge, p. 34.

should be the relationship between Europe's own process of integration and the development of the Atlantic security order?"[13] One does not need to be a NATO enlargement critic to find these questions relevant for cohesion of the Alliance and long-lasting Euro-Atlantic security. Yet, what some of the critics of NATO's eastward enlargement omitted or failed to see is that in this particular stance the agency of the states in Central and Eastern Europe as independent states that could decide on their own fate, was completely ignored. After all, if the basis of the argument about NATO's "expansion" was boiled down to the balance of power debate and maintaining best possible relations between the United States and Western European powers with Russia, why Poland or Romania, not to mention Georgia or Ukraine, should be even involved in building a joint Euro-Atlantic security? Unsurprisingly, these arguments were predominantly raised by realism representatives in international relations.[14] One of the direct policy-oriented consequences of framing NATO's enlargement in the "expansionist" terms was to put a responsibility on the Alliance and the new member states for any real and prospective destabilisations of the European security architecture.

While there is still no consensus in the debate about the consequences of NATO's eastward enlargement and the academic debate is ongoing, there are several articles that challenge the "NATO expansion" claims that perceived the decision to enlarge the Alliance as a move that is both provocative from Russia's perspective and harmful to NATO members. For example, Kimberley Marten admits that even though there is no question that NATO's geographic enlargement "was a major irritant to Russian leaders and contributed to the decline of the overall relationship between Russia and the West" there was also "little evidence that enlargement actually threatened Russia. Instead, NATO enlargement was a

---

13 Kupchan, Ch. A., 2000, "The origins and future of NATO enlargement", *Contemporary Security Policy*, 21 (2), p. 127.
14 Waltz, K. N., 2000, "NATO expansion: A realist's view", *Contemporary Security Policy*, 21 (2), pp. 23-38.

marker for Russia's declining status."[15] If putting Russia's rhetoric and propaganda aside, it seems evident that for Moscow the primary concern was not that NATO enlargement posed a threat to Russia's survival or prosperity, but rather a threat to its regional and global power and prestige. The issue at hand was Moscow's diminishing stature on the world stage and the perception that the United States (and its European allies) could act without any consideration to Russia's objections. NATO enlargement evidently epitomised Russia's weakened status and exacerbated these concerns.[16] Alexander Lanoszka in an article titled "Thank Goodness for NATO Enlargement" analyses the issue of agency of Central and Eastern European states and focuses on the regional geopolitical calculus while arguing that the 2022 war in Ukraine would have escalated into a broader conflict if not for NATO's prior enlargement and continued presence in Central Eastern Europe.[17] Considering the agency of the states in Central and Eastern Europe, most of which have liberated themselves from the shackles of the Soviet system, we can argue that the accession to NATO has clearly been their most significant achievement in their post-Cold war security policies and a necessary step on their path to integration with Western political and economic institutions. In practical terms, since Russia's full-scale invasion of Ukraine in 2022 the societies living in these states have showed that they appreciate membership in NATO even more. In Poland, for instance, trust in NATO reached an exceptionally high level, with 94 per cent of the respondents in an opinion poll survey carried out in the spring of 2022 by the national polling organisation, CBOS, supporting Poland's membership in the Alliance, which was a significant increase compared to just two years prior, when support for Poland's NATO membership hovered around 85 per cent.[18]

---

15 Marten, K., 2023, "NATO Enlargement: Evaluating its Consequences in Russia" in: Goldgeier, J., Shifrinson, J. (eds.), *op.cit.*, p. 212.
16 Marten, K., 2020, "NATO Expansion in Retrospect", *H-Diplo/ISSF Policy Roundtable* XII-1, 19 October, https://issforum.org/to/ir12-1 (Accessed: 15 May 2024).
17 Lanoszka, A., *op.cit.*, pp. 307-340.
18 Michnik, W., 2024, "How was NATO won? Assessing Poland's record in NATO after 25 years" *New Eastern Europe*, 25 March, https://neweasterneurope.eu/20

Tellingly, the latest NATO enlargement into the Nordic states adds another layer to the "enlargement versus expansion" debate. In both cases of Finland and Sweden, Russia's aggressive policies which peaked with the invasion of Ukraine, forced both states to change their long-standing neutrality and apply for NATO membership. For Finland, a state which experienced the Soviet invasion in 1939-40 and later struggled with Moscow's attempts to hamper its independence, 2022 was a watershed year. As a direct consequence of Russia's full-scale invasion of Ukraine Finland submitted its formal application to join NATO and became the 31st NATO member on 4 April 2023. This ground-breaking decision of the Finnish government was a product of the transition of its political elite that recognised the importance of NATO membership and the changing social attitudes regarding the country's security needs. The change in public opinion on NATO membership was striking, increasing from 24 per cent support for Finland's NATO membership in October 2021 to 85 per cent in October 2022.[19] Overall just like in 1999 also with Finland and Sweden joining the Alliance, NATO has been enlarged, not expanded. Both states have accessed the Alliance willingly (as all member states do), predominantly as a response to Russia's expansionist policies which led it to a territorial conquest into the independent state of Ukraine. If there was ever a decisive argument about using the term "enlargement" over "expansion" for NATO's policy, paradoxically, Moscow delivered it with the full-scale invasion of Ukraine.

Finally, one can argue that the term "expansion" has a subtly different connotation than the term "enlargement". While the former suggests that the process of bringing new members to NATO could be associated with aggressive moves of taking others' territory (as in a "territorial expansion"), the latter presents it for what it is—a mutual and consensual decision to increase the number of

---

24/03/25/how-was-nato-won-assessing-polands-record-in-nato-after-25-years/ (Accessed: 24 May 2024).

19 Black, J., Kleberg, Ch. and Silfversten, E., 2024, *NATO Enlargement Amidst Russia's War in Ukraine: How Finland and Sweden Bolster the Transatlantic Alliance*, Santa Monica, CA: RAND Corporation, https://www.rand.org/pubs/perspectives/PEA3236-1.html (Accessed: 24 May 2024).

NATO member states. Expansion might indicate a militaristic nature of the endeavour (act of spreading out), while enlargement simply promises "increasing in size".[20] This difference might seem marginal but in the heated debates about NATO post-Cold War enlargement it actually matters. Many of the critical sources on NATO enlargement refer to it as an "expansion". Interestingly, in a discourse about the European Union accession policies, the term "expansion" rarely occurs, as the process is referred to as the (EU) enlargement. In practical dimensions, NATO's Open Door policy which had brought the states of Central and Eastern Europe into the Alliance was not aimed at geopolitical "expansion" but rather of enlargement of NATO's political functions. In other words, NATO "was thus about not geopolitics, but democratic values."[21]

From "frenemies" to Cold War 2.0

In the aftermath of the Cold War, the West often treated Russia with hope, believing that it could contribute to the enhancement of pan-European security. While being a difficult partner in the 1990s, Russia was seen as part of a solution to the challenges that Europe faced, not recognised to be a part of the problem. This tendency seemed not to have change much until the 2008 Russo-Georgian War, which should have been the first wake-up call for the West. However, already the first round of NATO's eastward enlargement which took place in 1999 showed that from the early stages this process was a point of contention between NATO and the Russian Federation.

For the post-Cold War NATO, the eastward enlargement at first posed a large, to some controversial, question mark only to later become a strategic goal to broaden security and peace in Europe. Yet, it does not mean that this new situation was equally appreciated by all member states, not to mention Russia. As Michael Rühle pointed out "the twin goals of admitting Central and Eastern

---

20   Online Etymology Dictionary, 2024, "Enlargement" 10 April, https://www.etymonline.com (Accessed: 24 May 2024).
21   Rynning, S., 2024, *NATO. From Cold War to Ukraine, a History of the World's Most Powerful Alliance*, New Haven: Yale University Press, p. 289.

European countries into NATO while, at the same time, developing a 'strategic partnership' with Russia were far less compatible in practice than in theory."[22]

The Russian Federation, at least in the 1990s, although not as hostile to NATO as the Soviet Union, did not accept the new order in which it was not Moscow, but Washington DC, Brussels, Berlin and (eventually) Central and Eastern European states that would play key roles in establishing and maintaining the security architecture in Europe. Yet, the lack of that acceptance did not mean that NATO was (as some have tried to argue) the cause of all ills for Russia. As scholar of alliances Alexander Lanoszka emphasises: "NATO enlargement did not cause Russia's authoritarianism and aggressive foreign policy choices and did not make cooperation with Russia impossible." He indicates that numerous forecasts regarding Russia's behaviour after NATO enlargement have largely proven inaccurate. Contrary to expectations, NATO enlargement did not stifle Russian democracy in its infancy. Instead, other significant decisions, including those made by Western policymakers in the 1990s, bear more responsibility. In other words, Russia did not adopt its nationalistic, expansionist or anti-Western stances as a result of NATO enlargement. In fact, evidence indicates that the anti-Western trajectory of Putin's regime had predated NATO enlargement while the roots of Russian authoritarianism primarily stem from internal factors within the Russian society.[23]

The Kremlin obviously saw these developments differently. It viewed the so-called "post-Soviet space" through geopolitical lenses, treating the former Soviet republics as "buffer zones" that should make Russia feel more secure. Consequently, one of the main foreign policy goals that the Kremlin had identified and decided to implement was to keep and maintain these buffer zones. In Moscow's view, this security belt has yet been hampered primarily because "NATO expansion in 1999 and 2004 has brought the anti-Soviet alliance to Russia's borders". Following the same logic,

---

22 Rühle, M., 2014, "NATO Enlargement and Russia: Discerning Fact from Fiction", *American Foreign Policy Interests*, 36 (4), p. 237.
23 Lanoszka, A., *op.cit.*, p. 312.

Russia's desire to re-establish control over the post-Soviet space increased "the probability of discordant relations and conflict." (...) as Russia "wished to dominate the region for energy monopolisation, security, and prestige."[24] One of the consequences of such an approach, was the reoccurring theme in Russia's policy of treating enlargement as a bargaining chip in relations with the West and particularly with NATO.

The NATO-Russia Founding Act signed in 1997 was a document which stipulated the principles of mutual cooperation and establishment of a joint institution—the NATO-Russia Permanent Joint Council.[25] According to Sten Rynning this act was a cornerstone of the post-Cold War NATO. It defined and outlined contractual obligations in support of "a lasting and inclusive peace" as NATO offered to continue its transformation into "a broader and more political, open, and partnered organisation (...) while Russia agreed to continue its democratisation and economic transformation."[26] Russia's goal was to conclude an agreement, in a form of international treaty, that would guarantee that NATO's nuclear forces, troops or equipment would not be deployed, or stationed, on the territories of the Alliance's new member states.[27] NATO, on the other hand, wanted to have a politically binding agreement, not a treaty, which is what prevailed in the end. The Alliance thus proposed to enlarge politically rather than militarily. It was to grow bigger, but also softer. Russia was to keep its side of the bargain as well. NATO's precaution rested on its assertion that there was no anticipated necessity to modify the Alliance's nuclear strategy in the future, and its plans for conventional forces were tailored for the present and "foreseeable future."[28] Some commentators and an-

---

24 Maness, R., 2021, "Death by a Thousand Cuts: Is Russia Winning the Information War with the West", in: Cross, M., Karolewski, I. P. (eds.), *European-Russian Power Relations in Turbulent Times*, Ann Arbor: University of Michigan Press, p. 166.
25 Kupiecki, R., Menkiszak, M. (eds.), 2020, *Documents talk. NATO–Russia relations after the Cold War*, Warszawa: PISM, p. 10.
26 Rynning, S., *op.cit.*, p. 289.
27 Kupiecki, R., Menkiszak, M., *op.cit.*, p. 23.
28 Rynning, S., *op.cit.*, p. 290.

alysts argued that the Founding Act might have been too favourable to the Russian side. Henry Kissinger, for example, while sympathetic to the idea of enlargement, argued that NATO had conceded too much to Russia in exchange for its reluctant acceptance of the Alliance's enlargement, which Russia had limited ability to hinder.[29] Ultimately, with the annexation of Crimea in 2014 and the full-scale invasion in Ukraine in 2022, Russia made the NATO-Russia Founding Act completely obsolete. Retrospectively, we can say that perhaps it was too naïve and idealistic on the part of the West to assume that what Russia, under Boris Yeltsin as president agreed to would be honoured in Vladimir Putin's "New Russia". Yet, in the 1990s the political atmosphere favoured the thinking that NATO's aspirations to enlarge eastwards could not come at the cost of antagonizing Moscow. Whether it was a mistake on the part of the Alliance in general and the United States in particular (Washington DC was a main force behind NATO-Russia Founding Act) remains both debatable and controversial issue until today.

The first post-Cold War enlargement marked the beginning of a process of the opening of the Alliance's doors to the countries that were formerly part of the socialist bloc and were undergoing democratic transformations in the 1990s. Poland, the Czech Republic and Hungary's successful accession to NATO in 1999 was therefore not only seen as an achievement of these three states but also as a test of how former Warsaw Pact countries would integrate into the Euro-Atlantic security structures. Becoming a NATO member state also paved the way for Poland and other states in the region to later join the European Union, a process that would have been much more difficult, maybe even impossible, to complete had there been no security umbrella provided by NATO membership.[30]

While in the Cold War period NATO was mainly understood as an organisation created and committed to the defence of the West, in the course of the post-Cold War enlargement, the Alliance "arguably became an instrument that contributed to spreading and

---

29 Dodd, T., 1997, "NATO Enlargement", Research Paper 97/51, 8 May, House of Commons Library, https://researchbriefings.files.parliament.uk/documents/RP97-51/RP97-51.pdf. p. 32.
30 Michnik, W., *op.cit.*

supporting Western principles (democracy and liberal economy) and norms (international law) as well as to overcoming the post-Communist legacy in Central, Eastern, and South-Eastern Europe."[31] After 1999, the next rounds of NATO's enlargement by post-communist states included: Bulgaria, Estonia, Latvia, Lithuania, Romania, Slovakia and Slovenia in 2004; Albania and Croatia in 2009; Montenegro in 2017; and North Macedonia in 2020.[32] Seeing these developments from a time perspective and contrary to the opinions of some enlargement sceptics and critics we can now argue that overall NATO enlargements have created a more stable and secure Europe and a more peaceful Euro-Atlantic space. Since joining NATO in 1999, the new Central and Eastern European member states have sought to demonstrate that they are reliable allies by implementing political and military reforms and actively participating in allied operations.

Since 2008, Russia's aggressive policies toward its neighbours began to threaten their security and territorial integrity, prompting the governments in Central and Eastern Europe to place greater emphasis on defence, including collective defence, within NATO. Importantly, these states were among those NATO members that advocated for a more sceptical approach toward Russia and a firmer return to the Alliance's traditional defence and deterrence posture. These attempts were not always appreciated by other members of the Alliance, especially Germany and France that in the pre-2022 era advocated for dialogue or even "strategic dialogue" with Moscow.[33] Unfortunately, the illegal annexation of Crimea in 2014 first and the full-scale invasion into Ukraine second validated

---

31 Gotkowska, J., 2022, "Poland" in: Tardy, T. (ed.), *The Nations of NATO*, Oxford: Oxford University Press, p. 267.
32 Menon, R., 2022, "A new and better security order for Europe", 15 February, https://www.defensepriorities.org/explainers/a-new-and-better-security-or der-for-europe (Accessed: 24 May 2024).
33 Kunz, B., 2021, "There is No 'Europe': Disagreements within NATO are not Solely Transatlantic and Pertain to the Fundamentals of European Security" in: Blessing J., Kjellström Elgin, K., Ewers-Peters, N. M. (eds.), *NATO 2030: Towards a New Strategic Concept and Beyond*, Washington DC: Brookings Institution Press, https://sais.jhu.edu/kissinger/nato-2030-towards-new-strategic-concept-and -beyond (Accessed: 20 May 2024), pp. 165-167.

the fears of Russia that had been articulated by the states that had once been under Soviet rule. It also made Poland and other NATO states in the region play a key role in the shaping of the Alliance's responses, especially in the sphere of deterrence and defence. As a result, the role of NATO's so-called eastern flank became better recognised by other members of the Alliance. This role has further expanded after Russia's full-scale aggression against Ukraine in 2022. Since that moment on, Poland, the Baltic states and Romania became the so-called frontline states and are now playing a significant role in fortifying NATO's defence efforts.

Beyond the Soviet world and *Russkiy Mir*

In geopolitical and often simplistic terms the debate about NATO enlargement and escape from the Soviet world could be brought down to getting away from the shackles of the old sphere of influence. For Russia, maintaining influence over the former Soviet states and preventing their alignment with the West have been key priorities as NATO enlargement, EU and US sanctions, and asserting great power identity have been all prominent concerns for Moscow.[34]

Overall, the consequences of treating NATO enlargement as an expansion include a belief that in the 1990s and 2000s the areas of international relations were still framed by a Cold War style great power rivalry, in which the states of Central and Eastern Europe (and former Soviet republics) were just insignificant pawns on a greater global chessboard or served as a 'buffer zone" between the West and Russia. This belief indicated that regardless of whether it was Poland, Estonia, the Czech Republic or Romania, these countries had a limited role in deciding what kind of strategic alignment they could pursue. In the traditional Soviet fashion of world affairs, these states were deprived of their own agency. To Moscow they were irrelevant. Fortunately for many states in Central and Eastern Europe, this unsophisticated interpretation of security situation did

---

34 Mannes, R., 2021, "Death by a Thousand Cuts: Is Russia Winning the Information War with the West" in: Cross, M., Karolewski, I. P. (eds.), *op.cit.,* p. 166.

not prevail. They were able to gradually join NATO and the European Union. Yet, there were also states like Georgia, Moldova or Ukraine that due to a combination of domestic factors and complexity of the international dynamics were left on the outskirts of the Western integrational projects.

The convolution of the situation in Europe in the first two decades after the Cold War are aptly summarised in the following excerpt: "As the EU and NATO extended into the Balkans, non-NATO, non-EU islands formed to the south of Hungary, to the west of Bulgaria and Romania, to the east of Croatia, and to the north of Greece. Russian troops remained, as they had since 1991, in Moldova, a curious vestige of the Soviet empire. Moscow retained control over Kaliningrad, a non-contiguous bit of Russia that borders Poland and Lithuania. Belarus aligned with Russia, though it was not demonstrably less European than the Baltic republics, while Ukraine became Europe's wild card – less bound to Russia than Belarus but less bound to Europe than Poland. The Iron Curtain, terrible as it was, had been remarkably simple by comparison."[35] Within this complex environment, one of the ways forward for Central and East European states was an accession to NATO and the EU.

After the first round of the Eastern enlargement, critics of NATO's post-Cold War policy often argued that Moscow was "cornered" by the West, pointing to Russia's weaker "conventional military power and economy in comparison with the countries of Europe and North America". According to this claim "the expansion of NATO to its borders, US and EU influence in the post-Soviet space, and crippling economic sanctions have put Russia in a corner where it is now fighting back."[36] This view – quite popular in some Western academic circles – if taken a step further, blames the West for Russia's aggressive onslaught and subsequent war in Ukraine.[37] However, both, the real roots of Russia's aggressive policies and

---

35 Kimmage, M., 2024, "The Failure to Deter: U.S. Policy Toward Ukraine and Russia from the End of the Cold War until February 24, 2022" in: Brands, H., *War in Ukraine. Conflict, Strategy, and the Return of a Fractured World*, Baltimore: Johns Hopkins University Press, p. 74.
36 Maness, R., *op.cit.*, p. 179.
37 Mearsheimer, J., *op.cit.*

supposed responsibility of the West for "provoking" Moscow do not hold well against the scrutiny of facts. Given Russia's logic of not letting go its old "spheres of influence", it is hardly a coincidence that Georgia and Ukraine were targeted by Moscow when it decided to wage wars in 2008 and 2014. As Kimberly Marten explains, Russia may have chosen to establish "frozen conflicts" in each state partly to prevent them from meeting the criteria for NATO membership. Most likely even "more central to Russian military thinking, then, is the fact that through these operations Russia gained access to significant new chunks of the Black Sea coastline for its forces that are now based in Abkhazia and especially through its occupation of Crimea."[38]

From Russia's perspective, historically the concept of "great power" politics was intimately linked with its self-attributed leading role in "deciding fates of entire nations."[39] This strikingly audacious notion has justified Soviet and later Russia's imperial policies against smaller neighbours. Even though some analysts have argued[40] that the concept of "deciding fates of entire nations" was mostly exercised in the Caucasus and Black Sea region, the evidence of post-Soviet Russia's foreign policies from Central and Eastern Europe to Central Asia, have shown a different trend. Namely, the Kremlin has long been attempting to have a say in any strategic decisions of the countries that once were part of the Soviet Union or under its influence. The stakes seemed to have been even higher whenever these countries attempted to escape the sphere of control that was claimed by Moscow.

Consequently, and expectedly, the Soviet Union, and later Russia, did not hold a positive view of the formation and sustainment of NATO. Moscow has been seeing the Alliance as a "threat to its national security". A study of the NATO Enlargement from the Russian perspective that was carried out in 1998 by the US Army showed that the opinion of many of the Russian policy elite, media, academic institutions and military at that time was that

---

38 Marten, K., 2020, *op.cit.*
39 Samokhvalov, V., 2021, "Power, Identity, and Circumstances: Three Factors in the Ukrainian Crisis" in: Cross, M., Karolewski, I. P. (eds.), *op.cit.*, p. 247.
40 *Ibidem*, pp. 247-248.

NATO was no longer needed. It had, as the authors of the study quoted, "served its purpose and, with the dissolution of the Warsaw Pact, could claim no bona fide justification for its continued existence."[41] Thus, when it became clear that not only NATO did not cease to exist but actually found a new life in enlarging the zone of peace and security in Europe, policymakers in Russia could not take this information lightly.

While the Soviet world referred to the politically and geographically established space, the term *Russkiy Mir* (the Russian world) seems to be its phantom successor. Indeed, as a concept this phrase is much more elusive and arguably more dangerous then what was understood as the Soviet world. In the realm of geopolitics, *Russkiy Mir* was conceived as a "Russian diaspora empire". Thus, the authors of this term put strong importance on the "Russian enclaves" in Russia's "near abroad". The latter are the former Soviet republics, such as Ukraine or Moldova, while the areas with large Russian-speaking populations, meaning the "Russian enclaves" include such places as Crimea, Donbas, and Transnistria.[42]

While the Soviet world after the Cold War might have been treated as a desperate attempt to hold on to an old-fashioned imperial idea and sphere of influence, the *Russkiy Mir* seems to be much more revisionist in nature. It uses the Russian speaking minorities, diasporas and neighbouring states to justify a new version of Russian imperialism. Subsequently, it would be difficult to overlook the fact that nearly every country on the post-Soviet space has experienced territorial disputes with Russia which are rooted in linguistic and identity factors. The explicit adoption of Russia's *Russkiy Mir* doctrine, including the "official" annexation of new foreign territories, prompts a closer examination of the fundamental significance of the *Russkiy Mir* concept.[43]

---

41   Milano, J., 1998, NATO Enlargement from the Russian Perspective, Carlisle: US Army War College, p. 1.
42   Meister, S., 2016, "*Russkiy Mir*: 'Russian World' On the genesis of a geopolitical concept and its effects on Ukraine", German Council on Foreign Relations, 3 May, https://dgap.org/en/events/russkiy-mir-russian-world.
43   Sadohin, S., 2022, "What is behind Alexander Dugin's 'Russian world'?", *New Eastern Europe*, 9 November, https://neweasterneurope.eu/2022/11/09/what-is-behind-alexander-dugins-russian-world/

Overall, *Russkiy Mir* is based on exclusive notion of targeting nations, societies and states that used to be part of (or closely associated with) the Soviet Union. Furthermore, it is a concept that is defined solely on the basis of self-identification. In 2014 the Kremlin embraced this idea for "forming a nationalist narrative about the necessity of Russia's revival as a great power and its revanche in the post-Soviet space."[44] Given this, it is quite clear that a panacea, or at least effective defence mechanism, against Russia's imperial tendencies can be found nowhere else but in joining inclusive Western institutions that have broaden a sphere of freedom in Europe after the end of the Cold War. Both NATO and the European Union have played this role.

Ukraine's escape attempt?

With the exceptions of the Central and East European states, few Western powers saw the significance of Ukrainian political changes between 2004 and 2014. Even fewer envisioned Russia's aggressive turn that was heralded with the war in Georgia in 2008. In March 2014 Russia invaded and subsequently annexed Crimea; and a few months later it invaded eastern regions of Ukraine. In 2015 Russia launched a military operation in Syria, challenging the US policy in the Middle East. In the same year Moscow started its long covert campaign to meddle in the 2016 US presidential elections. All these: the annexation of Crimea, entering Syria, interference in American domestic politics should not be treated as isolated events.[45] They were all a part of Russia's long-lasting imperialist strategy.

For Ukraine, especially after it was invaded by Russia, NATO accession became both a priority and a necessity for a peaceful and stable future. In the long term NATO remains the only viable security organisation in the Euro-Atlantic area that is able to offer steadfast security for Ukraine. Hence, beyond bilateral security arrangements, NATO appears to be the only collective security option for

---

44 Zevelev, I., 2016, "The Russian World in Moscow's Strategy", Center for Strategic and International Studies, 22 August, https://www.csis.org/analysis/russian-world-moscows-strategy.
45 Kimmage, M., *op.cit.*, p. 78.

Ukraine. This reality appears to be well-understood both in Kyiv and NATO frontline states which, not accidentally, were instrumental in separating the region from post-Soviet and Russia's influences. Additionally, Ukraine's close ties with the Alliance that would eventually lead to an enlargement would symbolise the country's final escape from the Soviet and Russian world.

From NATO 's perspective, the Alliance's relationship with Ukraine goes beyond the straightforward decision to offer Ukraine membership. In fact, for both the organisation as a whole and its individual member states, the undivided security of Europe is a cornerstone of the Euro-Atlantic rules-based order.[46] Consequently, an independent and sovereign Ukraine is essential for the Transatlantic security. Yet, undeniably the most important factor that will affect NATO-Ukraine relations in the foreseeable future is the shape and potential outcome of the Russian-Ukrainian war. As the most likely scenario predicts the war to be long and protracted[47], it will require strategic patience from Ukraine, NATO and its member states on the path to the enlargement.

Unsurprisingly, NATO officially sees its Eastern enlargements as a success story and inherently positive developments. According to this narrative, not only the enlargement contributed to peace and stability in the Euro-Atlantic area, but also NATO's open door policy has been perceived "as an expression of the Alliance's fundamental values and strategic interest". This assumption can be gathered from the latest NATO's Strategic Concept presented during the 2022 Summit in Madrid in which NATO clearly states that its door remains open "to all European democracies that share the values of our Alliance, which are willing and able to assume the responsibilities and obligations of membership, and whose membership contributes to our common security". The Strategic Concept

---

46   Encke, F., 2020, "An independent and sovereign Ukraine is key to Euro-Atlantic security", *NATO Review*, 8 July, https://www.nato.int/docu/review/articles/2020/07/08/an-independent-and-sovereign-ukraine-is-key-to-euro-atlantic-security/index.html (Accessed: 24 May 2024).
47   International Crisis Group, 2023, "Why the War in Ukraine May Be a Long One", 7 July, https://www.crisisgroup.org/europe-central-asia/eastern-europe/ukraine/why-war-ukraine-may-be-long-one (Accessed: 8 May 2024).

underscores something that many of the critics of NATO enlargement tend to overlook, namely that "decisions on membership are taken by NATO Allies and no third party has a say in this process."[48] Yet, with a long and contested path of Ukraine to full membership in NATO, the Alliance's cohesion and determination to continue enlargements will be tested.

The NATO Summit in Vilnius in July 2023 resulted, among other things, in some important accomplishments including a closer NATO-Ukrainian partnership and a greater chance for Ukraine's future membership in the Alliance. As evidence to that the NATO-Ukraine Council was established[49] and NATO reaffirmed its membership invitation to Ukraine.[50] The members of the Alliance also reaffirmed and reinforced their commitment to supporting Ukraine and bringing it into NATO. The Summit communiqué thus read that the Alliance "will support Ukraine (…) on its path towards future membership", as NATO "will be in a position to extend an invitation to Ukraine to join the Alliance when Allies agree, and conditions are met."[51]

The established NATO-Ukraine Council has been (and will be) acting as an important platform for consultation, decision-making, and crisis meetings between the two sides. The issue of NATO's cooperation with Ukraine, the Alliance's support for Kyiv in the ongoing war against Russia and prospective Ukraine's membership will likely become central themes of NATO-Ukraine relations, as long as the war continues. For Ukraine, even though the results of the Vilnius Summit might have been unsatisfactory as Kyiv was not offered membership in the Alliance, this cooperation marks another

---

48 NATO, 2022, *Strategic Concept*, https://www.nato.int/nato_static_fl2014/assets/pdf/2022/6/pdf/290622-strategic-concept.pdf (Accessed: 24 May 2024).
49 NATO, 2024, *NATO-Ukraine Council*, 8 May, https://www.nato.int/cps/en/natohq/topics_217652.htm#:~:text=The%20NATO%2DUkraine%20Council%20was,bringing%20Ukraine%20closer%20to%20NATO (Accessed: 24 May 2024).
50 Garamone, J., 2023, "Agree to Expedite Ukraine's NATO Membership", *DOD News*, 11 July, https://www.defense.gov/News/News-Stories/Article/Article/3455199/leaders-agree-to-expedite-ukraines-nato-membership/ (Accessed: 24 May 2024).
51 NATO, 2023, *Vilnius Summit Communiqué*, 11 July, https://www.nato.int/cps/en/natohq/official_texts_217320.htm (Accessed: 24 May 2024).

step on its path to NATO and takes Ukraine further away from Russia's imperial grip. To put the progress of the relationship between the Alliance and Ukraine in time perspective, in January 2022, such close cooperation between the two sides would have been unthinkable. In 2021, NATO would not put Ukraine's membership on the top of its agenda, even though it also did not want to yield to Russia's demands to commit to "no further enlargement of the Alliance, including in particular to Ukraine."[52]

In another ironical twist of events, one of Vladimir Putin's official explanations for launching the so-called "special military operation" against Ukraine on 24 February 2022 was Ukraine's attempt to come closer to Western institutions, the European Union and NATO. By invading Ukraine and unleashing a full-scale war against it, Russia has accelerated this process. Today, Ukraine and many of its Western allies believe that Ukraine has earned militarily and morally its place in NATO. Indeed, membership in the Alliance, though by no means imminent, now seems to be closer than it has ever been before.

Conclusions

NATO has no offensive aims or record of aggression. Even more, membership in NATO is voluntary (and subject to the ratification by all member states). It would thus be difficult to refer to NATO's open door policy and subsequent rounds of enlargements as "expansion". Simultaneously, the only sphere of NATO's activities that might be labelled as expansion are NATO's increased functions and tasks that the Alliance has undertaken since 1990s and 2000s. They include: conflict management, "out of area" operations or cooperative security, responsibilities that did not necessarily created a more cohesive alliance.

As argued throughout the chapter, calling NATO's enlargements an "expansion" seems inaccurate and indeed erroneous. Not

---

52 Pifer, S., 2021, *Russia's Draft Agreements with NATO and the United States: Intended for Rejection?*, Washington DC: The Brookings Institution, 21 December https://www.brookings.edu/articles/russias-draft-agreements-with-nato-and-the-united-states-intended-for-rejection/ (Accessed: 24 May 2024).

only does this term blur the lines between the voluntary process of enlargement and the supposedly expansive policies, but it also diminishes the agency of the new member states presenting them as just objects of great power politics. What the debates about NATO's expansion, instead of enlargement, omit to expose is that the perspective of NATO enlargement for Central European states has been a true escape from the old world — one that was created by the Soviet Union and apparently attempted to be recreated in a new version by Vladimir Putin in the first quarter of the 21st century.

This escape from the Soviet world — not only in symbolic but also physical terms — seems to have reached its final stages with Russia's full-scale invasion of Ukraine. With the bombing of Ukrainian cities, the targeting of civilians, mass murders and ethnic cleaning, Russia has brought a total destruction and a large-scale war that Europe has not experienced since the Second World War. The war sent shockwaves across the continent. Only those whose ancestors lived under the ironclad rule of the Soviet Union or within the so-called Soviet sphere of influence were not surprised. However, slowly but steadily, even the most unconvinced European states have started to see Russia for what it truly has been for the last 20 years, a destructor of the European security and peace. France's president Emmanuel Macron has been among those who opened his eyes to the true nature of Russia's regime when he pointed out that Europe was not defined by its territory only, but by a "unique relationship with freedom and justice". Macron specified the realm's territory as ranging from "from Lisbon to Odesa", which is a complete shift from his 2019 call for a Europe "from Lisbon to Vladivostok."[53]

Also, the two biggest Western European powers — France and Germany — seemed to have finally changed their approach to both Russia and the states that have been trying to get away from Moscow's consistent attempts to maintain its long-gone empire. The new war reality has indeed marked a striking difference in Berlin and Paris's policies, especially when compared to their previous

---

53 Macron, E., 2024, "Europe Speech", 24 April, https://www.elysee.fr/en/emmanuel-macron/2024/04/24/europe-speech (Accessed: 24 May 2024).

positions towards Georgia and Ukraine's NATO membership as they were articulated in 2008. Since then until 2022, both Germany and France believed in the necessity of dialogue with Russia and were highly suspicious of any further enlargements of the Alliance, arguing for the need of "a strategic balance in Europe". The outcome of these intra-NATO debates in 2008 was a (bitter) compromise articulated during the NATO Summit in Bucharest.[54] Rather than granting them a Membership Action Plan (MAP), NATO issued a vague statement asserting that Georgia and Ukraine "will become members of NATO" without specifying the timing or conditions for this to occur.[55] Unfortunately, it took Russia waging a full-scale war against Ukraine and atrocities against the Ukrainian nation for many in the West to finally wake up.[56] As a result, the Transatlantic community (both the EU and NATO) have seemed to embrace this decisive moment and assist the states and societies of the Eastern Europe in their struggle to end the Soviet world and stop *Russkiy Mir* within its Russian borders. They can do it by committing resources to support Ukraine, economically and militarily and by enlarging the area of free, prosperous and stable states through offering Georgia, Moldova and Ukraine a clear path to both the European Union and NATO.

All told, one of the results of Russia's attack on Ukraine is a realisation that the process of escaping the Soviet world, even if started as an individual exercise, has now become a group effort. In other words, the guaranteed security and well-being of the states of Central and Eastern Europe depends on the situation in Ukraine, but also in Georgia and Moldova. As long as Russia is able to destabilise them the security of the entire region may suffer from severe consequences. NATO's frontline states (i.e. Poland, Romania, Finland and the Baltic states) understand that the outcome of the war in Ukraine, but also possible attempts by Moscow to freeze the

---

54 NATO, 2008, *op. cit.*
55 Larsen, H. B., 2023, *Research Handbook on NATO*, Cheltenham, UK: Edward Elgar Publishing, p. 311.
56 Michnik, W., 2023, "The West's Rude Awakening: Lessons after the First Year of War", *New Eastern Europe*, 2 (56), pp. 57–66.

conflict, will have long-lasting implications also on their own security. Finally, if the prediction that in the coming years "the balance of power within NATO will change in favour of Central and Eastern Europe"[57] holds true we may expect a greater understanding among the members of the Alliance that NATO and/or EU enlargement is the ultimate way to escape the Soviet world and fence off *Russkiy mir*.

---

57 Stolarek, J., 2023, "Credible partner on NATO's eastern flank—Poland's new role in security policy" 29 September, https://pl.boell.org/en/2023/09/29/credible-partner-natos-eastern-flank-polands-new-role-security-policy (Accessed: 24 May 2024).

Westernisation vs Easternisation

Kinga Anna Gajda

The concepts of Central Europe and Eastern Europe (or even East Central Europe) have traditionally been used in reference to the territories located between Germany and Russia. Accordingly, the region's diverse populations were perceived to inhabit a transitional space, an "isthmus" between East and West. The countries identified as "Central" European typically include: Poland, Czechia, Slovakia (or, depending on the time in history: Czechoslovakia), Hungary, but also, although less often, Austria, Ukraine and even Lithuania, while the group labelled as "Eastern" Europe is more complicated. Overall, since 1999 and especially since 2004, that is the moment when Central European states became members of NATO and the European Union, the name "Eastern European" has been used for those states that are East of Poland and that are not members of NATO or the EU. These are the former Soviet republics such as Ukraine, Belarus, Moldova, etc. At the same time, the term "Eastern" Europe, especially in the non-European discourse, is still used in regards to countries such as Poland, meaning those which are members of the EU and have never been a part of the Soviet Union. This inconsistency in terminology reflects the lack of familiarity with the developments in the region and a tendency to orientalise what is regarded as Europe's periphery.

The East vs West dichotomy

Historically speaking, the concept of Central Europe gained recognition in the 20th century after the First World War when the countries which emerged from the collapse of the European empires (especially the Austro-Hungarian empire) started the process of state-building. In the second half of the 20th century, thanks to the essay *The Tragedy of Central Europe* by Czech writer Milan Kundera (1984), this term became more widely known in the West. It was used mostly by Polish and Czechoslovak political émigrés, to counterbalance what was associated with the communist-ruled Eastern Bloc. Following the collapse of communism in the late 1980s, the discourse on Central Europe returned to the internal debate in the states it referred to, becoming integrated into official foreign policy discourse, especially the discussions on NATO and EU membership.

Central Europe is thus a concept which is not linked to a specific nation or country. As such, it has been more often used to unify a group of states rather than divide them. Yet this does not mean that the debate on what constitutes Central Europe as well as Eastern Europe has been completed. Many questions regarding these concepts are still being asked, including whether the states from this region actually belong to the European cultural community or are separate from it.[1]

Proponents of the idea of Central Europe naturally point to the region's historical and cultural ties with Western Europe. Their intentional contrasting of Central but, also — although to a smaller extent — Eastern Europe with Russia reveals a certain degree of moral superiority and attachment to European values which are opposed to the axiological systems that come from outside of Europe and are primarily associated with the East. In this way the discourse on Central and Eastern Europe contributes to some marginalisation of Russia, which is perceived as the "other" civilisation.[2] While the distinguishing features of Western Europe, as Walter D. Connor points out, include the Latin alphabet, Roman Catholicism and the legacy of the Renaissance and Enlightenment, they are juxtaposed with what constitutes Eastern civilisation.[3] This includes the usage

---

1 Neumann, I.V., 1998, *Uses of the Other "The East" in European Identity Formation*, Minneapolis: University of Minnesota Press.
2 *Ibidem*.
3 Connor, W.C., 2000, "Europe West and East: Thoughts on History, Culture, and Kosovo", in: Gitelman, Z., Hajda, L.A., Himka, J.P., Solchanyk, R. (eds.), *Cultures and Nations of Central and Eastern Europe. Essays in Honor of Roman Szporluk*, Cambridge, MA: Harvard Ukrainian Research Institute, p. 75.

of Greek and Cyrillic alphabets, Byzantine cultural influences, Orthodox Christianity, and perceived economic stagnation, which is said be found in Eastern Europe, but in Russia as well.[4]

Despite criticism, geographical divisions, such as West vs East, have also been used in normative assessments of the countries' and region's development. This explains Attila Melegh's observation that Eastern Europe has never fully integrated into the modernisation discourse. Instead it has fallen into an intermediate category of a region of "almost developed" countries while the adjective "Eastern" has become synonymous with "almost".[5]

Some scholars see the East and West dichotomy through the prism of the centre vs periphery relationship. Among them is Polish sociologist Tomasz Zarycki who has analysed the unequal spread of cultural, intellectual and material resources across the European continent. Its centre (the West) is characterised by higher concentrations of capital which the periphery (Central and Eastern states) compensates with cultural resources. This situation, Zarycki warns, creates a certain sense of in-betweeness but also inequality in Eastern Europe (periphery) where culture turns into a compensatory mechanism for deficient economic capital. Yet an excessive focus on cultural capital can also be used to cover up economic and political weaknesses, especially vis-à-vis the West.[6]

Thus, the term East, also linguistically, implies inferior status, especially when compared to the West. It is used as a label for the European "other", which is constructed and filled with stereotypes of underdevelopment.[7] Eastern Europe, by contrast, can be defined

---

[4] Smith, A., 2000, "Imaging geographies of the 'new Europe': geo-economic power and the new European architecture of integration", *Political Geography*, 21 (5), pp. 647-670; Lukacs, J., 1991 "The 'Other' Europe At Century's End", *The Wilson Quarterly*, 15 (4), http://archive.wilsonquarterly.com/sites/default/files/articles/WQ_VOL15_A_1991_Article_04_2.pdf (Accessed: 14 March 2024).

[5] A. Melegh, A., 2006, *On the East-West Slope. Globalization, nationalism, racism and discourses on Central and Eastern Europe*, Budapest, New York: Central European University Press, p. 69.

[6] Zarycki, T., 2009, "Socjologia krytyczna na peryferiach", *Kultura i Społeczeństwo*, 80 (1).

[7] Gajda, K.A., 2020, "Eastern Europe's Orientalised", in: Balazs, A.B., Griessler, Ch., *The Visegrad Four and the Western Balkans*, Baden-Baden: Nomos.

as "otherness constructed by the West" or, as Joshua Hagen suggests, "a product of Western imagination".[8]

Even though the role of the "Other" is not equivalent to that of the orient, Eastern Europe shares some identity traits with former European colonies. As such it has become subject to orientalisation, which is exposed not only through language and construction of stereotypes, but also self-stereotyping. However, unlike other former European colonies, for example India, states such as Ukraine, Belarus, and Moldova have been dominated by more than one foreign power. These were the Polish-Lithuania Commonwealth, the Austro-Hungarian Empire, the Kingdom of Romania, but also Russia (formerly the Russian Empire or the Soviet Union). The latter, matter-of-fact, colonised, at some point in history, all of the Eastern European states.

Exploring the topic of colonial legacy in Eastern Europe, American historian Larry Wolff argued that the discourse on the region is constructed in such a way that it conceals the shortcomings of the European model.[9] Instead, it projects immaturity, aggression, insecurity, underdevelopment, and inconsistencies onto the eastern parts of the continent. In Wolff's view this is aimed at justifying Western colonialism. In other words, the deficiencies of Western systems (political and economic) are projected onto Eastern European states which are put in a situation where there is "no escape" from the identity they "receive" from the West. Ukrainian writer and intellectual, Oksana Zabuzhko while analysing the interplay between East and West concluded that one of the undesired outcomes of this process is a tendency of the West to impose its values and norms upon the East. Zabuzhko argues that this imposition reveals a colonisation tendency wherein the West positions itself as the standard by which the East is evaluated.[10]

---

8   Hagen, J., 2003, "Redrawing the imagined map of Europe: the rise and fall of the 'center'", *Political Geography*, 22 (5) pp. 489-490.
9   Wolff, L., 1994, *Inventing Eastern Europe. The Map of Civilization on the Mind of the Enlightenment*, Stanford: Stanford University Press.
10 Zabużko, O., 2022, *Planeta Piołun*, Warszawa: Wydawnictwo Agora.

The shedding of the Soviet past

Throughout history Central and Eastern European nations have experienced interactions with both Western and non-European cultures and influences. Germany, for example, played a significant role in the area of education, publishing and the legal system, while Italian artists and their work primarily influenced the aesthetics of many cities in the region. Concurrently, Russia was also active in imposing its standards and cultural codes on the nations of Central and Eastern Europe. The latter took the form of occupation or dominance over the territories that fell under the control of the Russian empire, or later the Soviet Union. The Soviet times, especially, saw the suppression of the cultural identities of Central and Eastern European states in favour of a unified identity which corresponded to Russia's imperial ambitions.[11] However, as stated before, the reaction within the region brought also opposite results. Among others, they have been reflected in the term Central Europe.

The post-Soviet states, which predominantly belong to the category of Eastern Europe, have experienced the imposition of the communist system through coercion which, in many cases, has left a long lasting legacy on their functioning and preferences of their societies. The most striking example is Belarus, but also Ukraine up until the Orange Revolution. Yet as the cases of these two countries show, affiliation with Western culture and value systems is what the societies desire, even if they are being suppressed. In Ukraine this desire for greater Westernisation has been stronger than in Belarus and now also takes the form of the European integration process which Ukraine has officially been on since 2014.

Unlike in Eastern Europe, where the legacy of the Soviet era significantly differs across the states, in Central Europe we see a more cohesive cultural community whose states all rejected communism and started democratisation, although for varied reasons.

---

11 Chodubski, A., 2012, "Europa Środkowo-Wschodnia wobec integracji i dezintegracji cywilizacyjnej świata", in: Stępień-Kuczyńska, A., Słowikowski, M., (eds.), *Na gruzach imperium. W stronę nowego ładu międzynarodowego i społeczno-politycznego w regionie Europy Środkowej i Wschodniej*, Łódź: Wydawnictwo Uniwersytetu Łódzkiego, pp. 219–230.

Among the latter was the regime's repression of national cultural and religious traditions, which infringed upon these nations' freedom and sovereignty[12]. As a result, the perception of communism as an externally-imposed and anti-democratic system has prevailed throughout Central Europe until today. This sentiment is now also observable in Eastern European states, although to varying degrees.

From 1989 onwards, Central European states embarked on the arduous task of constructing new identities, replacing elements of their communist/Soviet past with what constitutes freedom and democracy. While initially embracing almost all Western European influences to signify their departure from the Soviet world, these nations retained a strong sense of national identity, despite decades of Moscow's influence. The process of shedding the communist past and preparing for EU accession has showed the resilience and determination that was built within these societies even when they were oppressed under the previous system.

While in Central Europe communist regimes did not manage to completely eradicate the national identity, the situation in Eastern Europe was different. The process of uniformed Sovietisation was strongly enforced, with a variety of instruments used to eliminate all elements that could cause a threat to the regime. Naturally, a strong national identity was perceived as one such cause. However, since the 1960s even these countries experienced a certain degree of revival of national (usually folk) culture, which eventually catalysed their transformations in the late 1980s and early 1990s. Following the system change which in Central Europe started in 1989 and in the former Soviet republics in 1991, the countries of both regions embarked on the process that was aimed at bringing them closer to Western Europe. As its result they were meant to shift their Eastern identity as far away from the core, meaning the Soviet world, as possible. Once this process was started the marking of what constitutes Eastern Europe has become more fluid and

---

12 Wandycz, P. S., 2003, *Cena wolności. Historia Europy Środkowowschodniej od średniowiecza do współczesności*, Kraków: Znak.

subject to change. For example, Ukraine before the Orange Revolution and Ukraine today are two completely different states, just as different is today's Belarusian society from the Belarusian society before the 2020 protests.

The West as an ideal

Vast research shows that in post-Soviet countries it is through revolutions and protests that societies start resisting Sovietisation and push their political elite to embark on a Western path. Therefore, it is first and foremost the protesters and activists who draw the attention of the society at large to the importance of European values in state-building. Their call for a return to Europe thus means a need for departure from the communist past and reaffirmation of European roots. In today's terms this translates into the need for adoption of political culture that is free from violence and respectful towards the rule of law and universal human rights. The lack thereof is especially visible in Lukashenka's Belarus as well as Putin's Russia. Therefore, the war that the Russian Federation started in Ukraine and which is aimed at this country's occupation is often interpreted as a war between East and West. In other words, the Ukrainian rhetoric which states that while fighting Russia Ukraine is defending European values expresses the belief that in today's world Westernisation means building a peaceful community, while Easternisation brings on aggression and war.

In Central Europe the breakthrough moment for the pursuit of a Western future and departure from the Eastern path was the fall of the communist system. It also took place as a result of revolutions, albeit less violent than the ones which happened in the post-Soviet states. However, unlike in Eastern Europe, the collapse of the communist regime in Central European states not only marked the beginning of the free market economy but also a multilayered approach to democratisation. Crucial to this process was the aspiration of Central European societies to align with Western European countries whom they saw as beacons of democracy, prosperity and modernity. Beyond geopolitical considerations, Central

Europe's yearning for Western recognition was also rooted in its cultural affinities and historical ties to the West.

The allure of Western lifestyle surely fuelled the aspirations of the people in Central Europe to cement their integration with the West. It can be argued that this fixation with the West has led these societies to the weakening of what is "Central" or "Eastern" in them. While describing this phenomenon, Polish researcher, Wojciech Śmieja, wrote that "what Western Europe naturally produces, we [Central Europeans] adapt".[13] We may thus say that the Central (but also Eastern) Europeans' perception of Westernisation as an ideal and the West as a stable point of reference explains why the notion of the East, if it is to survive, has to defend itself. Adam Daniel Rotfeld described this Western path in Central and Eastern Europe as post-Soviet syndrome. In his view, it entails emerging from a quasi-religious world of distorted reality.[14]

Westernisation as a security guarantee

Without a doubt, geopolitical considerations have played an important role in shaping Central Europe's quest for Western identity. Situated at the crossroads of Europe, the region has historically been a battleground for competing powers vying for influence and control. For that reason, Central European countries have opted to align themselves with Western institutions such as NATO and the European Union, viewing them as guarantors of security, stability, and prosperity.

This choice, although backed by the majority of the societies and achieved with the efforts of the political elite, was not the only option that the countries emerging from the communist system had. There were alternatives which varied across the states. In Poland, for example, we can point to five different paths that were discussed at the early stage of its system transformation. They all

---

13 Śmieja, W., 2013, "Do Wschodu wracam jak łosoś na tarło ... " in: *Patrząc na Wschód. Przestrzeń, człowiek, mistycyzm*, Białystok: Fundacja sąsiedzi, p. 252.
14 Rotfeld, D. A., 2022, in: Brysacz, P., Morawiecki J., (eds.), *Ani żadnej wyspy, Rozmowy o Rosji i Ukrainie*, Kielce: Paśny Buriat, p. 236.

had supporters, although they differed in terms of size and influence. The first path was based on the assumption that despite communism's collapse Poland was still strongly connected with the East (the Soviet world). Its supporters believed that for this reason Poland should pursue its interests in the former communist bloc. This viewpoint reflected certain scepticism towards the feasibility of rapid Western integration, an opinion which was heard in the early phase of its transformation. The second path was based on the so-called "Piast approach". Deriving its name from the first Polish dynasty, its supporters advocated for Poland's alignment with Western states, especially Germany.

The third path, which in a way competed with the second one, was based on the so-called "Jagiellonian approach". Recognizing Poland's historical heritage and legacy in Eastern Europe, mainly due to the memory of the Polish-Lithuanian Commonwealth, it postulated a greater cooperation with Eastern European states with whom Poland could build new bridges and regional alliances. The fourth path was that of being a leader of Central Europe, which later became known as the Visegrád Group. Lastly, the least popular, yet still articulated, vision was that supporting close ties with the Soviet Union, first, and the Russian Federation, later. This vision was attractive only to those who felt some communist nostalgia.

Polish scholar Jędrzej Morawiecki, while analysing the variety of these paths, argued that the pro-Western aspirations that were expressed during Poland's transition and the final choice for opting for Westernisation by Central European states were the result of the societies' fear of the East. At the same time, the researcher points out that until this day there are individuals in the region who dream of constructing an alternative to the West, which they do somewhat in defiance.[15] Yet it also needs to be said that these Pan-Slavic tendencies have remained rather dormant than subject of a wide public debate. This, of course, is not the case in Russia where the Eurasian movement has played an important role in shaping of Putin's foreign policy and Russia's current war doctrine.

---

15   Morawiecki, J., 2013, "Rosja jest gdzie indziej" in: *Patrząc na Wschód. Przestrzeń, człowiek, mistycyzm*, Białystok: Fundacja sąsiedzi, p. 121.

As stated earlier, in the early stages of Poland's transformation, the priority was given to the Western choice. However, with time, the regional orientation based on the Jagiellonian approach has grown in dynamism and intensity. This explains Poland's increased activity in the democratisation of Eastern Europe and its role in supporting political transition of the former Soviet republics. It took the form of Poland's President Aleksander Kwaśniewski's engagement in the Round Table negotiations that allowed for a peaceful end of the Orange Revolution in Ukraine, President Lech Kaczyński's support for Georgia during the 2008 Russo-Georgian war and the 2009 Eastern Partnership Programme which was championed by Poland's Foreign Minister, Radosław Sikorski, together with the Swedish politician — Carl Bildt. Despite these engagements Polish debates on foreign policy were never free from voices that were critical of Poland's activities in Eastern Europe as well as those that were calling them too reactive and not adequately responding to the local needs.

A turn towards the East

Polish writer, Andrzej Stasiuk, claims that once Central Europeans started to rid themselves of their Easternness they began to feel like orphans, traitors, or renouncers of their own identity. In his words this transformation resembled "poor villages pretending to be Europeans, just like our rural ancestors were pretending to be townsfolk, which they never were."[16] More explicitly, Stasiuk states that in Central Europe people "have disowned East and because of it they are now condemned as provincials". In the same manner, Maria Janion was right when she metaphorically said that we (Central Europeans) were wrongly baptised. For this reason, our Westernness resembles an eternal attempt to catch up with the West and please it. It is a perpetual wagging of a tail, a masquerade. At the same time, Stasiuk points out that the attempts to construct an au-

---

16 Stasiuk, A., 2013, "Rozbić namiot na Gobi, patrzeć jak Bug płynie", in: *Patrząc na Wschód. Przestrzeń, człowiek, mistycyzm*, Białystok: Fundacja sąsiedzi, p. 14.

thentic identity, which is free from this obsessive pursuit of Westernness, can turn into what he calls provincial nationalism. In such situations, the East serves only as nourishment for an unjustified national contempt. Thus, for Stasiuk it was the experience of communism that has shaped Central and Eastern Europe and which remains incomprehensive to Western Europeans. In fact, the chasm that communism has established between Europe's East and West is something which may not get overcome.

A certain turn towards the East which researchers have recently observed in Central Europe has to some degree been influenced by a series of crises which took place in the last two decades. First was the 2008 financial crisis, which — as Bulgarian political scientist, Ivan Krastev, argues — led people to doubt whether their children would live better than their own generation. The 2015 migration crisis, which followed the financial crisis, triggered a mass panic related to the sense of threat that for some people brought a vision of more culturally diverse communities. The 2020-2021 COVID-19 pandemic revealed the dark side of globalisation while simultaneously convincing many Europeans that they were entering a new era of authoritarianism. The full-scale war in Ukraine which started in 2022 shattered the illusion that the European continent was free from threat of an armed conflict and that security could be taken for granted.

These five crises share several common characteristics. They were all pan-European and perceived as existential threats. Although similar in terms of continental scale, they have different geographic locations and divided Europe in various ways. For example, the annexation of Crimea by the Russian Federation confronted Russia's apologists — France and Germany — in the West with Central and Eastern European countries (especially Poland and the Baltic states). The pandemic and climate change exposed generational divides within European societies. More importantly, the crises have created new identities and explain the political choices that do not fit into traditional divisions between left and right, pro- or anti-immigration, establishment or populists, or East versus West.[17] As a result of these changes, also Central European societies began to notice their Easternness but, instead of denying it as they did in the past, they began to juxtapose it with the West.

From *Homo Sovieticus* to post-Soviet identity

Historically, Central Europe was firmly entrenched within Western Europe. However, after the Second World War, when the new order was established in the world, the countries of Central Europe saw that the earlier strong Western influences started to yield to the dominance of the communist ideology. This marked the beginning of the over 40-year long period of Eastern influence in the history of Central Europe.[18] Many scholars characterise communism, and especially its first phase—Stalinism—as a period of malaise that afflicted Central Europe, leaving it scarred and disconnected from the broader European context.[19] As emphasised by researchers and journalists[20] one of the curses of the communist regime was that it made the boundary between East and West not merely based on a geographic demarcation but also established them within people themselves, affecting their value systems and perception of the world.[21] Belarusian writer and Noble Prize Winner, Svetlana Alexievich, who analysed how communism attempted to transform humanity, claims that this plan has succeeded.[22]

---

17 Krastev, I., 2024, "Pushed to the brink by more than a decade of crises, the continent is at a tipping point", *European Voices*, 1, pp. 10-15.
18 Baranov, N., 2018, "Central-Eastern Europe in the European political and historical-geographical context", *Politeja*, 6 (57), p. 54.
19 Garton-Ash, T., 1989, *The uses of adversity: essays on the fate of Central Europe*, New York: Random House; Kundera, M., 1984, "A Kidnapped West or Culture Bows Out," Granta, March 1, https://granta.com/a-kidnapped-west-or-culture-bows-out/ (Accessed: 14 March 2024).
20 Radziwiłowicz, W., 2013, "Rosję rozumem ogarniesz", in: *Patrząc na Wschód. Przestrzeń, człowiek, mistycyzm*, Białystok: Fundacja sąsiedzi, pp. 224–245.
21 Gajda, K. A., 2023, "Eastern Europe as a Community of Values", in: Gajda K. A. (ed.), *The Heritage of Central and Eastern Europe*, Berlin: Peter Lang.
22 Alexeivich, S., 2014, *Czasy secondhand. Koniec czerwonego człowieka*, Wołowiec: Wydawnictwo Czarne, Wołowiec, p. 7.

Her works show how in the laboratory of Marxism-Leninism, the red man—*Homo Sovieticus*—was bred. Recognisable by everyone, but understood only by his/her own, today the "Soviet" resides in different countries and speaks different languages. Yet, he/she still carries marks of redness. For Alexievich, whose study of the Soviet people is one of the most important ones, the red man is a person of great ideas and wars, as well as the drills. He/she is a hardened individual, incapable of understanding freedom, existing in isolation, and living like a houseplant. At the same time, the purpose of her/his existence is an imagined idea rather than materialistic needs and consumption. The Soviet man does not need to possess material goods but to suffer for his/her nation and speak the language of suffering.

Among the numerous concerns of the observers of the post-communist transformation in Central and Eastern Europe, there was some recognition that that the entrenched mentalities and coping strategies which were shaped under the previous regime and which are described as the "*Homo Sovieticus* syndrome" could undermine the effective transition to liberal-democracy and capitalism.[23] Thus, the terms "Homo Sovieticus" and more recently also "Homo Post-Sovieticus" have been widely employed to characterise the prevailing mindset in the societies that have been transitioning from communism to democracy and market economy.

It suggests that the communist system shaped specific attitudes and perceptions over its 45-year rule in Central and Eastern Europe. It is thus perceived as an infection deeply affecting individuals who lived, learned, and worked during the communist system, blurring the boundaries between what is considered "healthy" and what is deemed "infected". Despite extensive empirical research and theoretical reflections on post-communist transformation, cultural and mental barriers inherited from the communist era remain significant challenges.

The concept of *Homo Sovieticus* was deeply analysed by the philosopher József Tischner in his writings from the 1990s. More

---

23　Morawska, E., 1999, "The Malleable Homo Sovieticus", *Communist and Post-Communist Studies*, 32 (4), pp. 359-378.

broadly, however, this term is known thanks to the texts written by the Soviet philosopher Aleksandr Zinovyev, who portrayed *Homo Sovieticus* as a collective entity devoid of individuality, finding purpose solely in the collective. Thus, we may state that more than anything else the concept of *Homo Sovieticus* allows for an examination of the lasting legacy of communist ideology in post-communist societies. However, its utility in understanding social attitudes and behaviours during transition remains a subject of debate, with some scholars questioning its explanatory power and ideological underpinnings. It may thus be more correct to say that what we observe today are some of *Homo Sovieticus* traits that are still noticeable in many Eastern European but also Central European societies. However, to use the term *Homo Sovieticus* to explain the negative social attitudes, also towards the West, whose causes lie more in the present than the communist past, would be an oversimplification.

The bipolar vision of transition, which assumes that eventually the old *Homo Sovieticus* will die out as a result "civilisational" progress that has come with the process of opening up to Western culture, is also too linear and overly optimistic.[24] Just as erroneous is treating the communist period as "point zero," a moment when a new reality and a new human being were created, as if nothing had existed before. In reality, social transformations are never free from influences of cultural heritage and value systems which are passed down by generations. That is why even during the most intense moments of ideological mobilisation in the countries of the former socialist bloc traditional values that were transmitted by primary groups such as family, neighbours and friends, but also the Catholic Church played a very important role.

Today, we should rather speak of certain elements of *Homo Sovieticus* present in the social reality of the post-Soviet states than a "pure" form of *Homo Post-Sovieticus*. In fact, any attempts to attribute negative traits to *Homo Sovieticus* stem more from a simplified model of human behaviour than correspond with reality.[25] The

---

24 Tyszka, K., 2009, "'Homo Sovieticus' Two Decades Later", *Polish Sociological Review*, 168, pp. 507-522.
25 *Ibidem.*

truth is that over three decades of changes that have taken place in the former Soviet republics, and which often took the form of protests and revolutions, have rendered the idea of *Homo Sovieticus* obsolete, especially in a country such as Ukraine.

Russia as the main threat to regional security

To this day, Central and Eastern Europeans grapple with conflicting ideas and values. On the one hand, they show a strong inclination towards Western civilisation and European integration, while on the other hand, many of their members are still deeply attached to local traditions and hold more conservative values. Thus while the adoption of democratic systems in post-communist states could indeed be interpreted as their departure from the previous era, it has not been free from challenges and tensions. Among others, they took the form of democratic backsliding and the rise of populist or nationalistic tendencies. These, in turn, have been both recognised as the leading factors in the emergence of hybrid regimes (ones that combine elements of democracy with elements of authoritarianism) which we have seen in some countries in the region.[26]

Despite internal tensions, numerous scholars emphasise that support of Central European states, especially Poland and Czechia, for the promotion of democracy in former Soviet republics and Western Balkan countries is significant, especially when compared with the Western European member states of the European Union.[27] By supporting further EU and NATO enlargement to the East, Central Europeans confirm their strong opposition to cementing non-democratic regimes in their immediate neighbourhood and advocate for similar stances among other EU member states.[28] Central European states have also been vocal critics of human rights viola-

---

26 Pietraś, M., 2019, "Podziały przestrzeni Europy Środkowo-Wschodniej", *Rocznik Instytutu Europy Środkowo-Wschodniej*, 17 (1), pp. 11–49.
27 Petrova, T., 2011, "The new Role of Central and Eastern Europe in International Democracy Support", *Democracy and Rule of Law*, Washington DC: Carnegie Endowment.
28 *Ibidem*.

tions and breaches of democratic norms in Russia. More than anything else, they perceive the authoritarian system of the Russian Federation as the main threat to their own security as well as stability in the region.

The memory of the Russian/Soviet occupation in Central Europe is a multifaceted and constitutes its contentious heritage. Until today it influences the socio-political dynamics of the countries in the region. For example, the authoritarian policies of the Soviet Union which extended to Central Europe, resulted in political repressions against those who showed signs of dissent and opposition. This repression of freedom imposed by an external force (the Kremlin) remains in the memory and history teaching in countries such as Poland, Czechia, and — although to a smaller degree — Hungary. It is thus not surprising that the societies of these countries react when they only notice any signs of a possible repeat of history. The same can be said about their experience with the Red Army, which during communist times was presented as the army of "liberators". The wrongdoings of the Soviet soldiers in Eastern and Central European states which took place during the Second World War have left a long-lasting wound on many men and women who were violently deprived of their possessions and dignity. Stories of brutal use of force stayed in many families which explains why for many Central Europeans the mere mentioning of Russia generates fear.[29]

This fear was the main reason why before the full-scale war in Ukraine countries from Central Europe (especially Poland) and the Baltic states were alarming Western politicians about the threat that authoritarian Russia was posing to the region. Initially, their voices were interpreted as manifestations of Russophobia. This was especially the case when Central European experts were pointing to the danger that the Russian Nord Stream gas pipelines was posing to European security. Their statements were yet falling on the deaf ears of Western decision-makers. It had to take the full-scale war in Ukraine to turn the voices of Central European and Baltic states

---

29 Kurczak-Redlich, K., 2022, in: *Ani żadnej wyspy, Rozmowy o Rosji i Ukrainie*, Kielce: Paśny Buriat, p. 22.

from expressions of phobia to insights which were deriving from the region's earlier experiences with Kremlin-imposed policies.

It is also not surprising that in reaction to Russia's full-scale invasion in Ukraine, the people of Central Europe reacted quickly and showed solidarity with the victims. Demonstrating massive empathy towards Ukrainians fleeing from a war-torn state they offered them immediate and extensive support. In these acts of solidarity one could see traces of collective memory of the harshness of the Soviet regime and the victimisation that was once endured by Central European nations from the Russian aggressor.

Also, in the initial phase of the war the spreading of information about the threats that Russia was posing towards other post-Soviet states immediately increased fear also among Central Europeans. To reduce it, representatives of the region became vocal advocates for NATO's intervention in Ukraine. Their widespread calls for military assistance included support for such initiatives as closure of Ukrainian airspace. Individuals in Central Europe were also less shocked than their Western counterparts when they learnt about the violations of international law by the Russian Federation and the deliberate targeting of innocent civilians by the Russian army. For many people in the region information about the war crimes inflicted by Russian soldiers on the Ukrainian population resembled the stories they have heard at home and which date back to the experiences of their families during the Second World War.

The experience with pervasiveness of Soviet propaganda in former communist states also fostered higher awareness among Central European nations of the scale and intentions behind the Kremlin's disinformation efforts. It is thus justified to formulate a thesis that it is the experience of the communist regime that explains the common perception across the region of Russia as a threat.

To a large degree, the war in Ukraine has confirmed the existing divide of Europe between the East and the West. Not only did it demonstrate to Central and Eastern Europeans that they are different from Western Europeans but also showed some additional divisions that were previously invisible and seldom discussed. As

Krastev wrote: Putin's invasion of Ukraine united Europeans during the first 18 months of the war. However, over time, it transformed from an event that was regarded as an existential crisis for the entire Europe into a crisis that was primarily affecting Ukraine and some of its closest neighbours.[30]

The war may not have separated East from West as much as it divided Central Europe, which no longer is a region speaking with one voice. Illustratively, while Poland has been interpreting the Russian attacks on Kyiv as a threat to its existence, Hungary emerged as Putin's closest ally within the EU. Prime Minister Viktor Orbán made it clear that he was more willing to sacrifice Ukraine than see an increase in bus ticket prices in in his country. Similar sentiments could be found in Bulgaria, Slovakia, even Romania. On the opposite side are the earlier mentioned Poles, Estonians, Latvians, and Lithuanians, who are among the most fervent supporters of Ukraine. Back in 2001, Grażyna Borkowska argued that within the political and Europe's cultural framework, regardless of whether it is Western, Central or Eastern part of the continent, there is no place for Russia).[31] The escalation of conflict in Ukraine has shown a resurgence of this narrative.

Navigating Westernisation and Easternisation

The concepts of Westernisation and Easternisation, as discussed in this text, encompass the intricate processes of cultural, geopolitical and historical transformation in Europe which came to the fore with the full-scale invasion in Ukraine and the changing landscape in the post-Soviet space. These concepts are therefore deeply intertwined with notions of identity, power dynamics and the interactions which can be observed among different regions and peoples of Europe as well as their relations with Russia.

---

30 Krastev, I., *op.cit.*, p. 15.
31 Borkowska G., 2001, "Wschodniość, rosyjskość, orientalność. Porządkowanie pojęć", in: G. Borkowska, J. Wójcicki (eds.), *Pogranicza literatury. Księga ofiarowana Januszowi Maciejewskiemu na jego siedemdziesięciolecie*, Warszawa: Instytut Badań Literackich PAN, p. 277.

Westernisation involves the adoption, or emulation, of Western cultural, political and economic norms, values, and practices by societies in Central and Eastern Europe. This process often stems from a desire for modernisation, progress, and integration into the broader European and global community. It entails embracing Western ideals such as democracy, capitalism, individualism, and liberal values. The text illustrates how Central and Eastern European countries, following the collapse of communism, sought to align themselves with Western Europe, viewing it as a symbol of prosperity, freedom, and technological advancement. Their pursuit of Westernisation is surely rooted in historical experiences, cultural affinities, and admiration for Western achievements.

Easternisation, on the other hand, can be explained as a reaction, a response, to Westernisation. It is particularly visible in the analysis of Central and Eastern European identity and self-perception. It entails reaffirming Eastern cultural, political, and historical legacies in the face of Western influence. Despite aspiring to adopt Western ideals in their states, Central and Eastern European nations thus grapple with a sense of in-betweenness and ambiguity regarding their position on Europe's map. Easternisation encompasses efforts to assert unique cultural identities, resist homogenisation, and reclaim agency in shaping regional narratives. It also involves critiquing or challenging Western-centric perspectives and hegemonic power dynamics.

Both Westernisation and Easternisation represent complex and multifaceted processes that reflect the dynamic nature of European societies and their interactions. They point to the ongoing negotiation of identity, belonging, and aspiration within a region that is historically marked by geopolitical divisions and cultural diversity. Moreover, they highlight the enduring legacy of historical experiences and the lasting impact of power dynamics on shaping regional trajectories.

Characteristically, the contemporary landscape of Eastern Europe is deeply entangled in a complex interplay between Westernisation and Easternisation. The concept of *Homo Sovieticus*, originating from the communist era, continues to cast a shadow over Eastern Europe's contemporary identity. While the collapse of the Soviet system signalled a departure from the communist rule, its lingering effects have persisted, shaping social behaviours, attitudes, and perceptions. Thus until now, the legacy of communism intersects with broader societal dynamics, influencing values, and norms, albeit with variations across generations and countries within the region.

All said, Eastern European societies exhibit a blend of Western aspirations and Eastern legacies, reflecting a complex cultural landscape that is characterised by historical trauma, resilience, and aspirations for freedom. The current war in Ukraine has only further highlighted Central Europe's distinct identity and historical consciousness, prompting solidarity with Ukraine and heightened awareness of security threats coming from Russia. Moving forward, Eastern Europe faces the task of reconciling its past with aspirations for the future, forging a path that honours its cultural heritage while embracing opportunities and challenges of globalisation.

Westernisation and Easternisation are complex phenomena with varying interpretations. While some view Westernisation as a positive advancement towards modernity and progress, others perceive it negatively as a loss of traditional values and cultural identity. Similarly, Easternisation elicits diverse responses. The war in Ukraine while highlighting differences between the East and the West prompts consideration of whether it may lead to a greater understanding or adoption of Central and Eastern European way of thinking about Russia. Thus, the extent of Easternisation becomes a relevant question today.

Distinguishing between the mechanisms facilitating Easternisation and Westernisation is crucial. Westernisation often occurs through exertion of power by the West over other civilisations. In contrast, Easternisation must transpire through different means, as there is no dominance of the East over the West. This distinction hinges on the openness of a group to external influences, often indicative of dissatisfaction with their own culture or lifestyle. This dissatisfaction underpins the essence of Easternisation, suggesting a departure from traditional Western civilisation or its predominant ideologies.

This research has been supported by a grant from the Faculty of International and Political Studies under the Strategic Programme Excellence Initiative at Jagiellonian University.

Part II
Ukraine and Its Departure from the Soviet World

Ukraine's Integration with the European Union

Kataryna Wolczuk

Since the collapse of communism, Ukraine has been of marginal importance for the European Union (EU). For three decades since the break-up of the Soviet Union, geopolitical considerations and security of Ukraine have barely played a role in structuring relations between the EU and Ukraine. This reflected the post-geopolitical identity of the European project, with its focus on economic and functional integration with non-member states, while neglecting the more challenging issue of security in wider Europe, including relations with Ukraine. From the moment of Ukraine's emergence, as argued by British Minister for Europe from 2002 to 2005, Denis McShane, "the EU had very little idea what to do about Ukraine, and no obvious ambitions".[1]

Paradoxically, by 2022 Ukraine had turned into one of the most important internal and foreign policy challenges the EU faces. Russia's invasion of Ukraine, first in 2014 and then, as a full-scale invasion in 2022, has shaken the very foundations of the European integration project. This is because Russia seeks to destabilise the EU member states both economically and politically and not only because Russia is also defying the EU as an international actor, seeking to nullify its influence in Ukraine. However, above all, Russia seeks to turn the clock back on the European continent with a return to old-fashioned imperialism and denying Ukraine's right to exist as a sovereign nation.[2] In essence, the Kremlin has waged war against the values upon which European integration has developed

---

1 McShane, D., 2014, "Eurosphere has lost Ukraine", *Kyiv Post*, 10 May.
2 Wolczuk, K., 2023, "Overcoming EU accession challenges in Eastern Europe: avoiding purgatory", Carnegie Europe, July.

over the past seven decades—Europe as a peace project which successfully overcomes wars, hostilities and rivalries on the continent.³

Therefore, Russia's aggression against Ukraine represents an abrupt end to the post-modern, post-geopolitical phase in European integration by forcing the EU to confront this blind spot.

To make amends in face of the invasion, the EU took an unprecedented step: after opposing Ukraine's membership aspirations for the last 20 years, within four months of Russia's invasion Ukraine was granted candidate status in an accelerated procedure. The EU member states showed exceptional unity in delivering symbolic support to Ukraine by immediately granting candidate status in the landmark decision of June 2022 and opening accession negotiations in June 2024.

Ukraine aspired to join the EU for over two decades prior to Russia's large scale invasion. Yet, Kyiv's membership aspirations were politely but firmly put to one side. Instead, the EU focused on technocratic aspects of relations with its neighbours through the neighbourhood policy—a low-politics, low-risk substitute for membership, focusing on market access, economic and functional integration, but conspicuously excluding full membership.⁴ However, the EU's offer of the new contractual arrangement in the form of the Association Agreement (with the Deep and Comprehensive Free Trade Area) was seized on by Ukraine as a stepping stone towards membership.

As the EU comes to terms with the regional and global ramifications of Russia's invasion, it is clear that Ukraine's inclusion entails consequences for the EU itself: the key challenge is how to balance the geopolitical imperative of Ukraine's membership against the EU's merit-driven demands of applicant states against the continued reluctance of many member states to admit Ukraine. Despite the massive symbolism of the decision, there is no actual consensus on Ukraine's membership nor the legal, institutional and financial

---

3   EEAS, 2022, "Europe in the interregnum: our geopolitical awakening after Ukraine", 24 March.
4   Dragneva, R., Wolczuk, K., 2015, *Ukraine between the EU and Russia: the integration challenge*, London: Palgrave Macmillan.

reforms which are needed to bring it about.⁵ As of 2024, the symbolism captured in the rhetoric of the EU's geopolitical "awakening" is not backed up by the shared commitment across the member states to actually prepare for enlargement and pave the way for Ukraine's accession. For many in the EU, the offer of membership is a symbolic gesture of solidarity rather than a meaningful commitment to admit Ukraine in a foreseeable future.

Therefore, the EU's resolve to ensure Ukraine's accession still remains to be proven. This is somewhat ironic: the EU leaders routinely refer to "homework" that the aspiring states have to do. Against the backdrop of the experience in the Western Balkans, the EU's credibility is rather low. In particular, accession of such a large country as Ukraine entails strategic trade-offs and complex interlinkages between different objectives, priorities and policy areas.⁶ Yet, the enlargement sceptics use the expected long timeline of Ukraine's accession as a justification for removing the urgency from the preparations inside the EU.

This paper traces EU-Ukraine relations to map their idiosyncratic and paradoxical nature by using the boundaries of order proposed by Michael Smith as an analytical handle on analysing the relations. Further, it is argued how the desire to avoid geopolitics prompted the EU to lower legal barriers with Ukraine by concluding the AA-DCFTA. While this was meant to bypass the vexed question of membership, now the experience of the AA-DCFTA puts Ukraine in a good stead for accession negotiations.

Yet, the decision on geopolitical enlargement of 2022 also exposes the EU's difficulties in enacting its geopolitical priorities. While presented as a technocratic process of meeting the membership criteria, the enlargement process is profoundly political, due to the very nature of the European project. European integration

---

5   According to French President Macron, it will take decades for Ukraine to join the European Union. See: Herszenhorn, D. M., von der Burchard, H., de la Baume, M., 2022, "Macron floats European 'community' open to Ukraine and UK", *Politico Europe*, May 9.

6   Youngs, R., 2022, "Ukraine's EU membership and the geostrategy of democratic self-preservation", Carnegie Europe, May.

was conceived to lower the political and economic boundaries between the few original member states and provide them with a stake in the internal market and access to various policies and sources of funding. This kind of economic integration and the accompanying financial mechanisms provides strong disincentives for admitting new members, especially when they are both large and poor. Therefore, to admit Ukraine, the geopolitical imperative needs to be enacted by the EU institutions and member states in various ways inside the EU. After being a marginal country for decades, Ukraine has become a defining challenge for the European project.

Boundaries of order

In the aftermath of the Second World War, hard power was to be transcended by economic, social and political integration to ensure security on the European continent. When Europe was bifurcated during the Cold War, European integration was launched to ensure cooperation and integration amongst western European countries.[7]

Ensconced by the NATO security umbrella, the project focused on economic and political integration as a way to overcome wars and rivalry between the member states. The EU was so effective in doing this that it developed a post-geopolitical identity – the project aimed to avoid using geopolitics as a lens through which to view relations not only between its member states but on the European continent as a whole.[8] If anything, the end of the Cold War and the geopolitical contest between the west and the communist bloc in 1989-1991 further reinforced this post-geopolitical self-identification.[9]

---

7   Moshes, A., 2022, "The war in Ukraine and Europe's external policy", FIIA Comment, Finnish Institute of International Affairs, August.
8   Auer, S., 2015, "Carl Schmitt in the Kremlin: the Ukraine crisis and the return of geopolitics", *International Affairs*, 91 (5), pp. 953-968.
9   Guzzini, S., 2012, "The framework of analysis: geopolitics meets foreign policy identity crisis", in: Guzzini, S. (ed.), *The return of geopolitics in Europe? Social mechanisms and foreign policy identity crises*, Cambridge: Cambridge University Press, p. 62.

The disintegration of the post-communist bloc clearly offered a renewed impetus to the European project. Indeed, the evolution of the EU since 1989 has been "a reflection of a normative consensus which provides at least some form of route map for those attempting to find their way in a disorderly and volatile continent".[10]

The shift of the border to the East meant that the EU had to somehow manage its relations with its new neighbours, cognisant as it is that they were potentially the source of great instability and threats. This interface between the EU, and wider Europe, has been characterised by Smith as "boundary of order", with four elements to it: geopolitical, institutional/legal, transactional, and cultural.[11] In the case of the EU the geopolitical boundary relates to territory and its demarcation from the disorderly and/or threatening world outside.[12] The legal boundary relates to the EU's engagement with outside countries in relation to the spread of EU's rules, *acquis communautaire*.

When it comes to Ukraine's relations with the EU, these boundaries of order have extensive utility, particularly the geopolitical and legal boundaries. Smith's framework sheds light on a complex and dynamic set of relations between the EU and Ukraine. Writing in the 1990s, Smith placed much emphasis on exclusion, especially vis-à-vis the post-Soviet states. Indeed, with regard to the geopolitical boundary the EU has been unbending in its refusal to offer Ukraine membership. However, at the same time, the EU made deliberate efforts to blunt the "hardness of the boundaries" — embodied in the "fortress Europe" metaphor — vis-à-vis the neighbouring states. The EU has endeavoured to dismantle the dichotomy of "ins" and "outs": "intensifying webs of interdependence have, since the 1990s, prompted a progressing blurring of the functional boundaries of the European Union".[13] Therefore, Ukraine-EU

---

10 Smith, M., 1996, "The European Union and a changing Europe: establishing the boundaries of order", *Journal of Common Market Studies*, 34 (1), p. 11.
11 *Ibidem*, pp. 5-28.
12 *Ibidem*, p. 14.
13 Lavenex, S., 2011, "Concentric circles of flexible European integration: A typology of EU external governance relations", *Comparative European Politics*, 9 (4-5), p. 372.

relations reflect a highly desynchronised process — different boundaries have been subjected to competing dynamics. The EU's approach to Ukraine exemplifies what might be called "fuzzy logic, whereby approximations and an inevitable dynamism are characteristic of boundary-building. The EU's approach leads to variety and lateral thinking, rather than linear development".[14]

Ukraine and EU's geopolitical boundary

As noted above, the origins of the European project — in its various stages of the European Economic Community (1958-1993), European Community (1993-2009) and European Union (established in 1993) have been designed to avoid using geopolitics as a lens through which to view relations between European states.[15] The fall of the Berlin Wall further reinforced this post-geopolitical self-identification of a successful peace project.

And yet, geopolitics retains its salience both for those aspiring to join the EU and those challenging the notion of an EU-centred Europe, meaning that the very existence of the EU has geopolitical implications: "[t]he initial drawing of the boundary was a function more of superpower confrontation than of the EC's independent action; the EC in a sense had simply accommodated itself to the boundary".[16] Yet, the emergence of the EEC/EC as a "bastion of stability" occurred during the Cold War, effectively producing "a geopolitical boundary between the Community/Union and the disorderly and/or threatening world outside".[17]

Against this backdrop, the disintegration of the two-bloc Europe and disappearance of the Iron Curtain in 1989-91 created considerable uncertainty for the EU but, ultimately, did not affect its self-defined identity in Europe. A geopolitical role became unavoidable as by early 1990s, East-Central European countries were desperate to join this "bastion" of stability, prosperity and security.

---

14 Smith, M., 1996, *op. cit.*, p. 22.
15 Auer, S., 2015, "Carl Schmitt in the Kremlin: the Ukraine crisis and the return of geopolitics", *International Affairs*, 91 (5), pp. 953-968.
16 Smith, M., *op. cit.*, p.14.
17 *Ibidem*.

Yet at the time, EU leaders and member states prioritised closer integration over opening to new geopolitical realities. In other words, "deepening" took precedence over "widening".

Moreover, in the early 1990s, the EU had already drawn a line between East-Central Europe and the three Baltic States on the one hand,[18] and the rest of the post-Soviet states in Eastern Europe, on the other. To Ukraine's dismay, the EU has persistently refused to extend its offer that far to the East.

Notwithstanding overall reluctance, the enlargement of the EU in 2004-7 was proclaimed the "most successful foreign policy of the EU", which ironically, exhausted the EU's willingness to engage in further enlargement. As Romano Prodi, President of the European Commission (1999-2004), put it in 2002 "we can't continue to enlarge forever".[19] The EU was acutely aware that further enlargement would require institutional changes, as well as the high costs of offering membership to large and poor countries, such as Ukraine, with its detrimental impact on the EU's cohesion and solidarity.[20]

Despite the EU's overt refusal to become a geopolitical entity, that is exactly what attracted Ukraine. The desire to constrain and indeed counteract Russia's influence led Ukrainian leaders to declare a European choice and proclaim EU membership as a foreign policy objective. This was in the face of Moscow's repeated attempts to reverse the disintegration of the Soviet Union through launching various integration projects such as the Eurasian Economic Union.[21] Yet the goal of EU membership has been endorsed by all subsequent Ukrainian leaders since 1998.

---

18   Thanks to their small size, historical and cultural factors, and the unwavering perseverance of their leaders, Estonia, Lithuania and Latvia succeeded in joining the EU together in 2004, despite the latter two starting negotiations later than Estonia.
19   Prodi, R., 2002, "A Wider Europe—A Proximity Policy as the key to stability", speech during the Sixth ECSA-World Conference, "Peace, Security and Stability International Dialogue and the Role of the EU", Brussels, 5-6 December.
20   See: Guicherd, C., 2002, "The Enlarged EU's Eastern Border. Integrating Ukraine, Belarus and Moldova in the European Project", *SWP-Studie*, Stiftung Wissenschaft und Politik, pp. 12-14.
21   Dragneva R., Wolczuk, K., (eds.), 2013, *Eurasian Economic Integration: Law, Policy, and Politics*, Camberley Surrey: Edward Elgar.

Ukraine's insistence for EU membership fell on deaf ears in Brussels, not least as it prioritised relations with Russia. Up to the mid-2000s, the EU pursued a "Russia first policy" and, like in the case of all post-Soviet states, the EU's relations with Ukraine were largely conducted in the shadow of relations with Russia.[22] An expert writing for a governmental think-thank in Berlin asserted that, notwithstanding pro-European aspirations of Moldova and Ukraine, "it is doubtful whether there are alternatives to *the Russian channel* to those countries' economic modernisation".[23] For Germany, Ukraine was to remain confined in the Russian "sphere of influence".

At the same time, it has to be said that Kyiv's focus on geopolitics distorted Ukraine's priorities in its relations with the EU. In the early years of independence, the Ukrainian elites cherished the idea that independent Ukraine's sheer size and geopolitical significance as a counterbalance to Russia guaranteed it an elevated status in the eyes of the West.[24] The failure of this belief to gain any traction in the EU resulted in a "dialogue of the deaf" and the growth of "Ukraine fatigue" in Brussels by the late 2000s.[25] However, some within the EU sought to soften the boundaries between the "ins" and "outs" by exploring ways of lowering the legal and transactional barriers by the completion of the Association Agreement, as will be seen below.

Russia's geopolitical contestation

Russia has tried to ensure control over Ukraine and dissuade Ukraine from pursuing closer ties with the EU by a variety of means. This was evident when Russia tried to derail the conclusion

---

22 Wolczuk, K., 2004, "Integration Without Europeanisation: Ukraine and its Policy Towards the European Union", *EUI Working Papers*, RSCAS No. 2004/15, European University Institute.
23 Guicherd, C., 2002, "The Enlarged EU's Eastern Border. Integrating Ukraine, Belarus and Moldova in the European Project", *SWP-Studie*, Stiftung Wissenschaft und Politik, p. 60.
24 Wolczuk, K., *op.cit.*
25 Wolczuk, K., 2008, "A Dislocated and Mistranslated EU-Ukraine Summit", *EU-ISS Opinion*, October.

of the EU-Ukraine Association Agreement in 2013-14. Using a combination of incentives and disincentives which exploited Ukraine's political and economic weaknesses and dependence, Russia was in effect demanding that Ukraine renounce the right to determine its own system of government.[26] The popular protests against abandoning closer ties with the EU culminated in Viktor Yanukovych's unceremonious escape to Russia in the final hours of the Revolution of Dignity, bringing new leadership to power.[27] In retaliation and in an ominous warning for the post-war world order, the Russian Federation annexed Crimea and started the occupation of the Donbas region in 2014.

The resort to military means, aggression and annexation in 2014 in response to economic ties between the EU and Ukraine represented a dramatic escalation in Russia's geopolitical contestation in Europe. Some argued that this challenge culminated in the reluctant but ultimately decisive "geopoliticisation" of the EU.[28]

However, the EU's approach remained distinctively oblivious to the geopolitical stakes and implications. This is because the EU was caught off guard with Russia's geopolitical tug-of-war over the Association Agreement with Ukraine. Accordingly, the response from the EU reflected its self-identity as that of a non-geopolitical, post-historic entity. Firstly, the EU has not and is not considering offering membership to Ukraine. The military backlash from Russia has not changed this and, if anything, reinforced the opposition to further enlargement. Moreover, apart from enhanced financial and technical assistance there was no upgrade of relations beyond the Association Agreement. In general, the EU's Eastern Policy was scaled down in scope and ambition.[29]

---

26 Hedenskog, J., 2014, "Ukraine—Challenges for the Future" in: Granholm, N., Malminen, J., Persson, G. (eds.), *A Rude Awakening: Ramifications of Russian Aggression towards Ukraine*, FOI, Stockholm, p. 52.
27 Wolczuk, K., 2019, "The Revolutions and Ukraine's European Integration", in: Kowal, P., Mink, G., Reichardt I. (eds.), *Three Revolutions: Mobilization and Change in Contemporary Ukraine, Volume I*, Hannover: ibidem-Verlag.
28 Allison R., 2014, "Russian 'Deniable' Intervention in Ukraine: How and Why Russia Broke the Rules", *International Affairs*, 90 (6), pp. 1255-1297.
29 Wolczuk, K., et al., 2023, "Mapping Changing Opportunity Structures and their Impact on Past EU Neighbourhood Policies", *ENGAGE Research Paper*.

Moreover, to placate Russia the EU sought functional solutions. In particular, the EU agreed to delay the implementation of the economic part of the Association Agreement and engage in trilateral EU-Ukraine-Russia negotiations on the bilateral agreement over 2014-15. The EU's readiness to engage Russia in this way reflected the EU's trust in technical solutions despite the fact that Russian concerns were neither legal nor technical. Russia's demands for far-reaching revisions to the agreement were about asserting its gate-keeping position vis-à-vis the post-Soviet countries in Europe.[30] The EU inadvertently legitimised Russian hegemonic aspirations within the "post-Soviet space".

Some argued that Russian aggression against Ukraine in 2014 was a wake-up call for the EU: "What Europe needs is a more hard-nosed realist approach, which recognises that Russia's expansionist ambitions can only be constrained by its own readiness and willingness to deploy power both politically and, if necessary, even militarily".[31] Yet lacking a meaningful foreign policy role, let alone the necessary military power to back up that role, the EU and its member states favoured a technocratic approach. Overall, in response to Russia's actions in Ukraine, the EU continued to stake its reputation as an anti-geopolitical entity.[32]

The implications of the EU's reluctance to re-draw the geopolitical boundary were profound. While provided with significant support for reforms, Kyiv was in effect left on its own to face Russia's attempts to divert Ukraine's westward drift in military and economic terms. Yet Moscow failed to stymie Ukraine's desire to integrate with the EU, while the deployment of force backfired in a variety of ways, including a fierce resentment across Ukraine towards Russian actions.

---

30 See: Dragneva, R., Wolczuk, K., 2014, "The EU-Ukraine Association Agreement and the Challenges of Inter-regionalism", *Review of Central and East European Law*, 39 (3-4); Dragneva, R., Wolczuk, K., 2015, *Ukraine between the EU and Russia: The Integration Challenge*, Palgrave Pivot.
31 Auer, S., 2015, "Carl Schmitt in the Kremlin: the Ukraine crisis and the return of geopolitics", *International Affairs*, 91 (5).
32 Mead, W. R., 2014 "The Return of Geopolitics", *Foreign Affairs*, 93 (3), May/June.

At the same time, paradoxically, Russia's limited war against Ukraine from 2014 to 2021 resulted in Ukraine's greater reliance on the EU. Russia's actions imbued the EU with a much stronger purchase over Ukraine, something which the EU's own policies—the European Neighbourhood Policy (ENP) and the Eastern Partnership—could not achieve. In the face of Russian military force, Ukraine was determined to be covered by the "geopolitical blanket" of the EU, despite the EU's own reluctance to offer it. To this end, Ukraine opted for massive, asymmetrical commitments vis-à-vis the EU by concluding the Association Agreement, as argued below. Ironically, this agreement puts Ukraine in a good stead during the accession process, a decision triggered by Russia's full-scale invasion of Ukraine in 2022.

The legal boundary between the EU and Ukraine

As the most densely institutionalised international organisation in the world, the defining feature of the EU is its clearly delineated institutional and legal boundaries. It has been considered a "community of law", in terms of internal functioning and external relations, codified in the Lisbon Treaty's obligation to promote its values and rules via foreign policy.[33]

The dense and pervasive set of institutions and rules governing the inside of the EU is one of the central boundary markers which differentiates it from the wider European environment. It is the law-based, highly-legislated functioning which accounts for much of the EU's attraction to outsiders, especially those with weak domestic institutions and rule of law. Yet, at the same time, as Smith argues, this law-based nature constitutes "a severe gradient or set of obstacles" to aspirants to the EU.[34]

In this sense, the geopolitical and the legal boundaries of the Union used to be closely aligned. However, the collapse of communism and demand for inclusion prompted the EU to lower the

---

33 Dragneva, R., Wolczuk, K., 2011, "EU Law Export to the Eastern Neighbourhood and an Elusive Demand for Law", in: Cardwell, P., (ed.), *EU External Relations Law and Policy in the Post-Lisbon Era*, TMC Asser Press.
34 Smith, M., 1996, *op.cit.*, p. 15.

legal boundary with its eastern neighbours. To this end, the EU came up with an alternative framework — the ENP. This was conceived in 2002-3 as a policy for the post-Soviet countries of Eastern Europe, and subsequently extended to the southern neighbours of the EU. In total, 12 countries to the East and South of the EU's border have participated in the policy, from Morocco to Armenia.

The ENP was a technocratic exercise which provided a bureaucratic answer to the question as to where the geopolitical and cultural boundaries of Europe lie. Ukraine was a key "partner" country for the EU. Ukraine's importance was not only a result of the fact that Ukraine was the largest ENP country to the East, but also because it was the country that was most dissatisfied with the framework for relations with the EU, having expressed membership aspirations since the late 1990s. Thus, placating Ukraine by providing an ambitious and yet feasible framework for relations (thereby bypassing the vexed question of membership) gave a strong impetus to the whole endeavour of developing the Wider Europe/European Neighbourhood Policy. From its onset in 2003-4, the ENP was inspired by the spirit of enlargement: advocating extensive domestic reforms in the partner countries, the essence of which is the adaptation of their institutions and policies to those of the EU.[35]

However, devising the neighbourhood policy was not a straightforward endeavour, as it exposed the competing pressures within the EU. On the one hand, the policy reflected the development of a normative, value-driven foreign policy, which was consolidated during eastern enlargement.[36] The explicit ideational dimension of foreign policies was evident in the way that the EU has

---

35 The modelling of the ENP on enlargement was conditioned by human resources within the European Commission and the time pressure under which the policy was devised. See: Kelley, J., 2006, "New Wine in Old Wineskins: Policy Adaptation in the European Neighborhood Policy", *Journal of Common Market Studies*, 44 (1), pp. 29-55.
36 Sedelmeier, U., 2006, "The EU's role as a promoter of human rights and democracy: Enlargement policy practice and role formation", in: Elgström, O., Smith, M. (eds.), *The European Union's Roles in International Politics. Concepts and Analysis*, Routledge.

been seeking to externalise its norms and values.[37] At the same time, the ENP was conceived as an alternative to enlargement, aimed at deflating membership aspirations of neighbouring states by offering economic and sectoral integration, thereby weakening the purchase of the EU over domestic reforms.

Despite Ukraine's dissatisfaction with the policy, Kyiv used the new policy to develop closer legal ties with the EU. Ukrainian officials insisted on a new contractual framework to guide Ukraine's integration with the EU, with a view to paving the way to a membership perspective.[38] At first, the EU showed considerable resistance to any new agreement, fearful of opening the "membership question" with regard to Ukraine. Thus, from the EU perspective, the Agreement was a political "gift" to Ukraine because, in terms of trade alone, the EU had little interest in integrating Ukraine; at the time it accounted for only 1.4% of EU exports thus, making it difficult to justify such an agreement on purely economic grounds.[39]

Subsequently, the Association Agreement with Deep and Comprehensive Free Trade Agreements (AA-DCFTA) were developed as a flagship instrument of the European Neighbourhood Policy. The Association Agreement aimed to foster a new type of relation between the EU and Ukraine: economic integration and political cooperation.[40] The reform agenda embedded in the AA-DCFTAs incorporated not only broad norms and values, such as democracy and human rights, but also required the adoption of the legal standards of the European Union as a whole, i.e. much of the

---

37 Bengtsson, R., 2008, "Interfaces: the Neighbourhood Discourse in EU External Policy', *Journal of European Integration*, 30 (5), p. 613.
38 Author's interviews with Ukrainian officials from the Ministry of Foreign Affairs of Ukraine, Brussels, September 2006 and September 2010.
39 Delcour, L., Wolczuk, K., 2013, "Eurasian Economic Integration and Implications for the EU's policy in the Eastern Neigbhourhood", in: Dragneva, R., Wolczuk, K. (eds.), *Eurasian Economic Integration: Law, Policy, and Politics*, Camberley Surrey: Edward Elgar.
40 European Commission, 2008, *Eastern Partnership*. Communication to the Council and to the European Parliament, COM 823 final: 4.

acquis communautaire. The agreement became a vehicle for an unprecedented degree of exporting of law — approximately 80-90% of trade-related *acquis* was included in the DCFTA part of the AA.[41]

Overall, with the ENP, the EU has devised "alternative forms of integration below the threshold of membership".[42] In this way the EU hoped to soften the legal boundary with European non-members and entice the eastern neighbours into domestic reforms, but without the risk of jeopardising deeper integration between the members.

The cautious stance vis-à-vis Ukraine was understandable as, in terms of rule-based behaviour, Ukraine has hardly been a credible partner for the EU. The above-mentioned focus on security distorted Ukraine's priorities in relations with the EU, to the detriment of political, legal and economic reforms.[43]

AA-DCFTA and EU's support for reforms in Ukraine

Notwithstanding the initial reluctance, the European Commission drafted a comprehensive, complex and ambitious agreement which provided for economic integration and enhanced political cooperation. The Association Agreement belongs to an exclusive group of integration-oriented agreements — there are few agreements that the EU has with third countries which allow for such advanced forms of integration into the single market.[44] To protect the cohesion of the single market, the AA contains extensive, detailed and binding provisions on Ukraine to align its laws and policies with those of the EU. The commitment of Ukraine as a non-member state to abide by EU regulations implies first and foremost an extension of the EU's legal boundary to include Ukraine.[45]

---

41 Duleba, A., Ben, V., Bilčík, V., 2012, *Policy impact of the Eastern Partnership on Ukraine: trade, energy, and visa dialogue*, Research Center of the Slovak Foreign Policy Association.
42 Lavenex, S., *op.cit.*, p. 373.
43 Wolczuk, K., 2004; 2008.
44 Van der Loo, G., Van Elsuwege, P., Petrov, R., 2014, "The EU-Ukraine Association Agreement: Assessment of an Innovative Legal Instrument", *EUI Working Papers*, Law, 2014/09.
45 Lavenex, S., *op.cit.*, p. 374.

Yet, in drafting and negotiations of the AA-DCFTA, little appreciation was given to the sheer scale of the task in terms of scope, depth and associated investments as well as political incentives to embark on extensive, costly and politically sensitive reforms for the partner countries.

The AA-DCFTA fostered closer cooperation as Ukraine was very open to the influence of the EU. This led to a particularly close engagement of EU officials in Ukraine, which paved the way for a more tailored support for broader reforms in Ukraine since 2014. In particular, EU officials and experts noted the gulf between extensive AA-DCFTA commitments and a limited state capacity of Ukraine, something which led the Commission to come up with some flanking measures of assistance to enhance state capacity in Ukraine.[46] Therefore, the AA-DCFTA implementation prompted the EU to support broader reforms under the banner of European integration than the narrowly defined "AA implementation". Overall, strengthening state capacity has taken a variety of forms as the EU focused on the fundamental preconditions for the implementation in terms of building state capacity over 2014-21.

For example, the EU supported decentralisation, thereby devolution of power to local self-government in Ukraine. Already in 2015, the EU launched a large-scale support measure, the "U-LEAD with Europe: Ukraine Local Empowerment, Accountability and Development Programme". With a budget of 102 million euros, this programme supported Ukrainian decentralisation: reforms to strengthen regional and local governance structures in Ukraine. In particular, U-LEAD covered capacity building and support to the amalgamation process for local authorities and enhancement of administration and service delivery at local, regional and central level.[47]

---

46 Wolczuk, K., Zeruolis, D., 2018, "Rebuilding Ukraine: An assessment of EU assistance", Chatham House Research Paper.
47 See: Mathernova, K., Wolczuk, K., 2020, "The Eastern Partnership: Between fundamentals and integration", *New Eastern Europe*, 5 (43); Wolczuk, K., 2019 "State building and European integration in Ukraine", *Eurasian Geography and Economics*, 60 (6).

As a result, after 2014 the EU's assistance to Ukraine became both more systematic and system-focussed in that it sought to strengthen the state's capacity to implement reform rather than merely facilitate legal approximation of the *acquis*.[48] From that point of view, the AA-DCFTA has provided a powerful stimulus for EU and Ukrainian officials to develop joint solutions to address long-standing weaknesses and challenges. The agreement indeed prompted deeper and comprehensive ties and assistance in the run up to Russia's war on Ukraine in 2022.

Russia's war against Ukraine and a shift of geopolitical boundary

With the full-scale Russian invasion of 2022, the context of EU-Ukraine relations changed profoundly. The Ukrainian authorities seized the moment to rapidly apply for membership. While the invasion sent shockwaves across the EU, the summit in Versailles under the French Presidency of the Council of the European Union in March 2022 hardly indicated a sea-change with regard to Ukraine. Yet, in the run up to the summit in June 2022, a last-minute decision was taken on providing a symbolic support to Ukraine by offering the prospect of membership. This was to signal a step change in the EU's response to the scale of Russia's aggression. As Nychyk put it: "The EU was always afraid to provoke Russia, but its caution did not prevent Russian unprovoked invasion of Ukraine in 2022. The EU's leaders' awareness about the need to change the strategy was growing. Eastern EU-member states' politicians had a real fear of Russian possible attack on their own countries and even Western Europeans felt Russian threat. It was the moment when European decision-makers agreed that the EU had to develop a stronger response to Russia and fostering relations with Ukraine was one of the new measures".[49]

---

48 Mathernova, K., 2019, *op. cit.*
49 Nychyk, A., 2024, "The renewed chance for the EU's enlargement by Ukraine", *Crossroads Europe,* 15 July. https://crossroads.ideasoneurope.eu/2024/07/15/the-renewed-chance-for-the-eus-enlargement-by-ukraine/

The Russian brutality and war crimes created a huge wave of sympathy among EU citizens and politicians, given the EU's self-definition as a defender of human rights, peace and stability in Europe. This framing exerted strong pressure to support Ukraine with all means, including the use of the Peace Facility to provide arms to Ukraine and large-scale macro-economic assistance. EU politicians felt the moral need to help Ukraine to deal with Russia's aggression by signalling that Ukraine could join the EU after the war ends.

Having said that, enlargement is never easy for the EU. The legal, economic and political design of the European project militates against widening of the project by bringing in new members. With all the above considerations in place, an offer of membership was largely a symbolic gesture, which did not require any immediate decisions and did not entail any immediate and major consequences for EU institutions and member states. It was rather that the threat to the EU and the moral obligation were crucial in the EU's decision to make Ukraine a candidate country within months of Russia's large-scale invasion. This upgrade was a sign of moral support for Ukraine with no expectation of fast enactment.

However, with Ukraine eager to seize the moment and the Commission efficiently making the preparations, the decision started to be enacted and by June 2024 the EU agreed to open the accession negotiations. As a result, the pressing question has turned to the process of accession and its complexities.

Ironically, the EU-Ukraine legal framework during the accession process does not present any challenge: the *acquis*-heavy AA-DCFTA has simply acquired a new relevance. Ukraine's exposure to the *acquis* and progress in adopting it has strengthened its case as a candidate country.[50] The use of AA-DCFTA not only offered an invaluable experience along a steep learning curve for Ukraine and the EU, but provided an adaptable tool for the upgrade to the accession country status. Ironically, in light of the fact that the AA-DCFTA was designed to bypass the question of membership, the

---

50 Dragneva, R., Wolczuk, K., 2024, "Integration and Modernization: EU's Association Agreement with Ukraine" in: Rabinovych, M., Pintsch, A. (eds.), *Ukraine's Thorny Path to the EU: From "Integration without Membership" to "Integration through War"*, London: Palgrave Macmillan.

agreement has become excellent guide for the road to membership as well as structuring relations during the accession process.[51] The lowering of the legal boundary as a result of Ukraine's demand for membership put the country in good stead when the decision on geopolitical enlargement was made in June 2022.

However, the broader challenges remain daunting, including the dysfunctionality of the enlargement policy and the necessary adjustments to the EU's institutions, budget and policies to welcome not only Ukraine but, potentially, up to 36 member states in total. The very nature of the European project makes it difficult to deal with geopolitical imperatives, due to its focus on functional integration amongst the member states. Even though the "peace project" was the very rationale for pursuing European integration, the EU's dense legal order and the gatekeeping role of the member states put steep hurdles for any aspiring countries to overcome even when war is yet again raging in Europe.

Dysfunctionalities of the enlargement policy

Given that the European project of integration has been attracting new member states for 70 years, it would be reasonable to expect that the process would be well-rehearsed and efficiently enacted. In particular, the 2004-7 enlargement was proclaimed the EU's "most successful foreign policy". Yet, despite extending the membership perspective to the Western Balkans in the early 2000s, the EU's enlargement strategy has hardly worked efficiently since then.

The process has become so stalled and dysfunctional that some regard it as "a showcase of duplicity and double talk".[52] This is because the enlargement process aimed at the Western Balkan countries has suffered from two problems: excessive technocracy and excessive politicisation.

---

51 Wolczuk, K., 2023, "EU Policy Governance Mechanisms of Georgia, Moldova And Ukraine – Initially Politically Under-Invested and Legally Overloaded, Now Their Time Has Come", *3DCFTA Project Paper*, Centre for European Policy Studies.
52 Herszenhorn, D. M., Bayer, L., 2021, *op. cit.*

Excessive Politicisation of the enlargement process

The successful 2004-7 enlargement was driven by the European Commission, with strong support from many member states. The Commission decided on progression, specified conditions, and ensured compliance during the accession negotiations. Member states were not involved in the intermediate stages (for example, decisions to open and close negotiating chapters). Since the 2000s, however, the member states have taken on a stronger oversight of the process. The member states, such as France, specifically requested this political oversight over enlargement to the Western Balkan countries. In practice, this means that since the early 2000s every stage of the accession process, including not only opening the accession negotiations but other technical decisions (such as, for example, opening and closing every one of 35 chapters in the accession negotiations) needs to be unanimously approved by all 27 member states. This procedure has given a readily available veto power to any member state for whatever reason. It is hardly surprising that right has been abused by some member states.

The veto power means that without the political will of all the member states, the technical process—however well led by the European Commission—remains largely inconsequential. Any member state can derail the process in pursuit of their own ends, unrelated to the membership criteria.

In this way, the enlargement process has become hostage to national interests and bilateral disputes, as was shown by the tensions between Slovenia and Croatia before the latter joined the EU, or more recently when the opening of the accession negotiations with North Macedonia was delayed by the successive vetoes of Greece, France and Bulgaria. As a result, having been granted candidate status in 2005, North Macedonia waited for 17 years to start accession negotiations. These delays were easily achieved as member states need to agree unanimously on an enlargement strategy and any progress decision for individual countries.[53]

---

53 Zweers, W., *et al.*, 2022, "The EU as a promoter of democracy or 'Stabilitocracy' in the Western Balkans", Clingendael Report, February.

Some reforms in the enlargement methodology to make the process more transparent and fair took place in 2020, yet results have been underwhelming.[54] As a result, membership negotiations amounted to "little more than rituals of opening and closure of [negotiations on] chapters, that drag on and which only the specialists are able to decipher".[55] Thus, "progress has not been related to merit for a long time, [...] and the motivation of candidate countries to carry out reforms has declined, the longer the process has been ongoing."[56] The political influence of the EU in the region waned as a result, even though the political elites routinely pay lip service to enlargement.[57]

Excessive technocracy

For nearly two decades, the European Commission tweaked and refined its enlargement strategy in order to ensure that the aspiring countries were ready to assume membership obligations. The aim was to make accession conditionality both comprehensive and stringent—in terms of focusing not only on the EU's *acquis* but also addressing the so-called fundamentals—that is, how the political and economic systems function. Stringency was introduced to ensure thorough preparation *before* countries are admitted.[58]

However, despite boosting political conditionality, the EU has in the Western Balkans failed to engage the political elite in pursuit of more profound political and economic change. Some argue that the EU conditionality provided "money, power and glory" to the

---

54 Stratulat, C., 2021, "EU Enlargement to the Western Balkans—three observations", EPC Commentary, November.
55 Mirel, P., 2019, "European Union-Western Balkans: for a revised membership negotiation framework", Robert Schuman Foundation, Policy Paper No. 59, September.
56 ESI, 2022, "The Balkan Turtle Race: Warning to Ukraine", European Stability Initiative Report, 13 July, p. 4.
57 See: Bechev, D., 2022, "What Has Stopped EU Enlargement in the Western Balkans?", Carnegie Europe, 20 June.
58 The most recent revisions are outlined by the European Commission, 2020, "Enhancing the accession process—A credible EU perspective for the Western Balkans", COM 57 final, 5 February.

self-serving ruling elites.[59] Faced with such political obstacles inside the EU and in the aspiring countries, the European Commission often focused on technical issues to give the illusion of progress in their annual reports.[60] In particular, rule of law reforms were treated as technical rather than political issues. As Richard Youngs put it, the EU ended up "offering accession as a distant prospect and then pushing for extensive technical harmonisation in the hope that this would suffice to resolve intensely political problems".[61] At the same time, the European Commission was rather technocratic in its approach to reforms and avoided addressing more important and sensitive political issues, such as corruption or democratic backsliding in the Western Balkans.[62] The failure of the enlargement process to promote democracy in the candidate states in the Western Balkans has been studied widely but it seems that the Commission and member states have not discussed and drawn the lessons. Against this backdrop, there is a real risk with Ukraine that opening the negotiations on various chapters with multiple benchmarks will continue to become a de facto substitute for real progress in accession negotiations.

Reforms of the institutions and policies

The EU presents the process as a merit-based technocratic act on both sides: the countries reform and the EU checks progress and ticks off boxes. This masks the real challenges ahead: what it actually takes for the EU institutions and its member states to agree to enlarge in general and to Ukraine, in particular. The technocratic framing implies that this is premised on the opening and closing of chapters and clusters within which various opening, interim and

---

59   Richter, S., Wunsch, N., 2020, "Money, power, glory: the linkages between EU conditionality and state capture in the Western Balkans", *Journal of European Public Policy*, 27 (1), pp. 41-62.
60   Kmezić, M., Bieber, F., 2020, "The Crisis of Democracy in the Western Balkans. An Anatomy of 'Stabilitocracy' and the Limits of EU Democracy Promotion", The Balkans in Europe Policy Advisory Group, March, p. 95.
61   Youngs, R., 2022, "Ukraine's EU membership and the geostrategy of democratic self-preservation", Carnegie Europe, May.
62   See Zweers, W. *et al.*, 2022, *op. cit.*

closing benchmarks need to be completed. This is necessary, but not sufficient. The decision is not conditional on implementing particular recommendations or reaching any prescribed standards. The EU's so-called absorption capacity is a function of its 27 member states' bargaining skills to forge a political compromise to underpin a political decision on admitting a new country to the exclusive club. Buras and Morina argue that:

> "The real measure of its absorption capacity is whether member states can reach any political consensus about when to enlarge and under what conditions. Various national interests, power relations, public opinions, and expectations regarding the end goal of the integration process inform this debate. These considerations are ultimately far more important than technical or legal ones. Unless member states can strike a grand bargain that takes into account their respective positions as well as the geopolitical context Europe finds itself in, the EU will not be able to accept new countries – even if they tick all the boxes in the commission's annual assessment."[63]

As of 2024, the understanding of how to fulfil this geopolitical goal of enlargement varies across Europe. The report by the Franco-German working group on EU institutional reforms sheds light on the type and complexity of possible changes. Indicatively, however, it devotes considerable attention to some aspects of "deepening", which are favoured by the authoring experts, such as ensuring EU-level democracy by harmonisation of EU electoral laws. This would hardly be regarded as an indispensable adjustment in preparation for enlargement in many member states.[64] Inevitably, this indicates that any discussion of enlargement provides a stimulus for those interested in deepening of integration to make enlargement conditional upon "deepening" of the Union. At the same time, at least the report "starts the ball rolling", when most member states seem to still be in denial about the inevitable trade-offs and the imminence of decisions required.

---

63   Buras, P., Morina, E., 2023, "Catch-27: The contradictory thinking about enlargement in the EU", European Council on Foreign Relations, https://ecfr.eu/publication/catch-27-the-contradictory-thinking-about-enlargement-in-the-eu/ (Accessed: 24 August 2024).
64   Report of the Franco-German Working Group of EU Institutional Reform, 2023, "Sailing on High Seas: Reforming and Enlargement the EU for the 21st Century", 18 September.

The discussions and tough but pragmatic decisions on institutional reforms, budgetary adjustments and changes to key policies, such as the Common Agricultural Policy, the Green Deal and Structural Funds, are all necessary to enable Ukraine to join. In parallel, the discussion on the failure of the enlargement process and the "costs of non-enlargement" needs to be discussed to highlight what is at stake not only for Ukraine but also the EU and the wider international order.[65]

Conclusions

From an inauspicious beginning in the 1990s, over time EU-Ukraine relations have become increasingly important for Ukraine. And since 2022, Ukraine has become a defining challenge for the EU. Until 2021, the EU offered a technocratic solution to the question of boundaries. Ukraine succeeded in lowering legal boundaries from the Union but the EU has failed to dismantle the geopolitical boundary. And it was the latter boundary that mattered most to Ukraine in the Hobbsian world of Russian geopolitics. Therefore, the legal forms of inclusion did not compensate for the geopolitical exclusion. The EU is now seeking to make amends because Russia's war on Ukraine jeopardises the entire European order, its peace and stability. Russia's aggression against Ukraine and other post-Soviet states have put into question core European values: democracy and the rule of law, the inviolability of borders as enshrined in the 1975 Helsinki Final Act and the broader international system with its established principles on the use of force. Thus, Ukraine becomes a defining challenge for the EU, as the crisis "strikes at the heart of the European project" (Adebahr, 2015).

As Russia's war on Ukraine poses formidable political and security challenges for Europe, it also provides a unique opportunity for policymakers to revive the idea of the EU as a peace project.[66] The EU member states showed exceptional unity in delivering symbolic support to Ukraine by immediately granting candidate status

---

65 Visegrad Insight, 2024, "Costs of non-Enlargement: Foresight Report on EU Enlargement and Neighbourhood" Strategic Foresight by Visegrad Insight.
66 Buras, P., Morina, E., *op.cit.*

in the landmark decision of June 2022. This act appeared to indicate that, with political leadership, a renewed sense of purpose and unity within the EU can emerge in a very short time: "successful integration will be crucial to the entire future European order and the new self-identification of the EU as a geopolitical actor. This becomes a priority for the EU's foreign policy".[67]

Yet this requires the EU to both restore the credibility of the accession process and embark on adjusting its own institutions and policies. Above all, the EU member states and institutions ought to become goal- rather than process-oriented in order to "make enlargement a success again" and thereby deliver on its "geopolitical awakening" rhetoric. To face the challenges that arise from Russia's aggression, the EU must reconcile a credible enlargement policy with changes needed to adjust the union's institutions, budget and policies to a larger number of member states. This agenda needs to be completed by the existing 27 member states. The process is expected to get bogged down along various technical hurdles, chapters, clusters, with multiple (opening, interim and closing) benchmarks. Return to the dysfunctional mix of excessive technocracy with overt politicisation remains a real prospect and, in fact, a hope of many EU member states. Therefore, the challenges that face the EU are likely to be as daunting as was the case back in the late 1980s, when communism collapsed in Central and Eastern Europe. In the meantime, the reunification of Europe remains an elusive idea.

---

67 Lang, K. O., Buras, P., 2022, "Partnership for enlargement: a new way to integrate Ukraine and the EU's eastern neighbourhood", Policy Brief, ECFR and Batory Foundation.

The Future of Political Technology in Ukraine

Andrew Wilson

Political technology has its origins in 1990s Russia.[1] It has some antecedents in Soviet "active measures" and even the police parties or "Zubatov parties" of the late Tsarist era. But it is characteristically post-Soviet: it is the "managed" part in a "managed democracy". It is also a means of keeping things post-Soviet, opposing challenges to the hybrid regimes of the post-Soviet order.

Ukrainian politics has also been distorted by political technology since the fall of the Soviet Union. If the home of political technology was a re-imperialising Russia, Russia used political technology to expand its influence in post-Soviet states. But also, without being redundant, many post-Soviet states including Ukraine shared the relevant aspects of post-Soviet political culture that provided fertile ground for the spread of political technology. Many post-Soviet states were competitive authoritarian states: and political technology is one of the key aspects of Levitsky's and Way's definition of states that allow political competition, but that competition is unfair.[2]

This paper has three aims. First, to explain why so much political technology was used in Ukraine before February 2022. Second, to show that, as the EuroMaidan became the Revolution of Dignity in 2013-14 — a revolution against the post-Soviet condition — political technology has been less used in Ukraine. Third, trends since February 2022, especially changes in public opinion and the decline of oligarchy, are making Ukraine a less receptive future environment for political technology.

First, however, a definition of political technology is needed. Political technology is ubiquitous in much of the post-Soviet world. It is the operating code of the political system in Russia. But the

---

[1] Wilson, A., 2024, *Political Technology: The Globalisation of Political Manipulation*, Cambridge: Cambridge University Press.
[2] Levitsky, S., Way, L.A., 2001, *Competitive Authoritarianism: Hybrid Regimes After the Cold War*, Cambridge: Cambridge University Press, pp. 3 and 5.

phrase is little used in the West. This is partly because Russian definitions of their own political technology are too broad. They tend to be too close to being synonymous for politics as a whole. According to analyst Valery Solovey, political technology is "the methods, means and techniques of realising politics".[3] The definition by the leading Ukrainian expert on disinformation, Georgy Pocheptsov, is that political technology is any "way of organising information, semantic and human resources to achieve political goals".[4] But defining political technology as politics or as all types of information politics does not identify it as a new subject. It does, however, tell you a lot about Russians if they assume that all politics is manipulation.

Therefore, my definition is imposed: political technology is "the supply-side engineering of the political system for partisan interests".[5] It is not about demand. It is something that elites do. Voters do not ask for it. They may be unaware of its existence and tactics. Political technology is engineering or reshaping the political system. This is the sense in which political technology is "technology". It may use actual technologies like troll farms or social media platforms. But there is not much technology in
"judicial technology" (bribing judges) or "candidate technology" (determining who stands in elections) — though both methods are highly effective. And political technology is done to serve private, corporate or state interests, not the common good. So defined, political technology is common in the former Soviet world, though engineering of the political system can happen anywhere.

Why was there so much political technology in Ukraine?

Ukraine since 1991 has been both post-Soviet and either imperfectly democratic or competitive authoritarian. But I would suggest six main reasons why so much political technology was used in Ukraine before February 2022. First, Ukraine shared many, but not

---

3   Solovey, V., 2020, "Message via Facebook", 5 October.
4   Pocheptsov, G., 2018, "Interview via Facebook", 16 September.
5   Wilson, A., 2024, *op. cit.*, p. 3.

all, post-Soviet features to Russia. It did not have a revanchist instinct or global Great Power ambitions that led it to use political technology against other states. Ukraine did not have a cult of the KGB and *siloviki*, or of statism, the power of the state. But Ukraine did have cynical elites. It did have corruption, or rather *koruptsionery* — politics-as-corruption and therefore the need for politics-as-disguise. It did have a too powerful Security Service (SBU) and Procuracy (GPU). Ukraine had an inverted legal culture of universal prosecutability: nobody could obey all of the complex and contradictory laws, everybody broke some laws; so the decision whether or not to lay charges was always political. Politics was for our "own" (*svoi*), our friends; enemies were excluded.

Second, Ukraine had a powerful oligarchy. Moreover, it had a system of oligarchs and state capture rather than what Madlovics and Magyar call poligarchs and oligarch capture, as in Putin's Russia.[6] There were effective cycles of oligarchic reproduction, wealth defence and regular regeneration of political influence. These cycles were both material and political technological. Material cycles of rent-seeking have been well-described by David Dalton.[7] But the political technology cycle was just as important. Almost three-quarters of the media audience was captured by oligarchic TV. Those channels were used to promote project parties and politicians. Once they won office, they did material favours which further cemented oligarchic influence, and the cycle continued; or oligarchs bought off independent politicians.

Particularly for oligarchs and informal networks of influence, covert representation was the most important political technology in Ukraine. Candidates for president can of course be sponsored. There are many strategies for legislative elections. One is collective investment in "shares" in the governing party, as was with the Party of Regions during its heyday from 2006 to 2014. Sometimes, oligarchs can invest in parties after they have been created or after they have won, as with the Servant of the People party in 2019.

---

6   Madlovics, B., Magyar, B., 2023, *Ukraine's Patronal Democracy and the Russian Invasion: The Russia-Ukraine War*, Volume One, Budapest: Central European University Press.

7   Dalton, D., 2023, *The Ukrainian Oligarchy After the Euromaidan: How Ukraine's Political Economy Regime Survived the Crisis*, New York: Columbia University Press.

Every Ukrainian parliament has seen new factions created after the elections. In the current parliament elected in 2019, that would be For the Future, Trust and Recovery of Ukraine (part of the OPFL has relaunched as the Platform for Life and Peace). Individual deputies can be bought as "bayonets".[8] Independents can be bought up. "Project parties" can be created to insert representatives in parliament. In the executive, "*smotriashchy*" (watchers) look after sponsors' interests. In the legal system, there are pocket courts, judges and prosecutors: "sitters" and "foundlings", either long-term or purchased for the occasion.[9]

This is one key factor explaining why both the Orange Revolution and the Revolution of Dignity were effective at stopping democratic deterioration, but not at deep democratisation. The cycle was not broken.

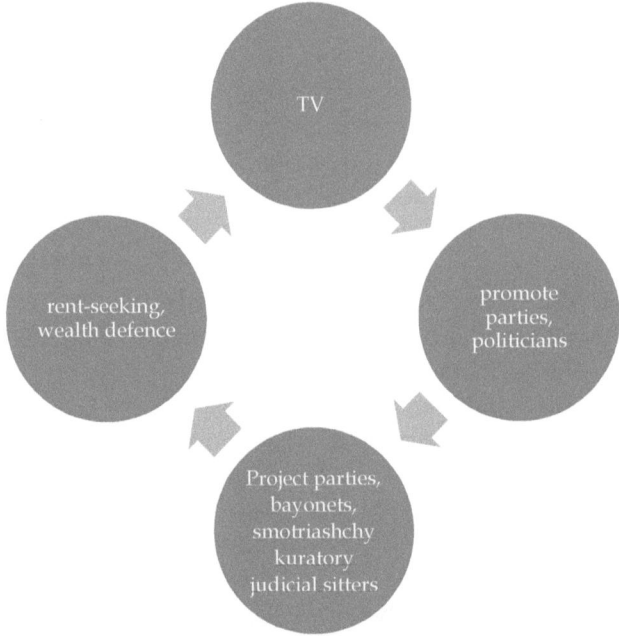

Figure 1: The chain of oligarchic influence

---

8 "Chotyry viiny Kolomoiskoho. Yak oliharkh povertaie svii vplyv", *Pravda*, 4 December 2019. www.pravda.com.ua/articles/2019/12/4/7233777/ (Accessed: 20 August 2024).
9 Wilson, A., 2024, *op.cit.*, pp. 355-7.

Third, Ukraine was the land of revolution and protest. Political technology was a key method for vested interests to protect themselves against it and blunt any drive for change. An uneasy counterpoint developed. Revolution was protest against all aspects of the post-Soviet condition, including political technology. But political technology was also a means to frustrate revolution. Least so with the Revolution on Granite in 1990, as political technology was then embryonic. But there was divide-and-rule of the student protest groups who led the revolution.[10] The Khmara affair (the arrest of a radical MP) was exploited to try and discredit Ukrainian nationalism. Political technology defeated many of the hopes of the 2004 Orange Revolution. It was not particularly successful in selling artificial parties in the 2006 and 2007 elections—though one, the Lytvyn Bloc, held the balance of power after 2007. But political technology was instrumental in building the Party of Regions; and in making oligarchs as powerful as politicians, as sponsors swapped between the three main political forces in 2005-10. Revolution only began to get the upper hand after 2014. But political technology attempted a "sweet counter-revolution"[11] (a pun on Poroshenko's chocolate business, but also because tactics were covert).

A fourth factor is money. Ukraine was the one post-Soviet state with the right combination of competition, size and money to create a big political technology market.

Fifthly, therefore, Ukraine became what I described in my book *Political Technology*[12] as a political technology hub state. The book tries to explain the globalisation of political technology. Certain states have more of it and are therefore importers and exporters. There is emulation from afar. There is the transfer of personnel between countries. There is a certain amount of technological de-

---

10 See: Kowal, P., Mink, G., Reichardt, A. and Reichardt, I. (eds.), 2019, *Three Revolutions: Mobilization and Change in Contemporary Ukraine II. An Oral History of the Revolution on Granite, Orange Revolution, and Revolution of Dignity*, Hannover: ibidem-Verlag.
11 Hrytsak, Y., 2017, "Sladkaya kontrrevolyutsiya", *Novoe Vremya*, 11 June. http://nv.ua/opinion/grytsak/sladkaja-kontrrevoljutsija-1288921.html (Accessed: 20 August 2024).
12 Wilson, A., 2024, *op.cit.*

terminism in aspects of political technology that involve more technology—Donald Trump's 2020 election app was modelled on India's NaMo, for example. There are national styles of political technology. Russia clearly is not China: the internet was not controlled there from its introduction, and it was relatively free until 2012. Hence the characteristic in Russian political technology of trolling the opposition. Israeli political technology is more about the political benefits of intelligence and surveillance. But hub states are importers that create their own alchemies. Hungary under Fidesz has American and Israeli political consultants. It has also learnt from Russia. Now it is exporting: in 2023 Fidesz political technologists unsuccessfully backed the Law and Justice (PiS) party in Poland, and more successfully Robert Fico in Slovakia.

Ukraine from 1998 to 2004 had a mass inflow of Russian political technologists. Then Americans like Paul Manafort were popular, with that popularity peaking in 2010 (with many veterans of the 2008 US election heading to Ukraine). But since then Ukraine developed its own political technologists and characteristic political technologies. *Grechka*, for example, means 'buckwheat'—that is, vote farming by supplying free goods or just cash. In Ukraine, *grechka* firms would organise pyramid networks to bind voters together and make sure they voted as promised. *Grechka* technologists then worked for export in countries like Moldova.

Sixth, as well as foreign and domestic political technology, Ukraine was also subject to Russian political technology. Initially, that was Russians working privately in Ukraine, who after 2004 were distrusted for failing to distinguish between their clients' interests and Russian state interests. After 2004, Russian political technology operations were increasingly run by the Kremlin or FSB; and were more clearly about trying to create a "Russian World" in Ukraine and a Russia-aligned Ukrainian foreign policy. Ukrainians were trebly unfortunate in that they were the object of domestic, foreign and Russian political technology.

Competition, not hegemony

Political technology in Russia is all about hegemony; in two senses. First, political technology is how Russian politics became fully scripted and controlled. Second, because political technology has spread into other areas: history, foreign policy, even church affairs. Political technology in Ukraine is not about hegemony. In fact, it is the opposite. Political technology has survived for so long because politics in Ukraine is brutally competitive. Political technology is what gives you the edge. The need for an edge and the need to out-fight your competitors motivate individual politicians and political forces to use political technology.

Typical political technologies in Ukraine

This also determines the characteristic forms that political technology takes in Ukraine. First was simple fraud. Initially simple, but then developing organised and professional forms. Like the "carousel" and companies that organise the carousel. (In south-east Europe known as the "Bulgarian Train" or "Indian String"). Large-scale fraud through the use of administrative resources was characteristic of the Leonid Kuchma era; but that has become more difficult since 2014.

Vote-farming or *grechka* (small-scale bribery) is characteristically Ukrainian. It operates through both supply and demand, as many voters want to sell their votes and/or get the best price.[13] *Grechka* firms promise to check that people actually vote for whom they promised to vote for. Technical solutions are imperfect: a photo of your ballot paper might be required, but you can always photograph someone else's. Better are schemes that embed voters within privatised, even entrepreneurial networks (*sitky* or "grids"), that are basically local vote-framing pyramid schemes. One-time Kyiv mayor Leonid Chernovetsky (2006-12) was notorious for his *grechka* politics. His operatives have helped spread the technology to Moldova and Georgia.

---

13 "Focus on Vote Buying" *Insajder*, 27 April 2016. https://insajder.net/en/site/focus/794/ (Accessed: 20 August 2024).

Man-marking or woman- marking was a largely unnoticed tactic in the 2019 election. Namely, harassing your opponent by creating or exploiting a clone candidate to depress their vote. Poroshenko was able to sneak past Yuliya Tymoshenko and Yuriy Boiko into the second round because both lost votes to clones. Volodymyr Zelenskyy did not. This tactic is described in the opening scene of Series 1, Episode 1 of Zelenskyy's *Servant of the People*. In the episode, oligarchs are plotting: "Gentlemen, aren't you tired of pointlessly wasting money? First, we spend millions to bring our candidates to the political forefront and then we spend twice as much to ruin our competitors".[14]

Ukraine also has competitive troll armies. Not the centralised Russian model of the Internet Research Agency/ Olgino Model, but bot and trolling operations named after individual politicians: Porokhoboty, Yuliboty, Ze lyudy.

Political technology under competitive conditions can have more than a marginal impact: as with the "Eastern Strategy" that did so much damage to Ukraine in 2005-14, as part of the comeback strategy of the Party of Regions. Paul Manafort arrived in Ukraine in 2005, just after the Orange Revolution, as a veteran of the US Southern Strategy — the use of culture politics and racial dog-whistling to shift the Southern States from Democratic to Republican support. Manafort did the same in Ukraine, but east-west; inking in and intensifying what were often only potential differences. These tensions were exploited by Russia in turn, both before and after Manafort, in 2004 and 2014. They have taken a long time to unwind.

Virtual political geometry

Political technology in Russia began with the creation, influence or direction of individual political elements, turning them into virtual political subjects. The first significant such party in Ukraine was the Green Party in the 1998 Rada elections. An effective national TV advertising campaign disguised the fact that an ecological party

---

14 "Servant of the People", 2015, Kvartal 95, Season One, Episode One, www.youtube.com/watch?v=HEvjsjvXQM4 (Accessed: 21 August 2024).

had been taken over by bankers and fossil fuel businessmen, winning them 5.6 per cent of the vote. Political technology in Russia then progressed to what I have called "virtual political geometry",[15] affecting or eventually directing how these political subjects move and relate to one another in political space. Ukraine has had elements of this, though never as full-blown as in Russia. The key transition election was 1999, the equivalent of how political technology saved Boris Yeltsin in Russia in 1996. Kuchma's 1999 campaign was structurally a copy of Yeltsin's in 1996. Because it was mainly run by a team of imported Russians, Tymofey Sergeitsev, Iskander Valitov and Dmitriy Kulikov.[16] They used the same four key plays as in Russia three years previously: split the opposition, ensure the ultimately unpopular Communist candidate was Kuchma's main opponent, split the "third force", and promote proxy candidates to hand over the "baton", i.e. their voters in the second round. The nationalist party Rukh was split. The moderate left was split: Socialist Party leader Oleksandr Moroz saw his path to the presidency blocked by a "clone" candidate Nataliya Vitrenko, leader of the political technology Progressive Socialist party, leaving Kuchma to fight against Communist Party leader Petro Symonenko. A fake grenade attack on Vitrenko blamed on Moroz's supporters was given wide coverage on oligarchic TV.

A would-be Ukrainian "third force", called the Kaniv-4, was disrupted just like in Russia in 1996: it included Moroz, who was double-crossed by at least two of the other three. One of them, Kuchma's proxy Yevhen Marchuk, came a strong fifth and was made Secretary of the National Security Council so that his supporters would transfer to Kuchma (dubbed a "relay race"). As in Russia-96, Communist leader Symonenko was first given an easy passage to the second round, and then an avalanche of black PR depicted him as bringing back the worst of the USSR. Fake KGB-style subpoenas threatened to call in citizens for questioning in the

---

15 Wilson, A., *op.cit.*, pp. 50-3.
16 Nebozhenko, V., 2019, "Na rozdorizhzhi istoriï", *Den*, 20 December. https://m.day.kyiv.ua/uk/article/podrobyci/na-rozdorizhzhi-istoriyi (Accessed: 20 August 2024).

event of a Symonenko victory.[17] To sum up: Kuchma was Yeltsin, Symonenko was Zyuganov, Moroz was Yavlinsky, and Marchuk played the part of Lebed.

Candidate	First round	Second round
Leonid Kuchma	38%	57.7%
Petro Symonenko (Communist)	23.1%	38.8%
Oleksandr Moroz (Socialist)	11.8%	
Nataliya Vitrenko (Progressive Socialist)	11.4%	
Yevhen Marchuk	8.5%	
Yuriy Kostenko (Rukh)	2.3%	
Hennadiy Udovenko (Rukh)	1.3%	
Against all	1.9%	3.5%
Turnout	70.1%	74.9%

The year 1999 in Ukraine launched the myth of the invincibility of political technology in the same way as Russia in 1996. But politics remained competitive. Elements of virtual political geometry were introduced, but no more. In the 2002 Rada elections, political technologists tried to create "third forces" to change the likely losing polarisation of the post-scandal Kuchma authorities versus the new popular opposition led by Viktor Yushchenko and Yuliya Tymoshenko (Moroz's Socialist Party was also then in opposition). A series of "brand parties" (women, youth) succeeded the Greens as a means of imitating the "new: and taking votes off the real opposition.

By 2004 the strategy was for Viktor Yanukovych to run for the presidency against extreme Ukrainian nationalists. Viktor Yushchenko wasn't one, so artificial nationalists were promoted on TV instead. This also counts as a "scarecrow" or lesser evil strategy. This is the subject of the rant by Zelenskyy's school teacher character in *Servant of the People*, that goes viral and makes him president. "There's no one to choose. We're choosing between two bastards! It's been like this for twenty-five years… Nothing will change this time! Do you know why? It's because you, my father and me will

---

17 Cheretun, D., 2021, "Vid hazet do teleserialiv. 30 rokiv evoliutsiï politychnoï ahitatsiï v Ukraïni", *Istorychna pravda*, 14 April. www.istpravda.com.ua/files/agitation30/page18249238.html (Accessed: 19 August 2024).

choose a bastard again! It's because, 'Yes, he is a bastard, but he is still better than the other ones!'".[18] The strategy often involves the exaggeration of evil, as with the ultra-nationalist Svoboda (Freedom) Party, covertly supported by elements around Yanukovych in 2010-12. One plan was to re-elect Yanukovych in 2015 by manoeuvring the leader of Svoboda to be his main opponent.

Artificial polarisation or lesser evil strategies can lead to the demand for a "third force". But that can be staged as well. In the 2010 presidential elections, there were two: Arseniy Yatsenyuk ran a quixotic campaign with Russian political technologists trying to depict him as a strong hand, which did not really appeal to the Orange electorate. Serhiy Tihipko was a more effective moderate outlier to Yanukovych, running another "relay race" to hand his votes over in the second round.

Other types of new faces or radical third forces are fake populists and/or challengers to the system. In the post-Maidan elections in 2014, Ukrainian nationalists at the centre of Russian propaganda won only 1.9 per cent (presidential election) and 6.5 per cent (Rada). The populist neophyte (others like Tymoshenko could be classed as populists) Oleh Lyashko was much more successful, winning 8.4 per cent and his Radical Party 7.5 per cent Lyashko was a creation of Akhmetov TV.[19] Serhiy Kaplin's Party of Ordinary People was accused of links to Russia and to Serhiy L'ovochkin.[20]

Russia moved on to a third phase, where all political subjects or "Kremlin parties" were controlled. The residual function of political technology was to police the boundaries of that system. Russia has now entered a fourth phase of no public politics at all. But Ukraine has remained at a partial phase two. There was much talk

---

18 "Servant of the People", 2015, *op. cit.*
19 "Systema Akhmeto-zabezpechennya: Yak Oleg Lyashko vyzhyvaie poza parlamentom", 2020, *Detector Media.* https://detector.media/kritika/article/1794 83/2020-08-09-systema-akhmeto-zabezpechennya-yak-oleg-lyashko-vyzhyvai e-poza-parlamentom/ (Accessed: 20 August 2024).
20 "Partyey prostikh lyudey: Kaplyna i narodnim kontrol'em, Dobrodomova rukovodyat iz Rossyy, — zhurnalyst", *iPress,* 9 August 2016. https://ipress.ua/ ru/news/partyey_prostih_lyudey_kaplyna_y_narodnim_kontrolem_dobrodo mova_rukovodyat_yz_rossyy__zhurnalyst_176473.html (Accessed: 20 August 2024).

of a new universe of the Ukrainian equivalent of Kremlin parties in 2010-12: but there was no strong second party to shadow the Party of Regions as its fake opponent. The best that political technologists could muster was Forward Ukraine! (Nataliya Korolevska) on 1.6 per cent in the 2012 elections.

Political technology needs narrative control, where there is a similar cycle of starting with individual elements: fake news, the toss or kompromat. Before progressing to controlling narrative geometry; and then to what Russians call a *dramaturgiya*, a hegemonic narrative that excludes all others. Ukraine would be halfway between phases one and two, with *dramaturgiya* partially creatable. More generally, "spin" is an outdated term. Modern media management is all about media delivery systems; and Ukraine has plenty of these, from oligarchic TV (before 2022) to Telegram. Ukraine used to be mistakenly praised for its marathon TV talk shows. They were not really about popular interest in politics. They were selling the soap opera of virtual politics: its characters, dramas and episodic ups and downs.

Securitisation

Unlike many other states, Russia especially, securitisation strategies have not really worked in Ukraine (to date). Political technology has largely been confined to domestic politics. Ukrainians were not committed enough to any given foreign policy to exploit it as a political technology, at least before 2014; although Manafort and the Party of Regions used anti-NATO campaigns successfully in the 2006 and 2007 Rada elections. Then, once Ukraine's Euro-Atlantic choice was constitutionally enshrined in 2019, it was too existential for political technology. Another factor is that securitisation strategies are rarely successful opposition tactics. They tend to be deployed by incumbents or those sufficiently entrenched in power to be called a "regime". But only one Ukrainian president has ever been re-elected, Leonid Kuchma in 1999. Petro Poroshenko tried with "Army! Language! Faith!" in 2019, but only won 25 per cent. There is some evidence that the Tomos (the Ecumenical Patriarch's official approval of the new Orthodox Church of Ukraine) may have consolidated some support.²¹ The "25 per cent" was a label of pride for some, who regarded Zelenskyy as naïve or soft on Russia (or even a Russian stooge). But Poroshenko lost heavily, in the middle of Russia's long war since 2014. Unlike Russia therefore, neither political technologists nor political technology have moved decisively into other areas like foreign policy or history, despite occasional forays.²²

Change since 2014

So how many of the conditions listed above as encouraging the use of political technology still applied after 2014? After the Revolution of Dignity, Ukraine introduced effective anti-corruption bodies. It had a very active and effective NGO sector. Media was freer, with effective investigative reporting in both media and NGOs (the fact that the latter were often harassed, and their methodology copied, was a tribute to their effectiveness). This meant the mass use of administrative resources was no longer possible. Unlike Russia, there were no real "controlled populations", not even the prisoners. Certainly not in the patriotic post-2014 Ukrainian army. Nor were there "controlled regions" like Chechnya in Russia. The Donbas was a one-party region, but was now half under Russian occupation. Rumours of mass fraud planned for the 2019 elections turned out to be only rumours.

Zelenskyy's election in 2019 could be seen as the triumph of one type of political technology over another. Or as the triumph of marketing over virtual political geometry. Zelenskyy soared above the man/woman making games with double Poroshenko's vote in round one. He recruited an online army for "participatory propaganda",²³ but also used bots. But he was also a transitional figure. Zelenskyy's marketing relied almost equally on social media and on 1+1 TV. Oligarchic media was still powerful. To take one example, Renat Akhmetov needed politicians to fend off challenges to

---

21   Brik, T., 2020, "Electoral Effects of the Tomos", *Baltic Worlds*, 13 (2/3), pp. 84-91.
22   Wilson, A., (forthcoming), *Russia's Propaganda State: How Russia Created the Propaganda that Helped Create the War Against Ukraine*.
23   Wilson, A., 2024, *op.cit.*, pp. 186 and 325.

his business interests in 2020-21. Dmitriy Razumkov, the leader of the Servant of the People and chair of parliament from the 2019 elections until October 2021, seemed to fit the bill. After he was removed as Rada head, he set up his own party *"Razumna polityka"* — a pun on "smart" — and was promoted on Akhmetov TV. His rating rose towards 10 per cent as Zelenskyy's dropped towards 20 per cent.[24] This now seems to be another time. Once the full-scale invasion started, by March 2022, Zelenskyy was at 75 per cent and Razumkov was on one per cent.[25]

Medvedchuk

Russian influence in Ukraine reduced significantly after 2014. But Russia had a multi-pronged strategy for re-establishing influence in Ukraine after the relative failure of the "Russian spring" in 2014. First, it shifted from direct appeals to support the Russian World to *fonovaya tekhnologiya* — "background technology" influencing a general narrative of disillusion.

This was also the strategy of "Medvedchuk 3.0". In his earlier periods of influence, Viktor Medvedchuk had first concentrated on media technologies (temnyky or "censorship notes") in President Kuchma's second term (1999-2005); on importing the "FEP model" of Gleb Pavlovsky's Foundation for Effective Politics in Russia, party media, think tanks and online attack sites; and party technologies (building the Social Democratic party). Medvedchuk 2.0 set up Ukrainian Choice to campaign against the EU in 2012, backed by friendly think tanks. Medvedchuk 3.0 under President Poroshenko involved new TV, and a "virtual chorus" or "backing vocals"[26] from an army of political technologists, "experts" and

---

24 KIIS, 2021, Public Opinion Survey "Omnibus". https://www.kiis.com.ua/?lang=ukr&cat=reports&id=1077&page=1 (Accessed:20 August 2024).
25 Sapiens, 2022, "Partiia Serhiia Prytuly vyishla na tretie mistse v reitynhu partii", 31 March. https://www.sapiens.com.ua/ua/publication-single-page?id=213 (Accessed: 20 August 2024).
26 "Bek vokal Medvedchuka: Golovni eksperty 112, Newsone ta ZIK", 2019 *Detector Media*, 26 October. https://detector.media/informatsiini-kanali/article/171883/2019-10-26-bek-vokal-medvedchuka-golovni-eksperty-112-newsone-ta-zik/ (Accessed: 20 August 2024).

NGOs. The message was "peace" in Donbas and any conspiracy theory to divide a war-weary population. In 2019, the new Russia-backed Medvedchuk-organised party projects Opposition Platform-For Life, with 13.1 per cent, plus for younger voters the Shariy Party at 2.2 per cent, were jointly two-thirds' more successful than the Opposition Bloc in 2014, with 9.4 per cent. Yuriy Boiko won 11.8 per cent in the presidential election, effectively marked by his clone Oleksandr Vilkul with 4.2 per cent. Hence the measures taken against Medvedchuk in 2021 — which deplatformed him as successfully as he had been platformed up.[27]

Change since 2022

Even more has changed since February 2022; and in ways that may finally break some of the cycles leading to the use of so much political technology in Ukraine. Leading oligarchs have lost around half of their wealth.[28] Many oligarchs' assets are/were disproportionately concentrated in eastern and southern Ukraine,[29] and/or suffered disproportionally in Russian attacks (energy, infrastructure), meaning they have fared particularly badly in terms of maintaining their asset base. Oligarchs have lost the pocket banks they once controlled. Several have fled abroad, mocked as the "Monaco Battalion" or "Vienna Battalion".[30] In November 2022, five of the largest companies were nationalised. Oligarchs with the closest links to Russia have been targeted: Medvedchuk, Firtash and Novynsky amongst others.

---

27 Wilson, A., 2024, *op.cit.*, pp. 464-5.
28 "Reyting naybagatshikh voennogo chasu", *Forbes*, 26 December 2022. https://forbes.ua/ru/money/reyting-naybagatshikh-voennogo-chasu-26122022-10741 (Accessed: 20 August 2024).
29 Tognini, G., 2022, "Ukraine's billionaires have lost $10 billion since Russia's invasion", *Forbes*, 5 April. https://www.forbes.com/sites/giacomotognini/2022/04/05/ukraines-billionaires-have-lost-10-billion-since-russias-invasion/ (Accessed: 20 August 2024).
30 "VIENNA BATTALION 2. Ukrainska Pravda tracks down Ukrainian fugitives, VIP refugees and VIP tourists", *Ukrainska Pravda*, 2023. https://www.youtube.com/watch?v=Yutvt8C4oFE (Accessed: 21 August 2024).

As well as losing assets, oligarchs have lost their main means of political influence. Their television companies have been included in Ukraine's national news collective. Oligarchs can no longer use them to promote favoured or artificially created parties and politicians. The national news marathon has lost audience; the once powerful TV debates are less political and have less impact. The state is stronger than it was before the start of the war, including at a local level where oligarchs often controlled key cities or regions.

Public opinion is less tolerant of corruption. It is more willing to back or participate in protest. It has higher expectations of politicians.[31] There are huge expectations for a different political culture after the war. As Zelenskyy has said, "No one at the front will understand those who, having any political weight or any position of authority, will try to return to the old life".[32]

Scenario one: Wartime and postwar conditions make it unlikely that Russia could return either to its model of influence before 2014 or to the model of Medvedchuk 3.0. Russia will have to use more indirect methods.

Scenario two: The self-reproducing oligarchy is diminished. But declining actors will still invest to protect their power. Ukraine is still a country of informal networks. Oligarchs can still use networks in the judiciary or SBU to protect themselves. The chain of influence (see figure 1) may be broken, but some links in the chain are still there.

Scenario three: The Presidential Administration (PA) may become the main user of political technology. The PA may consolidate control over the National News Marathon.[33]

---

31 See, for example, "Ukraine Wartime National Surveys", 2022, Mobilise Project, 1 June. https://mobiliseproject.com/2022/06/01/ukraine-wartime-national-surveys/ (Accessed: 20 August 2024).
32 "Shcho prezydent skazav u zvernenni do VRU", *Radio Svoboda*. https://www.radiosvoboda.org/a/shcho-prezydent-skazav-u-zvernenni-do-vru/32197509.html (Accessed: 20 August 2024).
33 "Telemarafon: Iedyni novyny", 2023, *Detector Media*, 15 September. https://detector.media/infospace/article/216877/2023-09-15-telemarafon-iedyni-novyny-rezultat-na-tablo/ (Accessed: 20 August 2024); "Ukrainski zmi", 2023, BBC Ukrainian. https://www.bbc.com/ukrainian/features-64112594 (Accessed: 20

Scenario four: More politics in Ukraine is happening online. A lot of political technology is now online. According to Olga Onuch's Mobilise project data, TV was the main source of news for 58 per cent of Ukrainians in 2019; by 2023 that was only 21 per cent. Social media has taken over; rising from 11 per cent in 2019 to 54 per cent in 2023.[34] This provides some opportunities for Russian disinformation and propaganda.

Scenario five: Ukraine is still a hub state. Even if political technology declines at home, it can be reimported. Russian political technologists have lost their market in Ukraine. But Israeli and US strategists are still likely to be popular. Given Zelenskyy's global prestige, many global political consultancy firms would love to work on Ukrainian elections. (From a research perspective, elections, leading to the launch of new political forces, are very unlikely to be held in 2024.)

Scenario six: Because of the war, securitisation strategies might work better in the future. Particularly negatively, i.e. defining political enemies as pro-Russian. Or indirectly: asserting that opponents' actions or strategies—such as too much criticism or internal disunity—serve the Russian interest.

Scenario Seven: The Future of Protest in Ukraine: In the post-Soviet political technology era, protest was often fake. The Russian word massovki means both film extras and hired rally extras. Putingi are organised pro-Putin meetings (mitingi) or counter-rallies to oppose real demonstrations—equivalents can be organised in support of any other leader (see Belarus in 2020 or Georgia in 2024). Ukraine has long had astro-turfed rallies and protests, particularly during periods of democratic regression and public disillusion. The first thing that protestors did in 2013 was therefore to proclaim: "we are not paid". But they still had to contend with the

---

August 2024); "Monitoryng spilnogo telemarafonu: Iedyni novyny za 10-11 sichnya 2024 roku", 2024, *Detector Media*, 19 January. https://detector.media/shchodenni-telenovini/article/221930/2024-01-19-monitoryng-spilnogo-telemarafonu-iedyni-novyny-za-1011-sichnya-2024-roku/ (Accessed: 20 August 2024).

34 "Analytical Report May June 2024 Graphs May June 2024", 2024, Mobilise Project. https://mobiliseproject.com/2022/06/01/ukraine-wartime-national-surveys/ (Accessed: 20 August 2024).

propaganda myth of "Maidan proplachennyi" (in Russian "paid-for Maidan"). And the dismissive concept of "mitingovaya demo-kratiya". In reality, it was the anti-Maidan that was more likely to be paid and orchestrated. But it was often hard to tell what was fake and what was real in split-screen reality – real politics coexisting with a fake one. In post post-Soviet Ukraine, it will be clearer what is and is not real. Moreover, if Ukraine is genuinely post-Soviet, there will be no more Maidans. Just normal protests; not existential struggles against a "regime".

Conclusions

Ukraine is supposed to be fighting a war that is in large part about opposing political cultures: Russian autocracy and propaganda against Ukrainian democracy and truth. Ukraine's Deputy Prime Minister and Minister for Digital Transformation Mykhailo Fedorov defined this to *Time* magazine in March 2022 as "our brand as one of an honest nation and an honest people trying to tell the truth".[35] It is important to be honest about how much political technology was used in Ukraine before February 2022. It is important to be optimistic that its use is now in decline.

---

35 Bergengruen, V., 2022, "'It's Our Home Turf'. The Man on Ukraine's Digital Frontline", *Time*, 15 March. https://time.com/6157308/its-our-home-turf-the-man-on-ukraines-digital-frontline/ (Accessed: 21 August 2024).

A Change Will Take Place in Russia Only When Ukraine Wins on the Battlefield

Garry Kasparov

No change will take place in Russia unless Ukraine wins the war on the battlefield. Vladimir Putin's fascist dictatorship thrives thanks to military victories. Thus, the only way to implement any change in Russia is the military defeat of the Russian Army. This is what Russian history has taught us.

I am shocked when I hear, quite often indeed, what people in the West say about Ukraine and its dire situation in the current war. For instance, there have been complaints about Ukrainian trucks not obeying EU regulations and unfairly competing with European carriers. Yet, the very same people, very rarely, if ever, admit that if it was not for the Ukrainian sacrifice and blood, Russian tanks would be deeper into Europe by now.

If not the miraculous battle of Kyiv, which we can compare to the also miraculous Battle of Warsaw in 1920 when Poland saved Europe from the Soviet invasion, the situation in the world would be very different and everything which is subject of public debate would be completely irrelevant. In fact, the very same governments which are pretending to be pro-Ukrainian would rush to Moscow to negotiate treaties with Putin.

As stated before, had there been no heroic defence of Kyiv, the Russian army could have taken the Ukrainian capital in three days. Putin was surely ready to take over the whole Ukraine. But what did the West do? Nothing.

Think about it: Alexander Litvinenko was murdered in 2006. How many British governments have blocked the British courts from pointing to Putin as the main suspect in the murder? At least five or six, but there could have been more. I have lost count. Or take France whose society in April 2022, that is two months into the invasion, voted in a majority (55%) for the political parties that openly support Putin. This shows that corruption is endemic, also in Europe. Therefore, Putin has managed to bribe Western politicians, from top to bottom, from right to the left. Having been on the verge of winning in Ukraine, the only thing that stopped him were the courageous Ukrainians and their incredible resistance. He was only a day away from the total dominance of Ukraine.

We should also remember that had there been no Ukrainians defending their state, there would be no NATO now. NATO would be dead. Instead, today the Alliance is stronger than ever before, as it is cemented by Ukrainian blood. Had there been no NATO, the Baltic states would already be under Russia's occupation. Poland would become a buffer state. All Putin needed was to win in Ukraine and to put his puppet, Viktor Yanukovych or Viktor Medvedchuk, or their likes, in charge and the West would have started negotiating with him. Thus the question is: who can save Ukraine?

Let's be honest, NATO was established in 1949 to save Europe from a Russian invasion. At that time, the threat was to be found east of the Rhine river. Today, it can be found east of the Dnieper river, but it's the same threat. Ukraine is the only country that has spilled its blood fulfilling NATO's purpose. And yet its membership in the Alliance is still being discussed and not certain. In my view, there is no doubt that Ukraine deserves to be a member of any organisation it aspires to, especially NATO.

It seems to me that the urgency of the moment is somewhat misunderstood, especially in the West. There is a lot of talk about the future and the past. But today we need to talk about the present—there is a war and Putin continues to destroy Ukraine. And yet, as stated before, I do not think that people realise the urgency of this moment. Thus, nothing will happen to Russia and in Russia, unless Ukraine wins the war. The alternative to this scenario is that the aggression will spread further. Indeed, we are already seeing a war and unrest, not to mention terrorism, in the Middle East.

Since the very beginning Putin has been very open about his plans. He has not been secretive at all. We all knew what his intentions were, and the Russians knew them too. I am not going to be an advocate for my compatriots, but I can say that their behaviour will be condemned by history. I do not like being called a "good Russian" because it reminds me of the term "good Germans".

To understand what Ukraine means to Russia it is suffice to bring back the late Zbigniew Brzezinski, American strategist of Polish origin, who once famously stated that there is no Russian Empire without Ukraine. Putin knows this truth all too well. That is why in 2005 he laid out his vision of Russia's future and claimed that the collapse of the Soviet Union was the greatest geopolitical catastrophe of the 20th century. The question again is: what did the West do over the course of these 17 years, that is from 2005 to 2022? The answer unfortunately is nothing. Instead, in 2008, the French President, Nicolas Sarkozy, negotiated with Putin, allowing him to take over 20% of Georgia's territory. It is unclear how Sarkozy was remunerated for this "gift", or maybe Putin had some compromising materials on him, but we know that when it comes to the 2008 war in Georgia the West did nothing to save this country from Russia's aggression.

The same can be said about the 2014 annexation of Crimea. Unlike Adolf Hitler or Saddam Hussein, Putin didn't even bother to come up with some diplomatic drumbeats. His forces just took over the peninsula and moved further. First they went to Donbas (still in 2014) where they established the so-called "people's republics" in Donetsk and Luhansk and later (in 2022) they started a full-scale invasion into Ukraine. Thus, today the future of the world is being decided on the battlefield in Ukraine. Yet, instead of focusing on that and what we can do to help Ukraine win, we are discussing whether Ukraine deserves to become a member of the European Union. This shows little recognition of the fact that if Ukraine loses this war, there will be no European Union. Putin will start destroying the community, while most of the Western leaders will rush to Moscow to negotiate.

Let's be honest about it. There's no leadership in the West. All we see is impotence and corruption. In this regard, the United States is not ideal either. Thus unless a Ukrainian flag is raised again in Sevastopol, there will be no change in Moscow. For the moment it is clear that there's no way that Putin will go somewhere else or stop the war altogether. Right now, Russia resembles Germany during the Second World War. The only difference between Putin's Russia and Nazi Germany is that there are many more Russians who are openly opposing Putin than there were Germans opposing Hitler back in 1944.

Again, the biggest problem with Russians, even those who would like to take a side, is that they cannot do it now. Why is that, we may ask? The answer lies again in the West, which is so good at not sanctioning the Russian oligarchs. The West has not sanctioned Putin, but it is sanctioning ordinary Russians. I have a Croatian passport, but many of my compatriots who would like to join me in the fight cannot do this. They have to stay in Russia because being Russian in Europe is a curse now. A few million Russians who could contribute to the free world economically, technologically and intellectually, are stuck in Russia because they don't know where to go. The reason for this situation is very simple. The West has no plan to win the war.

I'm still waiting for some Western leaders to decisively say that Ukraine must win. Just like Franklin Delano Roosevelt and Winston Churchill did in January 1943 in Casablanca when they demanded Germany's unconditional surrender. However now, the West still believes that one day it will be able to return to business as usual with Russia. I do not believe that this is what the future will be like, but I also cannot guarantee that a Ukrainian flag in Sevastopol will change everything. Yet without it, nothing will change at all. That is why I believe Ukraine's victory is inevitable.

Until now, we have implemented change in Russia four times. First it was in mid-19th century, after the first Crimean War (1853-1856). Our defeat in the war brought on the abolishment of serfdom, but also great liberal reforms. Later, under Alexander II, probably the greatest czar in Russian history, Russia faced a disastrous defeat in the Russo-Japanese War (1904-1905), which led it to the establishment of a constitutional monarchy in Russia. The 1917 revolution, which took place during the stalemate of the First World War, led, in turn, to the collapse of the Romanov dynasty. The year 1989, which marked the end of the Soviet-Afghan war (1970-1989) and the collapse of the Berlin Wall, brought an end to the Cold War, which for Russia was a big change too. All said, the four major transformations which took place in Russia were a result of direct geopolitical defeats, which were combined with Russia's military defeats. That is why, in my view, we are now also at the point in history where a military defeat could lead to the end of Putin's imperial Russia. We have to ensure that this war is the last war that is waged by Russia against another state.

In terms of its identity, Russia has actually dual roots. The primary ones come from the Principality of Moscow (1263–1547), popularly known as Muscovy, and include two historic experiences – that of the Golden Horde and the Byzantine messianic vision of the world. But there is also the forgotten heritage of the Northwest free trade republics that points to Russia's Kyiv roots, namely the Kyiv Rus'. For many of us, the war in Ukraine falls into the old Russian tradition of a fight between the European, or pro-European, world versus the Asian Golden Horde. For this reason, I think a military defeat in Ukraine would eventually reshape the perceptions of the Russian society towards Europe and influence those who are now incapable of accepting reality.

To explain the gravity of the current situation let me state that even if you put a person like myself on Russian TV, you would not achieve anything in terms of changing people's minds. It is almost impossible to break the spell that has been put on people's minds by Putin's propaganda machine. This can be explained in very simple terms: people watch Russian media coverage from the frontlines and they see the successes of the Russian army. Another thing is that Putin has indeed been successful in convincing Russians that the war in Ukraine is not a war that he has been waging against the West, but that this is a war between Russia and the West.

I do not pretend to be representing all 140 million Russians. Maybe I represent five million, but I still believe that it would be good if these people are given a chance. In fact, I think that the actual number of those who view this war as a war between Putin's regime and the free world is bigger than we assume. That is why these people should become a part of an anti-Putin coalition. Yet for this to happen, something else needs to take place. Something which is a taboo in Europe and in the US and which is expressed by the phrase "regime change". For this to change to have a chance to take place, however, the West needs to alter its strategy towards Russia.

On our side, that is, the Russian opposition, we need to build the matrices of future Russia outside of Russia. Nothing can happen inside. But if we offer an opportunity to hundreds of thousands of Russians, who now make the core of Putin's war machine, to travel outside the country and become a part of our community here, we could possibly make a much larger contribution. I call this idea "a Russian Taiwan". We need to start creating something outside of Russia for a simple reason: nothing can happen inside Russia today. We are indeed in a situation similar to which Nazi Germany was in 1943-1944. We do not expect people to rise just yet. In Russia the sense of fear dominates people's lives. The war is waged in people's minds. I have a few relatives who are still living in Russia and I can see that the situation inside the country is even worse than what we know about Nazi Germany in the 1940s. In fact, Goebbels could have only dreamt of all the mechanisms that Putin has at hand. Just to think that today's Russian propaganda is successful in the United States and that there are Americans who believe in Russian narratives more than they believe in the FBI is unthinkable.

The information situation inside Russia is even worse; people are constantly bombarded with propaganda messages and that is why so many of them believe that Russia is actually winning the war. That is why we have to stop fantasizing that something will happen in Russia and that Russia will undergo a change on its own. The earlier the West recognises this truth, the better. Only then will it be able to start acting. As of now sanctions do not seem to work because the West does not think it is at war with Russia. Meanwhile, Putin is convinced that Russia is at war with NATO; it is at war with Europe; and it is at war with the US.

The West will not win the war with Russia if it does not recognise that Putin represents an existential threat to Western civilisation. This also allows Putin to believe that he's winning the war. Observations of his reactions confirm that. Indeed, Putin may have panicked when the 2022 Kyiv offensive failed and Russian forces were forced to withdraw from Ukraine's capital, or during the first

Ukrainian counter-offensive in the summer of 2022 when Ukrainian forces took back the city of Kherson. At that moment Ukrainians could have won the war. Yet at the very same moment the West missed the opportunity to sufficiently supply Ukraine with the weapons and money that could have given it a greater advantage. Now we see a stalemate, but the stalemate will not last for long. Putin is preparing for the next massive assaults.

Realistically speaking, we have to start thinking about a strategy to win the war and how to effect change in Russia. A change in Russia means the end to the empire. It must cease to exist. This is my belief, but it is also shared by Mikhail Khodorkovsky, also in exile. We have to start from scratch. If some parts of Russia would like to go and become free, we will need to accept that. But we need to have a plan for it; a similar plan to what the West had for Germany and Japan back in 1943.

I would not like to make an impression that the only plan of the Russian opposition is to blame the West for not doing anything in regards to Putin. That is why we need to start thinking about what is possible and try to find out how we can get people who disagree with Putin to leave the country and join — as I call it — the "Russian Taiwan" in order to build the matrices of Russia outside of the country. We need to start thinking how we can use them, bring them to our side and start building Russia's future, for the moment outside of Russia. There's no other plan. Everything else is a fantasy.

Part III
The Unfinished Transformation

Unfinished Transformation
From Gorbachev's Failed Reforms to an Aggressor State

Iwona Reichardt

The dissolution of the Union of the Soviet Socialist Republics (USSR) was formally proclaimed on 26 December 1991 by Declaration № 142-H of the Soviet of the Republics of the Supreme Soviet of the Soviet Union. This document brought a formal end to the Soviet federal government. Its announcement was proceeded by a meeting of the leaders of the three of USSR's founding members, the Russian, Belarusian, and Ukrainian SSRs: Boris Yeltsin, Stanislav Sushkievich and Leonid Kravchuk. Collectively, on 8 December 1991 they declared the Soviet Union to no longer exist, establishing the Commonwealth of Independent States (CIS) as its successor entity. Shortly thereafter, they were joined by eight more republics, which led the Soviet leader and its last reformer, Mikhail Gorbachev, to resign and what was left of the Soviet parliament to end itself through a vote.

Soon after the process of transformation in post-Soviet states was about to start, leading the countries that emerged from the fallen empire towards liberal democracy and market economy. While, this transformation has been deemed successful in three Baltic republics, Lithuania, Latvia and Estonia where it was marked by their integration with western security, economic and political structures, and partially successful in others, such as Ukraine, Moldova, to some extent Georgia, which despite numerous difficulties have stayed on the official path towards western integration, it remains unfinished in the Russian Federation and Belarus. As a result, three decades after the Soviet collapse, these two countries have not only effectively abandoned their integration with the West, but also started a war against it.

Gorbachev's failed reform package and its legacy

The dissolution of the Soviet state was proceeded by a series of economic and military crises and political changes that had taken place both within the Soviet Union as well as in the countries that were under its influence. They included stagnation of the Soviet economy which, at the time of rapid technological development in the West, could no longer be addressed by the largely autarkic and command-based system. In addition, the political changes in Central European states, which brought an end to the monolith of the communist parties' rule there, resonated to the budding national movements in Soviet republics. This was especially true for the three Baltic republics (Lithuania, Latvia and Estonia), but also for Ukraine and Georgia where national movements had been in place throughout the 20th century and which had experiences of nation- and statehood building dating to pre-Soviet Union times.

The national movements, although to a smaller degree, were also present in other republics. In Belarus, it took the form of the Belarusian National Front led by Zenon Pazniak who also brought public attention to the discovery of mass graves of Stalin victims in the Kuropaty forest near Minsk,[1] while in Moldova it was the Pan-Romanian unionist movement which served as the main driving force behind the language laws that were introduced in 1988 and which allowed for the use of Latin alphabet in official writings.[2] Indirectly, these changes sent a message to the Kremlin that national ideals were gaining popularity throughout the republics and that Moscow was no longer the sole reference point for their development.

Under pressure of these and other challenges the leader of the Soviet Union, Mikhail Gorbachev, offered a response in the form of a reform package known as *glasnost* (openness) and *perestroika* (restructuring). Its introduction, led by the Communist Party of the

---

1 Pazniak, Z., Shmigalov, E., 1988, "Kurapaty—daroga smertsi," *Litaratura i mastactva*, 3 June; Pazniak, Z., 1988, "Kuropaty: narodnaia tragediia o kotoroi dolzhny znat' vse," *Moskovskie novosti*, 41, October.
2 King, C., 1994, "Moldovan Identity and the Politics of Pan-Romanianism", *Slavic Review*, 53 (2), pp. 345-368.

Soviet Union (CPSU), meant to save the weakening of the USSR's political and economic systems. They were envisioned to bring on some political democratisation (*glasnost*) and partial liberalisation of economic activities (*perestroika*). Nonetheless, the attempted reforms did not lead to the change they had been envisioned to lead. Instead, they proved to be disastrous to their own architect. While admired in the West, but also to some degree in Central Europe, where his image was that of a "Soviet democrat", Gorbachev was mistrusted domestically and his reforms brought on a fierce struggle between reformers and conservatives within the communist party.[3] The latter showed their mobilisation in August 1991 when the anti-Gorbachev putsch was organised in Moscow.

Aimed at depriving the Soviet leader of his powers and cementing (not reforming) the political system of the USSR, the coup led by Gennady Yanayev was yet ended without success after two days only. Its failure was attributed to the effective resistance of Russia's then President Boris Yeltsin—Gorbachev's ally and critic at the same time. The failure of the coup, which led to the immediate collapse of the CPSU was yet seen as one of the factors contributing to the dissolution of the USSR, which took place four months later. It surely sent the message to the peripheries that the centre was struggling with control.

Less attention was yet paid to the areas of internal discontent within the Soviet state and its political and security structures. Nor has there been enough recognition that this sentiment stayed beyond the collapse of the Soviet Union and actually turned into one of the most destructive forces of the further modernisation processes in Russia and Belarus first but other republics as well. Thus, while the enthusiasm of "history coming to an end" also on the territory of the former empire spread worldwide in 1991, few scholars remained cautious admitting that "after the initial shock opposition to the dissolution grew".[4]

---

3   Lewin, M., 1991, *The Gorbachev phenomenon: A historical interpretation*, Berkely: University of California Press, p. xi.
4   McFaul, M., 2001, *Russia's Unfinished Revolution: Political Change from Gorbachev to Putin*, Ithaca: Cornell University Press, 2001, p. 9.

Whether *glasnost* and *perestroika* brought an end, even partially, to the USSR remains subject of debate until today. The spectrum of opinions on this matter ranges from calling Gorbachev's reforms the main causes for the dissolution of the USSR to the viewpoint that they should not be considered any reforms at all. Regardless of our position on this spectrum it seems that a more relevant observation, also from the perspective of the unfinished transformation, is the one presented by US historian Stephen Kotkin who stated that "in the 1990s, the collapse was still called 'reform.'"[5]

Such semantics, given the negative interpretation of Gorbachev's reforms which the Moscow coup nonetheless revealed, points to a fertile ground that was formed as the basis for the construction of the new states. Therefore, from the beginning of the post-Soviet transformation terms such as liberalisation were assigned, through language and political discourse, negative connotations and indicated failure in regards to both the process and the end product. Evidently, this was caused by either lack of or limited positive experience with the implementation of reforms that was felt by the majority of the society before the Soviet collapse and right after it.

Until today, the closing down of enterprises and the falling living standards of large social groups, regarded as the work of Yegor Gaidar, acting prime minister in 1992 and the main architect of post-Soviet privatisation, remain in the memory of many former citizens of the Soviet Union as traumatic experiences, regardless of their earlier attitude to the Soviet state.[6] The cases of both Belarus and Russia show how effectively this linguistic but also emotional ground was used by those who wanted to bring back or preserve the Soviet-style reality.

This reality, despite being declared dead by an official act, was visibly alive in the minds and lives of many people of the former

---

5   Kotkin, S., 2001, *Armageddon Averted: The Soviet Collapse, 1970–2000*, Oxford and New York: Oxford University Press, p. 6.
6   The author agrees with S. Kotkin that to say that the lack of transformation in the 1990s was a result of neoliberal economic policies is an ideological simplification and that the scholars who blamed the West, particularly the US, for not coming up with a Marshall Plan for Russia, were in fact misguided.

Soviet republics, not to mention the working of their institutions. The former were often described as *Sovoks*, which negatively refers to Soviet/Sovietised people,[7] while the latter experienced many different forms of transformations: from moderate or gentle changes to a complete cover-up. In many cases, their cores remained completely intact. Such was the case of the education system but also the legal system and — most importantly — security services.

Their leadership and middle-level management, sceptical of Gorbachev's reforms, ensured conservation of Soviet practices already in the 1980s and continued to do so throughout the 1990s, disregarding the official change of the political system that took place after USSR's collapse. Thus, the main security agency of the Soviet Union, the KGB, which was officially closed as a result of the failed August 1991 coup, was succeeded (formally on 3 December 1991) by the Federal Security Services (FSB). It continued operations of its predecessor in the newly formed Russian Federation, where it established a power system in parallel to elected political institutions.

Since 2000, that is the beginning of Vladimir Putin's first presidency, these two systems have become tightly integrated, marking the start of the next stage of the unfinished transformation. Since that moment on the process of halting change was no longer limited to the need to reverse the unsuccessful reforms internally. It also included reactions to external processes that allowed for the completion of transformation in the three Baltic states and Central Europe, which could be repeated by other post-Soviet states. The risk of such a scenario, from the perspective of the Russian authorities, was that it could affect the social perception of reforms and, like domino effect, influence political processes within the Russian Federation. As a former KGB operative, Putin knew it had to be avoided at all costs.

---

7   Their fate was described in academic literature but also in the works of Svietlana Alekseivich whose *Secondhand Time* is a collective portrait of the early stage of the post-Soviet transition.

A similar process took place in Belarus, when after the introduction and initial implementation of market and democratic reforms, the lesser known politician, Aleksyandr Lukashenka, won presidential elections on a highly populist ticket. This moment marked the beginning of the end of transformation in Belarus, which lasted for only three years and which did not—as Lukashenka's election results indicate—gain popular support. The Belarusian context, believed to be the most unique throughout the post-Soviet space due to the society's highly traumatised memory of the Second World War and the overall positive experience of life in the Soviet Union, proved to be a prototype for what was to take place in Russia in the first decade of the 21st century.

Also, just like in the Russian Federation, the Belarusian system of state power first took a dual form consisting of two parallel branches: elected political institutions and security services. The latter have not undergone any significant change since Soviet times and continued operations, even with the same name—the KGB. Gradually, with the experience of repeated protests and opposition movements organised before and after subsequent presidential elections, when Lukashenka's system was no longer backed by the majority of people, the role of security services became even larger to finally—just like in Russia—become one integrated system of power and control.

From integration with western structures towards post-Soviet reintegration

Overall, the start of transformation from command economy to a free market and from authoritarianism to liberal democracy throughout what became known as the post-Soviet space took place at the same time. It also overlapped with the transformation of the states in Central Europe which started only a few years earlier, in 1989/1990. The completion of this process formally took place in 2004 with their membership in the European Union, and earlier NATO.

These two international structures, more than anything else, served as a seal of the former socialist states' western choice and as such became a compass for their transformations. The latter meant adoption of a liberal democratic system, elimination of corruption and introduction of competitive free market economy. In the group of the first countries that were once part of the Soviet bloc and after its collapse decided to join both NATO and the EU and thus completed their transformation were three former Soviet republics, now independent states: Lithuania, Latvia and Estonia. They joined these structures together with Poland, the Czech Republic, Slovakia, Slovenia, Hungary and Cyprus.

Accepting that membership in western structures is possible for countries that were once non-democratic, NATO and the EU created programmes also for other former Soviet republics, signalling to them that once they fulfil necessary requirements, they too could complete their transformations and become a part of the integrated West. Unlike in the case of Lithuania, Latvia and Estonia, the remaining post-Soviet states were not initially promised membership in the European Union. Instead, through the 2009 Eastern Partnership programme, the EU offered them integration. This policy was aimed at six non-EU post-Soviet republics that since 1991 had showed some interest in cooperation with the European Union and as such could establish bigger areas of exchange with EU's internal market. It was also envisioned to expand democratic practices in countries that were still struggling in their transformations and which were all located on the territory of the former USSR. The experience of the Soviet past was the sole common denominator for these states as since 1991 they had already diverged following their own development paths.

In the 1990s, a similar integration with a possibility of membership offer was presented to Russia. This path was envisioned through individually-tailored formats of co-operation between the Russian Federation and western structures, including the EU (in 1997 Russia and the EU signed the Partnership and Cooperation Agreement) and NATO (in 1994 Russia joined the Partnership for Peace programme), which reflected a popular at that belief despite being the former core of the Soviet empire, the new Russia could become part of the international system, on equal terms as other transforming states, as long as it agreed to cooperation with the West.

Quite soon it became visible that despite initial participation in these two EU and NATO cooperation programmes the Russian Federation could not accept an equal status in a multilateral system of international relations. Not only would such an acceptance require domestic reforms, it could also confirm that, in the long term, the dissolution of the USSR led to a liberalisation. With over a decade since the Soviet collapse it was possible that such thinking would get accepted by the new generation of Russian citizens.

To counteract it, a new rhetoric and policies were needed to generate emotions that would, once again, remind the society that the Soviet collapse was a failure and the transformation path that opened as its result should not be the preference of the Russian state and its people. Thus, with a goal to reach the domestic audience Vladimir Putin, in his annual state of the nation address to parliament in 2005 called "the collapse of the Soviet Union the greatest geopolitical catastrophe of the 20th century." Two years later he reiterated this message during the Munich Security Forum where he delivered a keynote speech to the international community of experts. From that moment on it has become clear, and Putin's own writings and speeches are best evidence of that but also other official documents issued by different agencies of the Russian government confirm this thesis, that since the second decade of the 21st century the focus of Russia's foreign policy was no longer integration with the West.

Perceiving western structures and the transformation they required from the Russian states as a threat, Moscow started pursuing the policy of reintegration of the former USSR. Militarily, as expressed by the 2010 and even more 2014 military doctrine of the Russian Federation, it meant preventing NATO's further expansion into Russia's neighbouring states. For this to happen, Russian authorities believed, Western structures had to come to terms that the former Soviet republics, now independent states, belong to the sphere where Moscow has special interests. As such, these states should not make any changes, including internal political changes, that are disapproved by the Kremlin. An inclusion of this assumption in the federal military doctrine meant that once Russia recognises political changes in neighbour states as threats to its own security it can militarily intervene on their territories. Such intervention took place in 2008 in Georgia and then in 2014 when the Russian Federation annexed Crimea and started an undeclared war in Ukraine. The full-scale invasion which was started in 2022 was thus the next step of this already implemented strategy of military intervention as a means of achieving the post-Soviet reintegration.

On the economic level, Russia has also made an anti-western turn, which took the form of the Eurasian economic integration project. First called the Customs Union, it was created in 2010, one year after the Eastern Partnership programme, to mirror the EU activities in post-Soviet space. First joined by Belarus and Kazakhstan, this Russia-led project, after establishing the Single Economic Space in 2012, saw its first "expansion" in 2015 when it was joined by Armenia, a state that Russia offered membership in the Customs Union as an alternative to EU integration which Armenia was about to start by signing the Association Agreement. The same offer was presented to Ukraine, before the 2013 Vilnius Eastern Partnership Summit, but it did not result in Ukraine's membership in the union once the Ukrainian society opposed President Viktor Yanukovych's decision not to sign the Association Agreement and started a mass protest in the centre of Kyiv, which turned into the last of its contemporary revolutions. Russia's reaction to this protest and its outcome was, as it was determined in the military doctrine, an intervention.

The birth of new national pride and Russia's next transformation

To build wide social acceptance for the policy of reintegration, which requires — as the war in Ukraine has showed — also the sacrifice of human lives in the name of the greater Russia — the language of failed reforms and the catastrophe of the Soviet collapse — was no longer enough. Just like during Soviet times a concept of a new Russian man had to be created and offered to the society as a model to adopt. It was neither going to be a replica of *Homo Sovieticus* nor – even more – *Homo Post-Sovieticus*, which was a term most often used in regards to the society in Belarus. These two categories are yet both anchored in the past, whereas the new Russian reality requires a new perspective and thinking about the future.

To achieve this, a plethora of modern social engineering techniques has been prepared and applied at all levels of public life, starting with schools and educational facilities, through media and modern information technologies. Collectively, their effort has created the "Z" generation, a term promoted by the *Financial Times* reporter, Ian Garner who attempted a wartime sociological portrait of young Russians in his latest book titled *Z Generation. Into the heart of Russia's fascist youth*. He described the generation that was born in the last decade of the 20th century or in the first decade of the 21st century and for whom the experience of both the Soviet collapse and post-Soviet transformation have been primarily known from family stories or literature. As such they are no longer relevant to the young people's lives who need new stimuli and new impulses to act.

In the era of digital technologies, such stimulations are found primarily online. For over a decade now, conspiracy theories and apocalyptic visions have been widely spread on Russian internet (known as ru.net). Their aim is to build in their recipients a sense of national pride, which now also inclines a rejection of western influences. The alternative, in the form of the pure Russian culture and traditional values, is widely promoted among this group to ensure the further transformation of the Russian state.

This time, however, the steered changes (it is difficult to call them reforms) are aimed at cementing the authoritarian system, which – as some Russia scholars argue – has already taken an almost totalitarian form. Messages sent to young people, online but also by means of an increasingly more violent pop culture – make references to the collapse of the Soviet Union which nonetheless is used as an inspiration to rebuild new Russia, which needs to be powerful and mighty. What it means and how it refers to the Soviet empire was best captured by Petr Akopov, a leading Russian nationalist, who in 2022 in an article for Ria Novosti wrote that:

"Again we will live in the Soviet Union. But not in the Soviet Union that Russia's opponents fear or the communists dream of. No, we will build a strong, just and sovereign Russia".[8]

References to fascism, also called russism, have been made by Russia observers since the start of the full-scale invasion in 2022. Yet, they are still far from receiving wide acceptance among scholars. Elements of a strongly authoritarian system can indeed be observed and identified in Russia, without much risk of an error. Thus, it is rather the constraints of proper terminology what limits scholars in their adequate description of Russia's political system.

Faced with these two challenges, that of an unfinished transformation in Russia that has allowed the largest of the post-Soviet republics transform itself from a weakened federation fighting for its place in the world affairs into an aggressor state, one that pursues authoritarian policies towards its own citizens and neighbouring states, but also that of the lack of adequate language to describe these changes, scholars of the current Russian transformation are in dire need for a theory that could lead them through the next stages of these processes. At this moment the only recommendation that seems appealing from the cognitive and methodological perspective is the decolonisation theory that from now on could be applied to Russian and post-Soviet studies, which as many proponents of this approach claim, has been long overdue.

---

8   Akopov, P., 2022, "Rossia buushechego-vpered v SSR", *RIA*, 22 March.

Belarus
New Society, Old State

Justyna Olędzka, Kacper Wańczyk

On September 9, 2020, a significant number of Belarusian citizens took to the streets of cities and towns to protest against the rigged presidential election. According to official figures, President Alyaksandr Lukashenka, who has held office since 1994, received more than 80 per cent of the vote. In contrast, the results presented by opposition NGOs documented something entirely different: it was estimated that the Belarusian leader did not get more than 35 per cent.

Weeks and months filled with dramatic events, unprecedented in the history of Belarus, began, and there was no shortage of voices saying that a real, albeit bloodless, revolution had begun in Belarus. A surprising characteristic was the scale and scope of the speeches, as well as the demonstration of political commitment, even by people who had previously been inactive in the public sphere and had been part of Lukashenka's stable electorate until 2020. The Belarusian protests can therefore be seen as an exemplification of a classic crisis of leadership legitimacy that stemmed directly from the rigged presidential election. However, the essence of the changes that occurred in Belarus appears to be more complex and rooted in a broader process: the not always publicly expressed ongoing lack of acceptance for the central institution of the Belarusian political system, symbolising the entire space of anti-liberal norms, values, and social beliefs that have dominated the country since 1994.

Changes occurring in Belarus after 9 August 2020, are difficult to categorise unequivocally, and this range of assessments reflects the wide spectrum of identification of the discussed events. Scientific and analytical works highlight different aspects of the events that occurred at that time. Numerous authors primarily emphasise the nation-building process that was initiated at that time,[1] while others focus on the awakening of civil society.[2] Additionally, some researchers view these events as a representation of late decolonisation or de-Sovietisation.[3] It can also be assumed that the political background of events was secondary to the economic foundation of this deep and long-lasting crisis of the regime.[4] Consequently, in order to operationalise Belarusian developments, various terms are used relatively freely and depending on the adopted research perspective: ranging from political or economic revolution, through democratic transition, civic and national emancipation, to the accelerated process of societal digitalisation and even the transformation of the traditional state into a digital Belarus.

The authors of this paper do not attempt to categorise the events that are happening in Belarus after August 9th, 2020. However, by identifying these events within the socio-political and economic space and showing their hierarchy of importance, they aim to evaluate the consequences of these events for the Alyaksandr Lukashenka regime and Belarusian society.

However, it should be stressed that perceiving Belarusian changes solely in terms of a significantly delayed democratisation process in comparison to some post-Soviet countries can be considered a rather anachronistic approach and does not fully reflect the complexity of the phenomenon, although the undisputed foundation of Belarusian changes is the aspiration of citizens to expand the socio-political sphere of freedom and, therefore, to reverse the democratisation regression that has been taking place in Belarus for the past thirty years.

---

1 Kazharski, A., 2021,"Belarus' new political nation? 2020 anti-authoritarian protests as identity building", *New Perspectives*, 29 (1), pp. 69-79. https://doi.org/10.1177/2336825X20984340 (Accessed: 20 March 2024).
2 Marozau, L., 2022, "Civil society in Belarus 2015-2021 / from stable development to new challenges" in: Shelest, A., Kazanecki, P. (eds.), *Civil society in Belarus 2015-2021: from stable development to new challenges*, Białystok-Warszawa: EkoPress Publishing Agency.
3 Saifullayeu, A., 2023, "The need for decolonisation", *New Eastern Europe*, 6 (49), pp. 167-174.
4 *Ibidem*.

It is worth noting that despite the expectations of many in Belarusian society and international political actors, the power system in Belarus has not disintegrated nor has there been a complete delegitimisation of Lukashenko's leadership after 2020. Therefore, the main research questions that this work aims to answer are: How was the power system in Belarus able to survive despite facing a significant breakdown, and what actions were taken to reduce the impact of the post-election protests, rebuild the sources of legitimacy, and minimise the risk of a similar crisis in the future?

Among the various approaches to explaining the functioning of the system created by Alyaksandr Lukashenka is the concept of "adaptive authoritarianism", coined by Matthev Frear (2019). In his analysis, such structure is characterised by personalist rule, neopatrimonialism, performance legitimacy, managerial pluralism and coercive capacity. An important part of the system is its pragmatism, which allows it to adapt to changing circumstances and continue to exist despite emerging threats to its existence. A system of this type constantly teeters on the edge, facing various external and internal threats to its existence.

Stephen Hall (2023) used Frear's framework to assess whether the events of 2020 have influenced the stability of the system. His research suggests that the system of adaptive authoritarianism has been shattered by the events of 2020–2021 and is slowly coming to an end. In particular, he highlights the growing independence of Lukashenka's inner circle and the system's limited financial resources, which reduces the space for manoeuvre in stabilising the economy.[5]

We believe that while this model explains many elements of Lukashenka's system's functioning post-2020, there are important elements that can only be assessed from a long-term perspective. We assume that although the regime, due to sanctions and the deepening of the integration process within the Union State, has significantly reduced its room for manoeuvre in terms of foreign,

---

[5] Hall, S., 2023, "The End of Adaptive Authoritarianism in Belarus?", *Europe-Asia Studies*, 75 (1), pp. 1–27. https://doi.org/10.1080/09668136.2022.2093332. (Accessed: 20 March 2024).

economic and military policy, the model of adaptive authoritarianism still retains functionality and can be used to analyse the Belarusian political space. However, after 2020, the concept of adaptability is only partly helpful in studying the social sphere, as many citizens view the political order as illegitimate and resist even the most flexible measures of power.

We argue that there was an important change in the behaviour of Belarusian society, which initially went unnoticed by the Belarusian authorities — the strengthening of grassroots movements. Emma Matteo (2020) shows how the non-hierarchical social networks helped to organise protests, while Volodymyr Artiukh (2021) presents how the lack of hierarchies helped to mobilise the labour movement.

Finally, we point out that the behaviour of Minsk authorities in economic policy is a result of a particular type of economic institutional framework. This framework, in our opinion, is best described by the "power-property" model.[6]

Furthermore, the adaptability of authoritarianism has not proven effective in the economic sphere, as the Belarusian economic model post-2020 not only failed to adapt to changing internal and international conditions but still relies on the triad of fundamentals: statism, Russian financial and resource support, and directly and centrally managed economic structure.

Social protest networks

When analysing the patterns of mobilisation during the 2020 events, Matteo aims at understanding why, in certain places, the protests began earlier and what the different reasons were for the dynamics of the events.[7] Her analysis proved that the crucial component that increased the possibility of the initiation of protests in

---

[6] Latov Y., Nureev R., 2016, *Ekonomicheskaja istorija Rossii* (opyt institucial'nogo analiza), Moscow: Knorus.

[7] Matteo, E., 2022, "'All of Belarus Has Come out onto the Streets': Exploring Nationwide Protest and the Role of Pre-Existing Social Networks", *Post-Soviet Affairs*, January, 1–17. https://doi.org/10.1080/1060586X.2022.2026127, pp. 1-2.

each location was the earlier existence of networks between members of a given locality.⁸ These networks exchanged information and coordinated activities mostly using internet communication network (Telegram).⁹ It shows that the strength of the protests of 2020 lay in the grassroots, widely self-organised network instead of centrally controlled protest activities. This argument is also confirmed by Matteo's other conclusion that the presence in a given locality of an event organised by Sviatlana Tsikhanouskaya's team did not significantly increase the possibility of a protest-like event.¹⁰

This grass-root character was visible in worker protests, which were another important element of 2020 events. Initially, most of the large-scale protests that took place in Belarus after 1994 were run by the representatives of intelligentsia, students, etc. There were occasional labour protests, however, these tended to be smaller and localised. The above characteristics can be observed in the protests of the potash miners in Soligorsk in 1992, transportation workers' protests in Gomel and Minsk in 1995, and a series of strikes connected to crises of the Belarusian economy in 1998–2001 and 2011–2013.¹¹ In most of the above cases, the actions of protests were strictly connected to social demands.

In 2020, however, this trend was broken significantly. According to Artiukh, between the beginning of the all-Belarusian protests on 10 August 2020, and 31 September 2020, different protest activities were observed in 88 state-owned or budget-financed organisations (his sample includes not only enterprises but also educational and medical institutions). He stresses that in this case, it is not possible to speak of strikes but rather of "labour unrest", as this term describes a wider range of types of labour protests.¹² Particularly

---

8   *Ibidem*, p. 10.
9   *Ibidem* pp. 12-13.
10 *Ibidem*, pp. 10-11.
11 Artiukh, V., Gorbach, D., 2020, "Workers' Struggles in Ukraine and Belarus – Rosa-Luxemburg-Stiftung", 4 November. https://www.rosalux.de/en/news/id/43290/workers-struggles-in-ukraine-and-belarus. (Accessed: 20 March 2024).
12 Artiukh, V., 2021, "The Anatomy of Impatience: Exploring Factors behind 2020 Labor Unrest in Belarus", *Slavic Review*, 80 (1), p. 52. https://doi.org/10.1017/slr.2021.26. (Accessed: 20 March 2024).

symbolic were the protest actions at large plants, which for many years had been a symbol of Belarusian economic stability. The authorities reacted by abolishing the remnants of the independent trade unions.

Artiukh underlines that this mobilisation was possible mainly because the workers of the "Belarusian working class protested as citizens rather than as workers."[13] It meant that the lack of a clear class (or social) agenda and the focus on protesting against the electoral behaviour of the authorities and further repression allowed faster unification of the protesters. Moreover, similarly to Matteo, Artiukh points out the spontaneous character of protests due to a lack of experience with strikes or proper knowledge.[14]

The policy of the Lukashenka regime in 2020–2023. From minimising losses to rebuilding legitimation resources

The political situation in Belarus after 9 August 2020, was determined by two main factors. One of these (of an endogenous nature) was the political protests that continued for at least nine months after the presidential elections. It should also be noted that although the post-election events in 2020 were an eruption of processes that had been running in the Belarusian socio-political bloodstream for years, one of their main catalysts turned out to be a non-political factor in the form of the pandemic, or more precisely, the attitude of the authorities towards it and the adopted state policy to fight COVID-19. The second factor (of an exogenous nature) determining the actions of the Belarusian authorities was the launch of full-scale Russian aggression against Ukraine from the territory of Belarus. Nevertheless, while this determinant strengthened the negative attitude towards Lukashenka's leadership in society groups activated after the presidential elections, it also reinforced the regime's mobilisation capabilities in moderately and strongly pro-Lukashenka

---

13   *Ibidem*, p. 58.
14   *Ibidem*.

groups. The propaganda tactic of highlighting Belarus' limited involvement in the conflict in Ukraine and gradually familiarising the public with the subject has yielded clear effects.

The chart below illustrates a cycle that occurred in Belarus during the discussed circumstances:

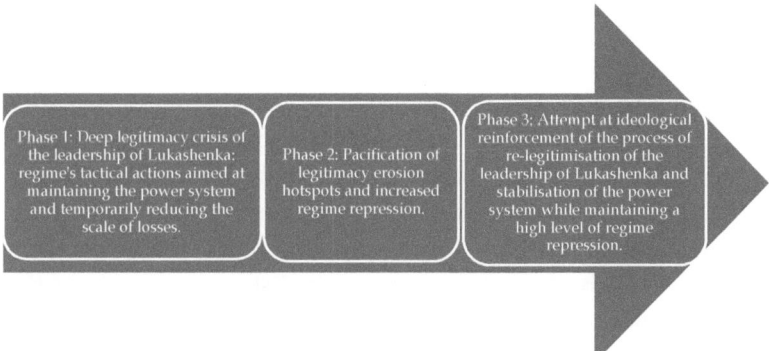

Source: Authors' own analysis

The Belarusian authorities relatively quickly recovered from the initial shock regarding the scale and intensity of the crisis. While maintaining a repressive state policy (over 30,000 people were arrested by the end of 2020), it also initiated comprehensive actions aimed at creating or refining legal solutions to curb the emergence or expansion of de-legitimisation outbreaks. Some of these activities included amending existing legal acts (as of 1 January 2022, amendments to the Criminal Code of the Belarusian People's Republic entered into force, followed by the adoption of the Law on the Genocide of the Belarusian People and the expansion of the grounds for imposing the death penalty), implementing practical violent solutions, and utilizing both existing and newly established special bodies, such as GUBOPiK (Central Office for Combating Organised Crime and Corruption of the Ministry of the Interior) or the Operational and Analytical Centre under the President of the Republic of Belarus.

Another example of the process of blocking the crisis space was the seizure of control over Belarusian information space. It is worth noting that this sphere had already suffered from a low level of autonomy due to the state's multi-stage process of dominating traditional media and establishing a state monopoly on Internet services since 1994. Over the years, the above process made it easier for the authorities to control information in the public space, especially in traditional media such as radio and television.

However, the year 2020 exposed the weakness of this project, as it turned out that the Belarusian authorities, recognising the hegemony of traditional media, underestimated the role of social media, which became an important tool for social mobilisation after the presidential elections. Therefore, an immediate systematic effort to combat anti-regime activity was launched, including surveillance on social media, establishment of new security organs for monitoring this environment, and blocking access to specific websites. Repression also affected the journalistic community in the form of organisations (Belarusian Association of Journalists, Belarusian PEN Centre) as well as individual members of this professional group. As of the end of December 2023, more than 40 journalists and media workers were in prison, and almost 500 Belarusian journalists had decided to emigrate.[15]

In 2024, a decision was made to establish a media holding company based in Moscow with only an office in Minsk. This is another step towards creating a unified and coordinated media policy within the Union State, thus representing a significant element of Belarusian democratic regression, wherein Belarusian society is to be subordinated to the information policy of a foreign state. The above measures are accompanied by a systematic restriction of freedom of speech and assembly.[16]

Actions aimed at combating "extremism" and "terrorism" have also become instruments in the fight against politically active opposition and tools of preventive politics. The number of individuals convicted on charges of forming and financing extremist groups has noticeably increased. The effectiveness of the repression

---

15 https://rsf.org/en/index
16 See the amendment to the 2021 Mass Events Act or the amendments to the 2023 Mass Media Act.

apparatus is evidenced by the data: the number of political prisoners in Belarus is at its highest in history, and the length of sentences imposed on "dissenters" is increasing.

Trials in absentia, introduced in 2022 by an amendment to the Criminal Procedure Code of the Republic of Belarus, and the possibility to revoke the citizenship of both native-born and naturalised Belarusians residing abroad became innovative instruments in the fight against citizenship. The increasing wave of emigration from Belarus after 2020 is not merely a side effect of internal transformations within the country but appears to be a deliberate action by the regime, thereby getting rid of citizens who do not accept the "new normality" proposed by the authorities in Minsk. As a result, according to various estimates, as many as 200,000 to 500,000 people ended up outside their homeland.

Whether assuming that this emigration is political-economic or a classic example of political exile, the result is that the Belarusian authorities effectively eliminated a group that could potentially oppose Lukashenka's rule and destabilise the new electoral cycle starting in 2024. Additionally, Belarusians living in emigration can neither extend the validity and exchange of their documents nor apply for new passports at Belarusian embassies and consulates. Entering Belarus to obtain documents may be dangerous for them. Belarusian émigrés are also practically excluded from the voting process, as polling stations are not open across borders, which deprives some Belarusians of actual influence on the political processes in the country.

Despite maintaining a high level of repression, the regime relatively quickly began seeking new non-coercive sources of legitimacy, indicating the system's departure from a critical stage of legitimacy crisis.[17] The very decision to maintain the scheduled electoral cycle demonstrates that the authorities succeeded in halting the process of erosion of legitimacy and then beginning a process of gradual regeneration and subsequent rebuilding of legitimacy

---

17 Dukalskis, A., Gerschewski, J., 2018, *Justifying Dictatorship. Studies in Autocratic Legitimation*, New York, NY: Routledge.

resources.[18] In 2022, a series of amendments to the Constitution were adopted through a referendum, introducing, among other provisions, the stipulation regarding the "ideology of the Belarusian state". This development signified an overture towards a new social contract, although in the case of Belarus, traditionally, the most essential object of the transaction between the authorities and society is still "peace and tranquillity". A "new normal" pervaded the Belarusian political scene, which meant changes to the Constitution, the electoral laws, as well as statutes governing the presidency, political parties, and social organisations. Lukashenka, by granting himself and his family lifelong immunity and introducing a two-term limit beginning with the next presidential election (which could mean entrenchment of the system until 2035), clearly manoeuvres towards ensuring a lack of alternatives and the political demobilisation of society.

The amendments to the Constitution also include regulations within the socio-cultural sphere, which are part of a broader trend of demonstrative valorisation of tradition and the elimination of national and sexual minorities. From a long-term perspective, these actions are coordinated with endeavours that can be characterised as a systemic socio-political de-modernisation rooted in anti-liberalism, fight against LGBTQ+ minorities, preservation of traditional values along the state-church axis and the cult of the institution of the family with at least two children, in opposition to the Western trend of childlessness deemed "fashionable".

In line with this sentiment, Lukashenka also issued a call for "cultural import substitution," aiming for Belarus to achieve full ideological and cultural self-sufficiency, facilitating a detachment from the West. In the ideological realm, the authorities began to promote the "return" of the state, i.e., the reinforcement of its presence in all spheres of life: the economy, education (with particular emphasis on historical education), public space, and popular culture. As part of their efforts towards social mobilisation, the Belarusian authorities declared 2021 as the Year of National Unity, 2022

---

18 Gerschewski, J., 2023, *The Two Logics of Autocratic Rule*, Cambridge: Cambridge University Press.

as the Year of Historical Memory, 2023 as the Year of Peace and Creation, and 2024 as the Year of Quality — amidst mass arrests and the ongoing armed conflict in Ukraine.

At lightning speed, with the support of a propaganda offensive and statutory changes, a pseudo-pluralist party system was launched. In practice, it meant reducing the number of party entities present in the system to four. In the parliamentary elections held in February 2024, which were the first real stress test of the power system after 2020, as many as 51 seats (out of 110 seats in the House of Representatives) were won by the newly established party, "White Ruthenia", described as the first power party in the Belarusian party system. Simultaneously, with changes in the political sphere, there was a vigorous simulation of grassroots and pro-state non-governmental initiatives intended to serve as substitutes for civil society organisations.[19] These actions starkly contrast with measures that restrict the activities of NGOs, hinder the functioning of religious organisations, reinforce the alliance between the altar and the throne, sustain the political role of the Church, and practically paralyse the operations of private schools and kindergartens, including education conducted in the Belarusian language and by national minorities.

The economy

The framework of the Belarusian economy

There have been recent interesting attempts at constructing the theoretical framework that would explain the functioning of the Belarusian economy. Nevertheless, it seems that the discussion could benefit from the application of the "power-property" concept, coming from the institutionalist school, that explains the functioning of the systems in which the ruler is in full control of assets.

---

19 Astapova, A., Navumau, V., Nizhnikau, R., Polishchuk, L., 2022, "Authoritarian Cooptation of Civil Society: The Case of Belarus", *Europe-Asia Studies,* 74 (1), pp. 1–30. https://doi.org/10.1080/09668136.2021.2009773 (Accessed: 20 March 2024).

The concept of "power-property" describes structures in which property rights ultimately belong to the political ruler. If they are transferred to another actor, this transfer is always reversible and temporary. Such structures are hierarchical; any initiative comes from the top, and the direct relationship between ownership and political power remains unchanged.

Latov and Nureev (2016) applied the concept in question to the analysis of the economic history of today's Russian Federation. In their research, the history is based on the constant tensions between "power-property" and forms of state economic policy, which attempted to introduce a system based on private property. However, the former model prevails in these tensions. While some elements of the "power-property" would change under the influence of different new ideas, its main features remain. The consequence of such an institutional arrangement is that there is a problem with introducing changes to the system. The ruler opposes any real change that would lead to a loss of control over property rights in the polity.

A decade of fluctuation

As measured by GDP dynamics over the last decade, the Belarusian economy fluctuated with an apparent tendency to flatten the fluctuation trend (Table 1). This represents the balancing act in the economy, as described by Frear and Hall. They were the result of policies of internal stimulation of demand by the authorities, maintaining production and the dependence of the Belarusian economy on external trade, as well as various types of economic support from Russia. In terms of property management, this kind of policy is possible because the Belarusian authorities can freely control assets in the country and move them to sectors when support is needed.

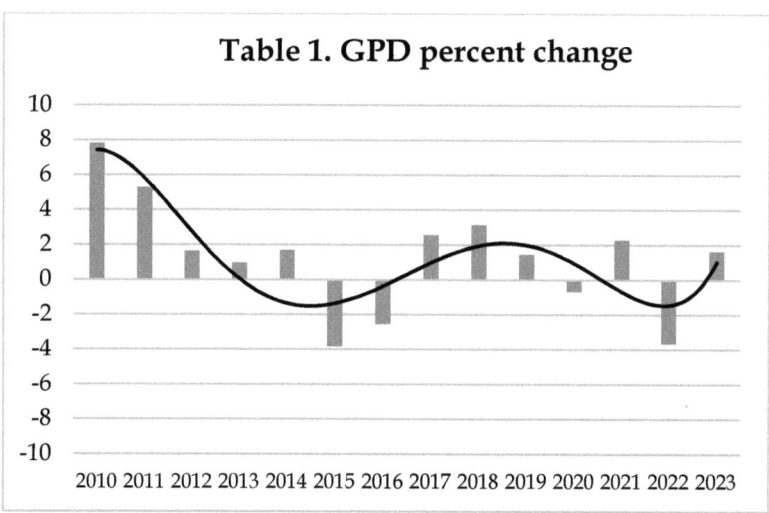

Source: International Monetary Fund, 2023 data / authors' own analysis

However, after the significant currency crisis, which led to a sharp rise in inflation in 2011 (Table 2), Belarusian economic policy became more restrained in terms of implementing domestic financial stimulus. Moreover, the traditional sectors of the economy (e.g. heavy industry) continued to underperform. The influence of the 2014-2016 Russian financial crisis on the Belarusian economy was another important factor affecting its performance. As a result, while GDP dynamics was losing its contradictory behaviour to some extent, it was also losing its ability to record extreme growth, which was always part of the picture of the "Belarusian economic miracle" depicted by Lukashenka.

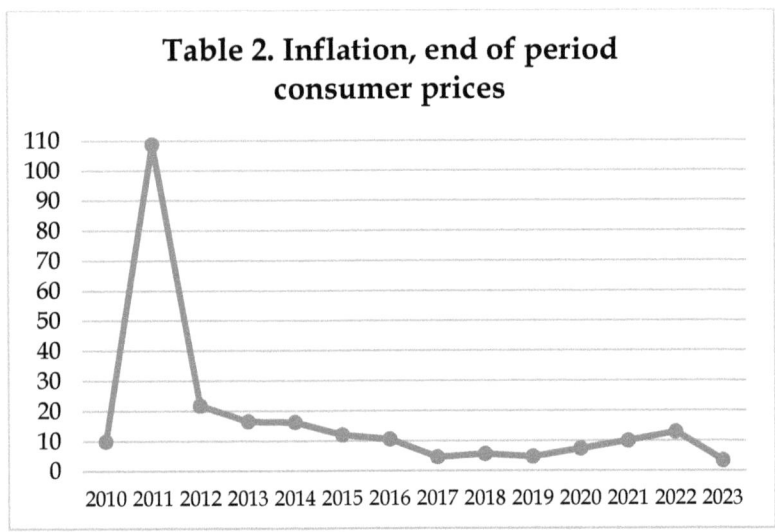

Table 2. Inflation, end of period consumer prices

Source: International Monetary Fund, 2023 data / authors' own analysis

During the same period, an interesting phenomenon could be observed: the growth of the Belarusian private sector, which now employs around 50 per cent of the workforce in Belarus. The history of this part of the Belarusian economy shows the characteristics of the "power-property" model.

Contrary to some other countries in the region, the private sector in Belarus developed not because of the support of the state but rather despite state policies. Minsk's policy in this area was limited to only pinpoint privatisation of enterprises and narrow reforms introduced after 2007, suggesting the strive to stimulate the expansion of the private sector.[20] As explained above, the privatisation and the expansion of private property would undermine the foundation of the "power-property system", with the property slipping away from the direct control of the autocrat.

As a result, instead of working in all sectors of the Belarusian economy and playing a complementary role to state companies,

---

20 Alachnovič, A., Korosteleva, E., 2023, "Stolen Decades. The Unfulfilled Expectations of the Belarusian Economic Miracle", in: Korosteleva, J., Petrova, I., Kudlenko, A. (eds.), 2023, *Belarus in the Twenty-First Century: Between Dictatorship and Democracy*, 1st ed. Routledge. https://doi.org/10.4324/9781003311454 (Accessed: 20 March 2024).

private companies seek niches in which the state is not interested or cannot fully control them. A good example of that is the explosive development of the Information and Communication Technology (ICT) sector, which could be traced back to 2005 to the creation of the High Technology Park in Belarus. The sector's share of Belarusian GDP was 5.5 per cent of GDP in 2018 and was expected to reach 10 per cent of GDP by 2023 in projections made before the 2020 events.[21]

This sector's development mainly resulted from two institutional characteristics of the system built by Lukashenka. Firstly, it had a great custodian in the person of Valeri Tsepkalo. This former Belarusian Ambassador to the US and one of the closest aides of Lukashenka was a driving force behind the creation of the High Technology Park in Minsk and the formulation of the legal framework, stimulating the ICT companies' development.

Secondly, most of the companies working in that sector were branches of companies registered abroad (in Cyprus, Luxembourg, the US etc.). As such, most of their assets were abroad: away from Lukashenka's control. Therefore, it is not visible in the "power-property" type of economy, where only the assets that could be seized and controlled by the ruler are essential. As it later turned out, despite the generally good performance of the sector, the Belarusian authorities did not hesitate to suppress it after 2020 because they did not see any real value for themselves in it.

Another crucial element of the Belarusian model is the deep economic connection with the Russian Federation. Russian markets traditionally accounted for about 30-40 per cent of Belarusian exports and about 50 per cent of imports. Moscow supplies natural gas at favourable prices and remains the dominant supplier of oil to Belarus.

Russia is also an important financial and investment partner. It is responsible for 50-60 per cent of all foreign direct investment in

---

[21] *Ibidem*, p. 71; Papko, A., 2017, "Informal Barriers to the Development of Small and Medium Enterprises in Belarus" Unpublished PhD dissertation, Warszawa, pp. 128-132.

Belarus. Around 80 per cent of Belarus' external debt is held by Russia. Russia also supported the rear and not very successful placement of Belarusian debt securities on foreign markets and allowed loans from the Anti-Crisis Fund of the Eurasian Economic Union.

The crisis hattrick

The COVID-19 pandemic did not affect the performance of the Belarusian economy as much as expected, nor as much as the pandemic affected neighbouring countries. More than the slowdown in economic activity due to COVID-19, external factors affected GDP dynamics in 2020. The fall of the prices of potassium fertilisers and another conflict with Russia on the deliveries of oil to Belarus were more significant.[22]

Source: International Monetary Fund, 2023 data / authors' own analysis.

Western sanctions introduced in June 2021 against Belarus were the first to have a direct impact on Belarusian foreign trade.[23] They targeted the export of two goods crucial for the Belarusian economy: oil products and potassium fertilisers, which before 2020 accounted

---

22 "'Vlijanije Pandemii COVID-19 Na Ekonomičeskie i Social'nye Processy v Belarusi", 2020, Friedrich Ebert Stiftung.
23 Council Regulation [EU] 2021/1030 of 24 June 2021.

for around 60 per cent of Belarusian exports to the EU. The EU was a target for around 78 per cent of Belarusian exports of these products.[24] The sanctions had a delayed impact because they affected only contracts concluded after the introduction of sanctions. Therefore, Belarus was able to record positive foreign trade dynamics in 2021 (Table 3.) and maintain a positive dynamic of the GDP. It was also partly due to the positive situation in the global economy (the increase in prices for exported goods).

Another weakening of the Belarusian foreign trade came after Minsk joined the Russian aggression against Ukraine. New restrictions lead to the blockage of other elements of exports to the EU: petroleum products, wood and wood products, metals, and chemical production. They also stopped imports of high-technology equipment used in heavy industry. Moreover, the measures included the restriction of SWIFT access for three Belarusian banks as well as transactions with the Belarusian central bank.[25] According to the EU's experts' assessment, the 2022 sanctions focused on goods that comprised 70 per cent of Belarusian exports to the EU.[26]

However, the real blow came from the other direction. Before the invasion, Ukraine was the largest single non-Russian Belarusian foreign economic partner. It was the largest single importer of Belarusian petroleum products. Belarusian data from 2020 (before the authorities started to restrict some data) shows that exports to Ukraine amounted to 45 per cent of total Belarusian petroleum products exports. Belarus, in turn, together with Russia, accounted for most of the supply of these goods to the Ukrainian market.

Belarus exported fertilisers such as potash, nitrogen and mixed fertilisers to Ukraine. According to Belarusian trade data for 2020, Ukraine was the third (and largest European) customer of Bel-

---

24 Aslund, A. Hagemejer, J., 2021, "EU Sanctions on Belarus as an Effective Policy Tool", *SSRN Electronic Journal*, p.16. https://doi.org/10.2139/ssrn.3991710 (Accessed: 20 March 2024).
25 Council Regulation (EU) 2022/398.
26 Guarascio, F., 2022, "EU Bans 70% of Belarus Exports to Bloc with New Sanctions over Ukraine Invasion", *Reuters*, 2 March. https://www.reuters.com/world/europe/eu-approves-new-sanctions-against-belarus-over-ukraine-invasion-source-2022-03-02/ (Accessed: 20 March 2024).

arusian fertilisers. Belarus also exported timber or automotive industry goods and food products. The southern neighbour also served as a transit country, for example, for Belarusian agricultural produce to China, which was routed through Ukrainian ports. All these ties were severed after Minsk joined Moscow in the aggression against Ukraine.

This cumulative effect led to a significant decline in foreign trade (Table 3.) and the general decline of the economy measured as GDP (Table 1.) in 2022.

Old tricks

Despite the significant changes in the external environment described above, Lukashenka continued to employ traditional economic policies. These are mainly based on three pillars: strengthening control over the economy, stimulating internal demand, and seeking support from Moscow.

On the internal side, the authorities started to tighten the grip on the economy by restricting private sector activities. Apart from the political reasons behind limiting the activities of any non-state-dependent organisations in Belarus, the resources at the disposal of authorities were shrinking, so there was a need to strengthen the position of the governmental sector.

The most visible was the case of the already-mentioned CIT sector. Given the fact that some of the businessmen working in that sector participated in or supported, to some extent, the protests in 2020, some companies were already under pressure from the onset of the events. A lot of specialists employed in the field had already left after the first repressions in 2020; the second wave came after the start of the Russian aggression against Ukraine. Belarus estimates that after the February 2022 Russian invasion on Ukraine until October 2023, around 22,000 IT experts left the country ("The Myth of Mass Political Emigration 2023"). Many companies relocated their operations to other countries (Georgia, Lithuania, Poland). According to a Belarusian expert, between the spring of 2022 and October 2023, 170 companies left the Belarusian High Technologies Park ("The Myth of Mass Political Emigration 2023").

Moreover, in 2022, the Belarusian authorities launched a series of inspections of private education and healthcare companies and introduced new measures regarding their work. This led to the liquidation of almost half of non-state education institutions. Allegedly, the actions in the healthcare system resulted in the subjugation of this part of the private sector to the entities close to Lukashenka.

Meanwhile, aiming at rebuilding the economic dynamics from the fall of 2022, Belarusian authorities returned in 2023 to their policies of stimulating internal demand. As in previous situations, this policy is conducted by widening society's access to cheap consumer credits. At the same time, however, the Belarusian authorities needed to curb the inflationary pressure that usually accompanies a policy of stimulating demand in Belarus. To do that, Minsk tightened the price control and introduced temporary limits on the export of food products to Russia.

Finally, Lukashenka continued to rely on support from Russia, which now remained the only close economic partner. Russian territory became a transit for Belarusian goods. Some shipments are transported by rail through Russia, and some through Russian Baltic ports. This may be confirmed by the data showing a drastic increase in exports to Russia. Russia is now responsible for around 90 per cent of Belarusian exports.

Moreover, Moscow agreed to keep the preferential price of gas from 2022 (USD 128/1,000 cubic metres) at the same level up until 2025 and agreed to Belarus' suspension of loan repayments (approximately US$3 billion per year). Finally, the two countries agreed to join high-tech import substitution projects: Russia is to borrow between US$1.5bn and US$1.7bn for them.

Conclusions

The concept of "adaptive authoritarianism" seems to explain well the political part of the functioning of the Belarusian system. However, it should be complemented with some observations concerning the changing character of Belarusian society and the stable character of its economic policies.

Belarusian society underwent a significant change through self-organisation and voluntary networking, which horizontally connected groups that had previously been isolated in their protests against the regime. This may further complicate the functioning of "adaptive authoritarianism" in the future.

Despite several waves of economic sanctions, the influence of the COVID-19 pandemic, and the cut of economic ties with Ukraine, the Belarusian economy is still able to maintain its volatile stability. The GDP dynamics of 2023 are better than the results of the crisis between 2014-2016, and the financial authorities are still able to maintain low inflation levels.

This is the result of the peculiarity of the Belarusian model of a "power-property" system that allows for almost complete control over the assets in the economy. In a crisis, Lukashenka can divert resources to where they are needed at any given moment.

Another important element of the puzzle is the support from Russia. Without economic cooperation with Moscow, Belarus would be almost completely cut off from external markets, which are crucial for its functioning. Preferential prices for energy resources and financial help also play a significant role. Despite repeated declarations and some concrete policies diminishing the support by Moscow it is still ongoing.

Therefore, instead of loosening the grip over the economy, Lukashenka tightened it, diminishing the private sector. Additionally, being cut off from other economies, Belarus agreed to deepen economic relations with Russia further. Therefore, this part of its policies cannot be seen as "change" or "adaptation". Despite significant changes in the external situation, the economic policies of the Belarusian authorities remain the same.

The true functionality of the Belarusian model of adaptive authoritarianism post-2020 could only be assessed from a long-term perspective. It seems, however, that despite the visible efforts of the authorities in Belarus, there is still a certain mental and axiological gap. The regime has, of course, attempted to adapt to these changes, as the legitimacy crisis following the presidential election brought about a collapse in Lukashenka's authority and the social groups on which the previous legitimisation strategy was based until 2020 (bureaucracy, employees of state-owned enterprises, pensioners) were partly replaced by loyal representatives of the power ministries.

Interestingly, despite the prolonged and drastic repressive measures undertaken by the authorities following the presidential elections, the Belarusian society attempted to manifest its disagreement with the political apparatus twice more (although the scale of these protests significantly differed from the events of the 2020/2021 breakthrough): after 24 February 2022, anti-war protests occurred in several Belarusian cities (promptly pacified), and in 2023, there were demonstrations against the constitutional referendum. Since 2021, the authorities in Minsk have been sending numerous signals of readiness to embark on various pro-state projects, thereby expanding their legitimisation resources with non-coercive ideological instruments.

However, they have yet to relinquish intensified repression and control. The government has weathered the crisis, yet it appears to remain in a state of constant readiness, especially since presidential elections are scheduled to take place in Belarus in 2025, and Lukashenka has already announced his intention to participate in them. It should be emphasised that Lukashenka's strength still lies in the weakness and fragmentation of the Belarusian opposition (including those in exile), political demobilisation, which has affected part of society following the outbreak of full-scale warfare in Ukraine, and the lack of realistic prospects for a change in power. Assuming that August 2020 had a huge potential for change and was a generational and formative experience for many Belarusians, even if a significant proportion of politically active people today choose internal migration or exile, it marks the emergence of a new society, and its transformation is irreversible.

The text was written in the framework of a research under the Preludium Grant 2022/45/N/HS4/02191.

Occupation in the Name of Destabilisation
Russia's Policies Towards Donetsk and Luhansk

Magdalena Lachowicz

On 30 September 2022, in an address to both houses of the Russian parliament, Vladimir Putin announced annexation of Donetsk, Luhansk, Kherson and Zaporizhzhia oblasts of Ukraine by the Russian Federation. The United Nations, Ukraine, as well as many other countries condemned the annexation, regarding it as a breach of international law. However, as of now, Russia has not paid a price for the unlawful takeover of Ukrainian lands. Instead the Kremlin has developed and implemented nationalisation policies that cement Russian presence in this part of Ukraine.

To achieve this, Russia has constructed a narrative centred on the myth of *Novorossiya* (New Russia). Historically speaking, this term referred to the area north of the Black Sea that was conquered during the 1768-1774 Russian-Turkish wars under Catharine the Great. Since 2014 the Kremlin has been using it as a name for around one-third of the territory of Ukraine (including Crimea), to which a large degree overlaps with the 19th century Russian acquisitions, which today's Russian authorities believe should belong to Russia.

Overall, the current myth of *Novorossiya*, as it is promoted by Russia, can be seen as an attempt to combine three ideological paradigms. They include: the "red" (Soviet) paradigm, the "white" (Orthodox) paradigm and the "brown" (fascist) paradigm.[1] Skillfully put together, they have served the Kremlin as an ideological framework for the transformation of eastern Ukraine. This process, nonetheless, has not ended successfully. The concept of *Novorossiya*

---

1 Laruelle, M., 2016, "The Three Colors of Novorossiya, or the Russian Nationalist Mythmaking of the Ukrainian Crisis", *Post-Soviet Affairs*, 32 (1), pp. 55-74.

has not yet been fully implemented and therefore it has been ignored by the international community.

In the early years of Russia's ongoing war against Ukraine, the promotion of *Novorossiya* played a significant role in shaping public attitudes in Russia toward Ukraine. It has also proven very useful for the Kremlin to legitimise its revisionist foreign policy and carry out military operations. In the opinion of the French sociologist and specialist on international relations, Marlene Laruelle, promotion of this concept has significantly contributed to an increased popularity of Russian imperialism and Messianism. Their development has been also facilitated by a noticeable imperial nostalgia and the mushrooming of ultraconservative Orthodox groups (the so-called conservative pivot) as well as some European fascist traditions. Metaphorically speaking, *Novorossiya*, means a battlefield, an area where a new revolution and the overthrow of old regimes takes place.[2]

Laruelle further argues that since the beginning of the war in Donbas numerous pro-Kremlin political movements have used the concept of *Novorossiya* to promote the idea of "genetic" unity between eastern and southern Ukraine and Russia. These organisations have included: the Izborsky Club, the Institute for Dynamic Conservatism, Institut de le démocratie et de la coopération (IDC), which is based in Paris but funded with Russian resources, www.orthodoxy.ru, the Cossack National Guard, and the Russian Spring movement.

At the time of the writing of this chapter, Russia continues to gain control over the Donetsk and Luhansk regions as well as Kharkiv, Dniepropietrovsk, Zaporizhzhia, Kherson, Mykolaiv and Odesa. The Kremlin justifies its claims to these places with social and demographic factors. Specifically, prior to 2014 the highly industrial Donbas region was inhabited by almost 45% of Ukraine's total population and generated around two-thirds of Ukraine's GDP.[3] The region's acquisition was thus perceived as a solution to

---

2 *Ibidem*, p. 56.
3 Basora, A., Fisher, A., 2014, "Putin's 'Greater Novorossiya' – The Dismemberment of Ukraine", FPRI. https://www.fpri.org/article/2014/05/putins-grea ter-novorossiya-the-dismemberment-of-ukraine/ (Accessed: 24 April 2024).

some of Russia's most pressing problems, especially the continued demographic crisis.

Despite gaining control of Ukrainian territories in 2014, Russia has not financially profited from their occupation. Its costs, especially in Crimea, have proven very high. To cover them the Russian state had to reallocate budget resources from other categories, including infrastructure projects in Siberia and the North Caucuses, as well as federal pension plans.[4] Given the scale of propaganda accompanying Russia's actions in Ukraine, along with the unreliable and incomplete data provided by Russian state agencies, it remains impossible to objectively assess the true costs of these occupations. For similar reasons, evaluating the impact of the economic sanctions imposed on Russia by Western states is also challenging.

Evidence shows that Russia has recognised that to maintain control over the newly annexed territories it needs loyalty from the local populations. To achieve this, the Kremlin has orchestrated activities that are aimed at aligning the administrative agencies on the ground with the Russian administrative model. This process has been accompanied by an intense propaganda campaign and investments in third sector operations. Altogether they make up a complex system of monitoring and controlling of the processes that, from the Russian perspective, are perceived as desirable. Responsibility for accomplishing these "desirable" changes has been put on certain pseudo-civil society actors that have been established in the region. It thus seems more correct to refer to them as "implants" than NGOs.

Consequently, the analysis presented in this article cannot be grounded in traditional civil society theory. Instead, it focuses on the Kremlin's central control in the annexed Ukrainian regions. Clearly, the space typically allocated to non-governmental actors in democratic countries is no longer accessible to these organisations in the territories controlled by Russia. This is due to the Kremlin's lack of trust in genuine non-governmental organisations, which it

---

4   Saivetz, C., 2014, "The Foreign Policy Essay: The Price of 'Novorossiya'", *Lawfare*. https://www.lawfaremedia.org/article/foreign-policy-essay-price-novorossiya (Accessed: 24 April 2024).

views as facilitators of unwanted democratisation that lie beyond the control of central authorities.[5] Therefore, it treats them as instruments of external influence and foreign intervention, while in countries such as Serbia, Kyrgyzstan, Moldova, Georgia and Ukraine it recognises them as a threat to Russian spheres of influence. Similar interpretation has been assigned to the NGOs that are operating in Russia but are financed with external resources.

Russia's political and legal engagements in Eastern Ukraine

In 2014 Russian paramilitary groups and special forces started taking control over public administration agencies in Donbas. The rebellion, which they orchestrated and which also took place in Crimea, was initiated and led by Igor Strelkov (real name: Igor Girkin) and Alexander Borodai. In eastern parts of Ukraine, it turned into a war. Despite international attempts to regulate the conflict in its early stages, Russian occupation of parts of Ukrainian territories continued. In February 2022, the war entered into the next stage. First, on 21 February 2022, the Russian Duma recognised independence of the so-called republics: the Donetsk People's Republic (DNR) and the Luhansk People's Republic (LNR). In the aftermath of their recognition these two entities facilitated the arrival of regular Russian troops and signed agreements with Russia on friendship, cooperation and mutual assistance.

The process of annexation did not involve any boundary delimitation or demarcation. Consequently, Russia's takeover of the annexed "republics" constitutes a violation of the principle of territorial integrity and the prohibition against interference in another state's internal affairs, as outlined in the United Nations Charter, the Helsinki Final Act and the 1994 Budapest Memorandum. The

---

5   Lutsevych, O., 2016, *Agents of the Russian World: Proxy Groups in the Contested Neighbourhood. Russia and Eurasia Programme*, Chatham House, pp. 4-8.

presence of Russian troops in Donbas is, in turn, proof of occupation and meets the criteria of aggression stipulated in the 1974 United Nations General Assembly Resolution 3314.[6]

Thus far, Russia's annexation of Ukrainian lands has included four oblasts (regions): Donetsk, Luhansk, Kherson and Zaporizhzhia. Their annexation, which — as stated above — is a breach of international law but has so far brought no legal consequences. Even more, the annexation's approval by the local population, obtained in pseudo referenda, allowed Russia's President, Vladimir Putin, to conclude agreements with the puppet authorities in these regions and thereby incorporate them into the Russian Federation.[7]

Russia-DNR and Russia-LNR agreements were ratified by both chambers of the Russian parliament on 3 and 4 October 2022. On 5 October 2022 constitutional laws regulating the annexation process were passed and signed by Putin. These acts are the legal basis that Russia uses to treat the occupied areas as part of its territory: the Donetsk and Luhansk regions are now regarded as Russian republics, while Kherson and Zaporizhzhia as regions. Even though the Russian army does not fully control all of these territories, the republics are demarked by the borders stipulated in their constitutions, while the regions by the borders that "existed at the time of their annexation", that is on 30 September 2022.

---

6   Zaręba, Sz., 2022, *Rosja uznaje "republiki ludowe" w Donbasie*, Warszawa: PISM. https://www.pism.pl/publikacje/rosja-uznaje-republiki-ludowe-w-donbasie (Accessed: 24 April 2024).

7   By deciding to annex four Ukrainian oblasts within their administrative boundaries (their total area is approximately 110,000 square kilometres, which constitutes 18.2% of Ukrainian territory), the Kremlin has created a situation of formal incorporation into Russia of territories which are not controlled by its own armed forces. According to Ukrainian estimates, until recently about 88% of Kherson Oblast, 67% of Zaporizhzhya Oblast, 57% of Donetsk Oblast and 99% of Luhansk Oblast were under occupation. Ukraine also lost 4% of the Mykolaiv region, an area Moscow annexed to the occupied Kherson region. A total of 327 municipalities (hromady) were under Russian control before the Ukrainian counter-offensive began in mid-September 2022. See: Menkiszak, M., Domańska, M., Żochowski, P., 2022, "Russia announces annexation of four Ukrainian regions", OSW. https://www.osw.waw.pl/pl/publikacje/analizy/2022-10-03/rosja-oglasza-aneksje-czterech-regionow-ukrainy (Accessed: 24 April 2024).

On that day, the Russian Federation granted citizenship to residents of the annexed territories, allowing them the option to renounce it within a month of the annexation. To discourage this renunciation, Russia offered employment guarantees exclusively to Russian citizens beginning in 2026. The same regulations stipulated the rules of establishing Russian administrative agencies and courts on the occupied territories and replacement of Ukrainian currency with the Russian rouble from 2023 on.[8]

Research methodology

The analysis presented in this chapter is based on official and secondary data obtained from agencies of the Russian Federation and Ukraine as well as statistical data. It also includes a review of the grants distributed by the President of the Russian Federation. Presented information comes from official websites of the earlier mentioned regions as well as the administrative agencies in Luhansk and Donetsk, Ukrainian state agencies and institutions as well as international organisations. The analysis thus contributes to the current state of research in the area of post-Soviet studies.

The scope of the analysis is focused on the territories that are not controlled by the Ukrainian government as they are occupied by the Russian Federation. In particular, attention is put on Russian practices of territorial incorporation and the inclusion of the residents of the annexed territories into the system of social policy of the Russian Federation, which is achieved by means of administrative mechanisms as well instrumentalisation of the third sector.

Research has shown that to effectively orchestrate social change activists and social movements need to play four different roles: that of a citizen, a rebel, an agent of change and a reformer. Each role has its own goals, requires different styles and skills, and

---

8   Zaręba, Sz., *op. cit.*; Żochowski, P., Nieczypor, K., 2022, "Pełzająca aneksja. Rosyjskie plany rozbioru Ukrainy", OSW. https://www.osw.waw.pl/pl/publikacje/komentarze-osw/2022-06-28/pelzajaca-aneksja-rosyjskie-plany-rozbioru-ukrainy (Accessed: 24 April 2024).

addresses varying needs. Moreover, each role can be executed effectively or ineffectively.[9] Social activists thus need to build their reputation among the so-called ordinary people, which is also dependent on the local traditions and political culture.[10] Recognising these, Russia has been actively engaging local, or pseudo local but loyal, organisations to support its activities aimed at territorial incorporation.

The Russian Federation has adopted new social policy instruments which allow it to complete the process of occupation and are aimed at integrating Ukrainian citizens/immigrants with the Russian society. The most effective tools in this regards have proven to be: social assistance and support systems which are offered to "new Russians" as well as "identity-building" projects that focus on: language, culture and historical education. Their promotion by the Kremlin verifies the thesis that from Russia's perspective social assimilation of the local population living in the newly annexed territories is a necessary condition for the long-term success of their integration with the Russian civilisation. For this to take place Russia relies on the so-called GONGOs (government-organised non-governmental organisations) and SONCOs (socially-oriented non-commercial organisations) which serve as a bridge between the regional authorities and Moscow, from where they are receiving money through the system of presidential grants. Distribution of significant financial resources to loyal organisations in annexed territories is aimed at minimizing the risk of a crisis that could emerge from low quality social services, especially those directed at seniors and youth.

---

9   Moyer, B., 1987, "The Movement Action Plan: A Strategic Framework Describing the Eight Stages of Successful Social Movements" https://www.historyisaweapon.com/defcon1/moyermap.html (Accessed: 24 April 2024).
10 Giugni, M., Grasso, M., 2019, *Street Citizens: Protest Politics and Social Movement Activism in the Age of Globalization*, Cambridge: Cambridge University Press, p. 3.

Migration as an element of Russia's social policy

As a result of the war in eastern Ukraine, several waves of internal and external displacement have occurred since 2014, including migration to the Russian Federation. Statistical data from early 2018 recorded almost 1.5 million internally displaced persons (IDPs) in Ukraine. Among them the largest groups were people from Crimea and eastern Ukraine. This war-related internal migration is evidenced to have generated some tensions within the Ukrainian society. Researching them, sociologists pointed to the following reactions: negative attitude towards IDPs, tensions within IDP groups and their accepting communities, increased conflict potential in regions, adjustment problems, confrontation tendencies.[11] Research has also showed that in the eyes of the residents of other parts of Ukraine, IDPs from Donbas were often seen as separatists. In parallel, on the occupied territories, some negative social trends were observed from the early stages of the war, including an increased level of mistrust towards the Ukrainian state.[12]

These facts have also been noted and interpreted accordingly by the Russian authorities. As a result, people living in the DNR and LNR have been offered an opportunity to become citizens of the Russian Federation through a simplified naturalisation procedure starting in April 2019.[13] Almost right away, as many as 550,000 DNR residents became holders of Russian passports. Their number doubled after 30 September 2022, when the separatist republics became annexed into the Russian Federation.

The process of mass naturalisation of Ukrainians by Russia on the occupied territories goes beyond foreign policy practice. It relies heavily on methods of manipulation, also of international public opinion and decision-makers. Thus, what international organisations regard as a breach of international laws and agreements that

---

11 Voytyuk, O., 2020, "Internal migrations from Crimea and Donbass after 2014 as conflict-triggering factors in the regions of Ukraine", *Athenaeum. Polskie Studia Politologiczne*, 67, pp. 155–159.
12 Interfax, 2017, "Half a million displaced persons returned to ORDLO not receive pensions – Grymchak", 30 November. https://ua.interfax.com.ua/news/general/465924.html.
13 Decree no. 183, amended in 2022 by Decree no. 440.

have been concluded to solve this conflict, including the Minsk Agreements, Russia called "humanitarian motifs" and a response to what it regards as a restrictive policy of the Ukrainian government. As a reaction to Russia's unlawful activities and the rhetoric accompanying them, the European Commission issued directives for EU member states not to recognise passports issued by the two separatist "republics".[14]

Russia, suffering from a serious demographic crisis caused by both natural and COVID-19 related causes, desperately needs new citizens. For this reason, the Kremlin actively promotes the concept of compatriot *(соотечественник)*, which is a reference to Russian-speaking persons living outside Russia. In practical terms, since 2006 the Russian state offers assistance to former Russian/Soviet citizens upon their return home. This programme was introduced by Decree no. 637 issued by the President of the Russian Federation on 22 June 2006. In addition, the Russian government has been implementing the State Migration Policy Concept of the Russian Federation through to 2025 which was approved by Vladimir Putin in 2012. Among other things, this document foresees the possibility of a "simplified" citizenship procedure for people who had once left the territory of the Russian Federation or the Soviet Union. The State Migration Policy Concept has served as a basis for the amendment to the law on Russian citizenship, which entered into force on 26 October 2023.[15]

Russkiy mir

After the Second World War the ethnic structure in Donbas changed significantly. The region's industrialisation was accompanied by a Russification policy which increased the number of ethnic Russian population and which explains a high approval of the idea of *Russkiy Mir* (the Russian World) on these territories. Created by

---

14 European Commission, 2022, "Proposal for a Decision of the European Parliament and of the Council on the non-recognition of Russian travel documents issued in occupied foreign regions", https://eur-lex.europa.eu/legal-content/EN/TXT/HTML/?uri=CELEX:52022PC0662 (Accessed: 25 April 2024).
15 Federal law no. 138-FZ passed on 28 April 2023.

Vladimir Putin's decree in 2007, the *Russkiy Mir* foundation is, in theory at least, tasked with the promotion of the Russian language and culture abroad. In practice, its operations are directed at Russian-speakers living outside Russia — the compatriots. They are the recipients of the Russian interpretation of history which inclines admiration for tsarist and Soviet heritage, focuses on the legacy of the Kyivan Rus' as the cradle of Eastern Slavic civilisation and the shared legacy of fighting against fascism during the Second World War. In eastern parts of Ukraine, the concept of *Russkiy mir* has been additionally promoted through the works of such organisations as: Rossotrudnichestvo, Intergovernmental Foundation for Humanitarian Cooperation of CIS countries, World Congress of Russian Compatriots, International Union of Russian Compatriots, Institute of Russian Compatriots, Anti-Globalisation Movement of Russia. Together, they have created an effective horizontal network of actors that are subordinate to the Kremlin, although operating in the third sector. Their narrative is in line with the Russian revisionist policy which has also been promoted, among others, by such organisations as the Foundation for Historical Perspective, World Without Nazism, International Antifascist Front, Russian Association for International Cooperation, Historical Memory Foundation.

The Presidential Commission of the Russian Federation to Counter Attempts to Falsify History to the Detriment of Russia's Interests, which operated from 2009 to 2012, focused on preventing any departures from the official Russian narrative, while its priority was to convince the Western world of Russian achievements in saving Europe from fascism. The key role in this regards was played here by the World Without Nazism coalition, which was set up in 2011 as well as conservative and Orthodox movements, including Russians Without Russia.[16] Among the proxy groups that were the most active in mobilizing fighters at the first stage of the annexation of Crimea and Eastern Ukraine was the International Eurasian Movement led by Alexander Dugin while the Russian Orthodox

---

16 Lutsevych, O., *op.cit.*, pp. 10-25.

Church and private business organised assistance to rebels in Donbas.[17]

According to the 2021 Freedom House report, Russian policy towards Donbas intensified significantly after the 2020 COVID-19 pandemic. This policy focused on political "integration", which, in practice, meant Russification and creeping annexation. Key elements of this process included issuing passports to Ukrainian citizens, obstructing their access to Ukrainian administrative services – most notably those that have an impact on the seniors – and orchestrating a deep crisis of democracy that deprived Ukrainian citizens of their basic political rights. These actions were further supported by extensive pro-Russian propaganda and manipulations of election results.

General elections were held both in DNR and LNR in November 2018. At that time voters were also asked to elect heads of both separatist "republics". The results of these elections were not recognised by the European Union nor the United States; they took place in questionable conditions with no real competition in place. What the 2018 elections yet showed is that since 2014 Russia has established a complex, non-transparent, network of control of the "people's republics" and thanks to that the Russian authorities can influence all aspects of people's lives, including their political engagements. Local media, schools, universities and public services as well as business structures got into the hands of people who proved their loyalty towards the separatists. Some of the key positions in the "republics" were given to Russian citizens. The political control over these territories is executed through secret ministries of "state security" which operate in both "republics".

While the constitutions of both the DNR and LNR stipulate equal rights, regardless of people's ethnic background, race, or religious belief, in practice representatives of ethnic or religious groups that are not connected with Russia, are excluded from political life and no segment of the society can organise itself independently in order to defend its political interests. Any form of pro-Ukrainian activity is regarded as a threat. Since 2014 there have

---

17   *Ibidem*, pp. 33-34.

been no independent media in the occupied parts of Donbas. According to Freedom House, believers who are not a part of the Orthodox Church–Moscow Patriarchate are persecuted.[18] This fits into a wider framework of Russia's activities that are aimed at fostering (or actually forcing) pro-Russian attitudes in post-Soviet states in order to promote and strengthen the so-called Eurasianism model, which puts Russia at the centre and which weakens the pro-European orientation in these countries.

Russia's social policy offer to DNR and LNR citizens

The Pension and Social Insurance Fund of the Russian Federation, which is an off-budget state fund established on 1 January 2023, has its divisions in the DNR and LNR. They offer services and provide financial resources to the disabled, veterans, medical personnel, blood donors, parents and pensioners. Benefits are granted based on the documents that were issued prior to the establishment of the fund but which were in accordance with the laws of the Russian Federation abiding on 30 September 2022 as well as the laws of the DNR, LNR and the Soviet Union. To access services, claimants and their children must be registered in the new unit of the Russian Federation, with this registration valid as of 30 September 2022, the day of the annexation. An exception applies to those seeking a one-time child benefit and subsequent monthly payments for their firstborn (or adopted) child; they must hold Russian citizenship. Additionally, holders of Russian passports without proof of registration (i.e., a stamp) can obtain confirmation of their DNR or LNR passports with the appropriate stamp. To prove residency in the "new territories," having a permit to reside in the Russian Federation is sufficient.

In 2022, Russian social policy agencies released information on the rules regulating access to Russia's social services for people who were forced to leave the DNR and LNR as well as the territory of Ukraine. These rules were regulated by the Presidential Decree no.

---

18 Freedom House, 2023, "Eastern Donbas. Freedom in the World 2022", https://freedomhouse.org/country/eastern-donbas/freedom-world/2022 (Accessed: 24 April 2024).

586 issued on 27 August 2022.[19] The types and amounts of social benefits that Russia offers to the above mentioned groups[20] include: 1) monthly pensions in the amount of 10,000 roubles[21] 2) monthly social benefits for disabled persons in the amount of 10,000, 3) supplement to monthly pension or social benefits for disabled persons with the first degree of disability, disabled children and seniors 80 years of age or older in the amount of 3,000 roubles, 4) monthly benefits for the veterans of the Great Patriotic War in the amount of 5,000 roubles, 5) lump sum payment for pregnant women in the amount of 20,000 roubles, 6) lump sum payment for the birth of a child in the amount of 20,000 roubles, 7) monthly child benefit in the amount of 4,000 roubles for each child under 18 years of age, or 23 years of age, as long as the child continues education, 8) monthly benefit in the amount of 15,000 roubles for each child under 18 years of age that is under care or guardianship, 9) monthly benefits for a single parent in the amount of 10,000 roubles for each child.

Third sector in DNR and LNR

The activity of GONGOs and proxy groups pretending to be NGOs yet operating without any formal structures, is widespread in east-

---

19 Decree of the Government of the Russian Federation No. 1547 of 02 September 2022 "On the procedure for providing payments to citizens of the Donetsk People's Republic, Luhansk People's Republic, Ukraine and stateless persons who were forced to leave the territories of the Donetsk People's Republic, Luhansk People's Republic, Ukraine and arrived on the territory of the Russian Federation", http://government.ru/docs/all/142953/; Decree of the President of the Russian Federation No. 586 of 27 August 2022, "On payments to citizens of the Donetsk People's Republic, Luhansk People's Republic, Ukraine and stateless persons forced to leave the territories of the Donetsk People's Republic, Luhansk People's Republic, Ukraine and arrived on the territory of the Russian Federation". https://government.ru/docs/all/142953/

20 In the four permissible categories, a citizen must meet one of the following criteria: 1) arrived in the territory of the Russian Federation after February 18, 2022; 2) has permanent residence in the Donetsk People's Republic, Luhansk People's Republic, or Ukraine; 3) temporarily resides in the territory of the Russian Federation; or 4) is not receiving similar social benefits under Russian Federation legislation.

21 Pensions are distributed to people who are entitled to work-related pension, workers' disability benefit, survivor's pensions.

ern Ukraine. It is aimed at increasing local support to Russian policies towards the DNR and LNR, which to a large extent resemble the Kremlin's policies towards Georgia and Moldova. The main goal is consolidation of pro-Russian forces, promotion of anti-Western rhetoric and traditional Orthodox values as well as permanent destabilisation of the region. At the same time, the activity of independent NGOs has been practically banned. The last independent non-governmental organisation that operated on the occupied territory was a volunteer group called "Responsible Citizens". It stopped its activity in 2016 and its leaders were deported. A similar fate fell upon the Czech organisation, People in Need, which received the status of an undesirable organisation and can no longer operate in the areas that are controlled by the Russian Federation.[22] The only organisations that are allowed to continue their operations on these territories are the International Committee of the Red Cross, UN agencies and the Organisation for Security and Co-operation in Europe (OSCE).

Russian non-state actors have played a significant role in destabilizing these territories. They employ both non-transparent and overt means of influence, which bear little resemblance to what the Western world considers soft power. For instance, many of the organisations that operate in the occupied territories have no official websites or publically available information about their work. Operating in a grey zone, they have been useful in Russia's hybrid warfare where non-military means of control are often applied. These non-state actors are thus classified as civil society implants which are instrumentally used by the Kremlin to legitimise Russia's aggressive policy towards eastern Ukraine and Crimea. Their networks are well integrated into the vertical system of power and financing.[23] Yet many of these organisations are sustained with completely non-transparent financial resources.

In the LNR the size of the third sector has been significantly reduced over the period of the war. In 2023, only seven NGOs and one social movement operating in this "republic" filed their annual

---

22 Freedom House, *op. cit.*
23 Lutsevych, O., *op. cit.*

reports to the Ministry of Justice of the Russian Federation (see: Annex, Table 1). Non-profit financing in 2023-2024 equalled to 22,361,080.12 roubles in LNR and was granted to 17 projects which, just like in the DNR, were implemented in the area of social policy, youth policy and propaganda activities. In DNR the third sector, as it is presented in the 2023 reports of the Ministry of Justice of the Russian Federation, is larger than in the LNR. It is made up of 54 non-profit organisations (see: Annex, Table 2). Altogether, 229 annual reports were filed in 2024. The financing that these organisations received in the 2023-2024 framework of presidential grants equalled to 35,732,909.61 roubles. Financial resources were granted to 13 projects in the area of social policy, youth policy and propaganda activities.

Ukraine's measures to counter Russian influence in the occupied territories

In 2019, Ukraine's Ministry of Internal Affairs presented a comprehensive plan of the de-occupation of Donbas, the so-called "Small Steps Mechanism". The document outlines the path for the regaining of Ukraine's sovereignty and territorial integrity as well as the reintegration of what the Ukrainian authorities call temporarily occupied territories. Ukraine's policy towards the residents of the areas that have been occupied by Russia includes the amnesty law. It is assumed that amnesty will be offered to a large majority of the population living under occupation, with the exception of criminals and war criminals. In addition, in March 2022, Ukraine passed a law on criminal liability for collaboration, establishing penalties for individuals cooperating with the aggressor state, its occupation administrations, armed forces or paramilitary formations.

From 2014 to 2019 attempts were made to establish an international peace mission and a demilitarised security zone in the occupied parts of Donbas. Until the start of the full-scale invasion in February 2022 the main priority of the Ukrainian state was to establish an interim administration which would cooperate with the government in Kyiv. This cooperation was foreseen to be based on reintegration procedures as they are formulated by Ukrainian laws.

Ukraine also recognises the threat of a potential environmental disaster that may affect the lives of the local population in this once highly industrious region, including the risk of poisoning from drinking water, pandemics, emissions and explosions of methane and other dangerous substances.[24] To ensure control over the region and the movement of people, Ukraine planned to establish a Special International Peace Mission and a State Border Service. In other words, it was assumed that Ukrainian border services would control the border together with the peace forces. The duty of ensuring law and justice was to be taken by Ukraine's police, the National Guard and UN peacekeeping forces (the "blue helmets"). Initially, plans were made to include local volunteers who would be representing local villages and city councils in all of these endeavours.

Most importantly, for Ukraine elections carried out in accordance with Ukrainian law are the main condition for bringing back Ukrainian state institutions and law enforcement agencies to the reintegrated territories. Only then would the reintegration process begin. In addition to demining and other activities aimed at eliminating physical threats, both caused by environmental and manmade factors, a programme of verification and reissuing of Ukrainian documents to all persons who lived on the occupied territories has been envisioned in the plan. This would require a special citizens' verification system which could be modelled on the one that has been developed by the Institute of Peace.

In the framework of Ukraine's de-occupation plan it has been envisioned that the right to run for public office will be brought back to the people who lived in the occupied areas, yet it will be granted to them no earlier than five years after the de-occupation

---

[24] The annex to the de-occupation plan indicates that there are over 1,200 sources of ionizing radiation across 65 facilities in the Donbas region. Experts warn that military activities, along with the uncontrolled operation and maintenance of these radiation sources, pose a significant radiation threat. Hostilities have compromised the integrity of radioactive waste storage facilities at the Donetsk Chemical Plant and the Donetsk Special Combine. See: https://mvs.gov.ua/en/ministry/projekti-mvs/deokupaciya-donbasu.

and reintegration. At the same time, it has been agreed that elections, also to Ukrainian central authorities, could take place only on demilitarised territory. Significantly, the period necessary for the refugees and the IDPs to return to the earlier occupied territories has also been established.

A key element of Ukraine's strategy was to institutionalise and formalise civil society structures which are seen as extensions of state agencies. The Ukrainian state openly formulates its goal to engage the third sector to support reintegration, social policy implementation, and the re-Ukrainisation of the occupied territories. In 2016, the Coordination Council for the Development of Civil Society was established as an advisory body to the president of Ukraine. Its members include representatives of the Council of Ministers of Ukraine and other state agencies, local governments, academic institutions as well as representatives of public organisations. The latter constitute 64% of the council's members. Ukraine's 2021-2026 strategy for civil society development, which was passed in 2021 by a presidential decree, stresses the role of the third sector in effective policy-making. This assumption reads as follows:

> "Civil society is an expression and defender of interests and aspirations of diverse social and civic groups. The civil society is able to make a significant contribution to the state's sustainable development by providing social services, ensuring social entrepreneurship, increasing workplace for people, including the self-employed, improving business environment, fighting corruption, promotion of transparency in the works of state authorities and local governments, as well as the implementation of other socially beneficial projects. Civil society organisations in Ukraine also play an important role in bringing back the territorial integrity of the state and building peace. Taking into account the role of the civil society in different spheres of public life, creating adequate conditions for its development and establishing relations with its institutions is an important task for state authorities and local government agencies."

In 2020, the Center for Democracy and Rule of Law, together with the Ukrainian Center for Independent Political Research and working in a consortium with ICAP Ukraine, presented a "Map of legal reforms for civil society in Ukraine". It includes a vision of the development of civil society and reforms in Ukraine for the period of 2022-2026. In that document, as many as 91 problems faced by the

Ukrainian third sector have been identified and 307 solutions to these problems have been recommended. The identified problems included: tax pressure on charity and volunteer activities, lack of NGO engagement in the provision of social services at the cost of state and local budgets, lack of online registration for all NGO actors, weakness of procedures aimed at engaging citizens in decision-making processes at the local government level (civic participation), lack of financial support from state budget to cover administrative costs of NGOs, high costs of operations, low institutional capacity, complicated and non-transparent system of humanitarian aid registration. The document also pointed to the negative consequences (lower social trust in the third sector) of impeding the works of the Coordination Council for the Development of Civil Society and criminal investigations against civil society activists.

The same recommendations have been included in the strategy of the development of civil society on the territory of the Donbas region which is controlled by Ukrainian authorities. Tilted "Regional targeted programme for promoting civil society in the years 2022-2026" the strategy first and foremost recognises that providing social benefits to the local population is a priority. The document also emphasises that reforming the local social security system must be integrated with Ukraine's decentralisation of state structures and local government reform. This approach will enhance citizens' access to social services and improve their overall quality. Additionally, it is essential, the document stresses, to establish, at the local level, a mechanism to foster partnerships between socially-oriented civil society organisations and local authorities.

Ukrainian policies towards increasing the third sector's role in fostering civic engagement

Ukrainian social policy was analysed in the "Civil Society in Donbas" report published in March 2021 by authors Volodymyr Lukichov, Tymofiy Nikitiuk and Liudmyla Kravchenko. They highlight the increased activity of civil society actors and civic initiatives in the Donetsk and Luhansk regions from 2016 to 2019, driven by support from national and international civil society organisations. During this period, the third sector in Ukraine underwent a structural transformation, evolving into a platform for dialogue and the exchange of best practices, both in-person (through civic hubs, cultural centres and civic platforms) and online. Numerous public initiatives focused on monitoring, oversight, and anti-corruption were established alongside specialised civic organisations aimed at addressing social issues and protecting marginalised groups, including internally displaced persons (IDPs) and those who were forcibly relocated. The number of members registered in public organisations was constantly on the rise (in the years 2014-2017 it doubled in the Donetsk region and increased six times in the Luhansk region). According to analysts, there are three main causes of this phenomenon: 1) the 2013-2014 Revolution of Dignity, which stimulated civic activism; 2) social and civic consolidation during Russia's occupation of Crimea and the war in Donbas, including the involvement of volunteer battalions and NGOs providing assistance; and 3) the development of the National Strategy for the Development of Civil Society for 2016-2020.

A review of the activities of 382 civil society organisations identified as active in the Donetsk and Luhansk regions in 2020 revealed five main priority areas: culture, education, specialised organisations (focused on infrastructure repair, micro-financing, and economic support), veterans, youth and sport. These areas align with Ukraine's social policy priorities. However, it is important to note that youth organisations often serve as key partners for cooperation with political parties and international organisations, including UNICEF and the Danish Refugee Council.

The priority is thus to foster an active civic policy driven by independent third-sector initiatives. This includes organisations like CivilM+, an independent international civil society platform dedicated to integrating civic initiatives aimed at restoring the Donetsk and Luhansk regions as peaceful, integrated and developed areas within a democratic Ukraine and a united Europe. Established in 2017 by civil society representatives from Ukraine, Russia, Germany, and France, this platform aims to facilitate the implementation of local grassroots projects. One example of its reintegration activities is "The Future of Donbas" — an information and expert support project for reintegration implemented in 2021. This initiative was carried out by the "Alternative" Luhansk Regional Human Rights Centre, the "Frontir" non-governmental organisation, and journalists from *"Реальная газета"* (*Real Newspaper*), with financial support from USAID. The project was based on the assumption that a deepening divide exists between the population living on the territory controlled by the Ukrainian government and those remaining in the temporarily occupied areas of eastern Ukraine. It was considered a priority to enhance social communication in the region, particularly with individuals outside Ukraine's legal, educational and information systems. Additionally, recommendations were primarily directed at representatives of the Ministry of Reintegration of the Temporarily Occupied Territories, which is responsible for shaping and implementing state policy regarding the temporarily occupied regions in Donetsk and Luhansk, as well as Crimea.

The authors of the report recommend pro-active and preventive measures for mainstreaming the position of the Ukrainian government among people living in the region and who are outside of control of the Ukrainian authorities. They include feedback-based communication, openness of civil servants, and transparency in public messaging, also those broadcast by the media. It was deemed necessary to have a systematic and reliable evaluation of the quality of communication and its effectiveness with quick implementation of the correction of the Ukrainian strategy in the future.

A recommendation was made to create permanent communication platforms that establishes open dialogue between the government and civil society actors, including those from territories not controlled by the Ukrainian government, to discuss ways to address the negative consequences of the conflict. The report highlights serious barriers that may be encountered when crossing the contact line between the Ukrainian and separatist sides. In addition to the challenges posed by disinformation policies, there are issues of fear, low trust in authorities and Ukrainian media, and a desire for a "return to normalcy". People living on the territories not controlled by the Ukrainian government often lack Ukrainian IDs, particularly passports. As a result, they have no choice but to rely on "local" or Russian passports and diplomas from "local" educational institutions, which heightens their fear of persecution by Ukrainian authorities.

Finally, the report emphasises the need to actively counter Russian propaganda, which exacerbates these negative trends. In practice, the recommendations presented remain largely theoretical. The authors noted positive actions taken by the Ukrainian government towards people living on the territories no longer under Ukrainian control, such as allowing access to Ukrainian schools and universities, providing social security services, including pensions, and facilitating online verifications. Additionally, Ukraine has stopped imposing fines on those who "illegally cross the border" and has adopted a Strategy for Economic Development for the Donetsk and Luhansk regions through 2030. However, the authors are correct to argue that these measures are not sufficient.

In the current context of Russian occupation in the so-called Donetsk and Luhansk republics, the administrative and social integration of eastern Ukrainian territories with the Russian Federation has intensified. The government-organised non-governmental organisations (GONGOs) in these areas actively legitimise Russia's aggressive social policies, aiming to integrate local communities with Russia and strengthen their sense of belonging to the Russian nation.

The instrumentalisation of identity and language within the "compatriot" concept accelerates a process of assimilation and acculturation, reinforced by an effective local and central administrative policy. With limited access to these regions by Ukrainian state authorities and international organisations, including those focused on human rights, this process risks becoming irreversible. Consequently, there is a strong potential for low public resistance to the Kremlin's actions in the region. Kyiv's efforts to reclaim these territories may face social resistance from local Ukrainian citizens who, due to loyalty shifts, may support Moscow. This situation arises from the Kremlin's targeted social policies, which primarily benefit the poorest, most impoverished, and marginalised groups. These groups receive substantial social assistance and benefits, while the Kremlin also offers financial incentives to the middle class, who are the main audience for cultural initiatives led by Kremlin-controlled NGOs.

This situation is worsened by the exhaustion of the local population, who have endured ongoing military operations since 2014. Under the guise of social activism, Russia is pursuing a policy of structural transformation in these areas to advance Russian policy priorities and cultivate "loyal, passive citizens." This strategy paves the way not only for the region's economic exploitation but for its eventual incorporation into Russia and potential border shifts, likely met with minimal resistance from a worn-down local population.

Despite active efforts by the Ukrainian administration and civil society, supported by international organisations, the ability to counter Kremlin policy in eastern Ukraine has shrunk considerably. This is due to the intense and volatile conditions on the eastern front, the depletion of Ukraine's defence capabilities, and the subsequently diminishing chances of reclaiming the region within its original borders. This makes the outlook for future developments in this region far from optimistic for the Ukrainian state.

Annex

Legal category/ status	Organisation (number and name)
State-public association	No. 1239400001631: Regional branch of the All-Russian public-state movement of children and youth "Movement of the First" of the Luhansk People's Republic (Russian original: Региональное отделение Общероссийского общественно-государственного движения детей и молодежи "Движение первых" Луганской Народной Республики)
Non-profit foundation	No. 1237700105763: Charitable foundation for helping people in difficult life situations "Thank You" (Russian original: Благотворительный фонд помощи людям попавшим в трудную жизненную ситуацию "БлагоДарите")

Public organisation	No. 1239400005250: Regional sports public organisation "Chess Federation of Lugansk People's Republic" (Russian original: Региональная спортивная общественная организация "Федерация шахмат Луганской Народной Республики") No.1239400009133: Interregional public organisation "Promotion of Patriotic Education "Unity" (Russian original: Межрегиональная общественная организация "Содействие патриотическому воспитанию "Единство")
Social movement	No. 1239400007054: Regional branch of the All-Russian public movement "PEOPLE'S FRONT "FOR RUSSIA" in the Luhansk People's Republic (Russian original: Региональное отделение Общероссийского общественного движение "НАРОДНЫЙ ФРОНТ "ЗА РОССИЮ" в Луганской Народной Республике)

Table 1: Author's analysis. Source; Ministry of Justice of the Russian Federation database. Accessed on 25 April 2024.

Legal category/ status	Organisation (number and name)
Autonomous non-profit organisation	No. 1239300015822: Autonomous non-profit organisation Training and Methodological Center "Expert" (Russian original: Автономная Некоммерческая Организация Учебно-Методический Центр "Эксперт") No. 1239300009750: Autonomous non-profit organisation "Center for the Development of Art, Culture and Sports "PROSVETANIE" (Russian original: Автономная некоммерческая организация "Центр развития искусства, культуры и спорта "ПРОЦВЕТАНИЕ") No. 1239300010223: Autonomous non-profit organisation "Center for the Development of Tourism, Sports, Cultural and Creative Leisure and Youth Initiatives "Konserva" (Russian original: Автономная Некоммерческая Организация "Центр Развития Туризма, Спорта, Культурно-Творческого Досуга И Молодежных Инициатив "Консерва")

	No. 1239300010168: Autonomous non-profit organisation "Center for Further Education "Origami" (Russian original: Автономная некоммерческая организация "Центр дополнительного образования "Оригами")

No. 239300006076: Autonomous non-profit organisation helping children with mental disabilities and their families "Mazhenika" (Russian original: Автономная некоммерческая организация помощи детям с особенностями ментального развития и их семьям "Маженика")

No. 1239300001544: Autonomous non-profit organisation "Resource Center for Support of Non-Profit Organisations of the Donetsk People's Republic" (Russian original: Автономная некоммерческая организация "Ресурсный центр поддержки некоммерческих организаций Донецкой Народной Республики")

No. 1239300003106: Autonomous non-profit physical culture and sports organisation of additional education "Helikon Sports School" (Russian original: Автономная некоммерческая физкультурно-спортивная организация дополнительного образования "Спортивная школа "Геликон")

No. 1239300009244: Autonomous non-profit organisation for the development of culture and theatrical activities "Kukolnikiki" (Russian original: Автономная некоммерческая организация по развитию культуры и театральной деятельности "Куколь ники")

No. 1239300013501: Autonomous non-profit organisation of social support and assistance to people in difficult life situations "Good Samaritan"
(Russian original: Автономная некоммерческая организация социальной поддержки и помощи лицам, попавшим в трудную жизненную ситуацию "Добрый самарянин") |
| Non-profit foundation | No. 1239300005328: Alexander Vladimirovich Zakharchenko charitable foundation (Russian original: Благотворительный фонд имени Александра Владимировича Захарченко) |

Social organisation	No. 1239300002710: Foundation for the Promotion of Spiritual and Social Revival "Svyatogorye" (Фонд содействия духовно-социальному возрождению "Святогорье")
	No. 1239300013677: Donetsk Republican branch of the All-Russian public organisation of small and medium-sized businesses "SUPPORT RUSSIA" (Russian original: Донецкое республиканское отделение Общероссийской общественной организации малого и среднего предпринимательства "ОПОРА РОССИИ")
	No. 1239300013677: Mariupol branch of the All-Russian public organisation "All-Russian Society of Disabled Persons" (Russian original: Мариупольская местная организация Общероссийской общественной организации "Всероссийское общество инвалидов")
	No. 1229300127209: Regional public organisation "Sports Club 'Fighter'" of the Donetsk People's Republic" (Russian original: Региональная Общественная Организация "Спортивный Клуб "Ратник" Донецкой Народной Республики")
	No. 1239300010509: Regional public organisation "Republican Federation of Motorcycle Sports" of the Donetsk People's Republic (Russian original: Региональная Общественная организация "Республиканская Федерация Мотоциклетного Спорта" Донецкой Народной Республики)
	No. 1229300123590: Regional public organisation "Wushu Federation of the Donetsk People's Republic (Russian original: Региональная Общественная Организация "Федерация Ушу Донецкой Народной Республики")
	No. 1229300123062: Regional public organisation "Judo Federation of the Donetsk People's Republic" (Russian original: Региональная Общественная Организация "Федерация Дзюдо Донецкой Народной Республики")
	No. 1229300124900: Regional public organisation "Sambo Federation of the Donetsk People's Republic" (Russian original: Региональная Общественная Организация "Федерация Самбо Донецкой Народной Республики")
	No. 239300005141: Donetsk branch of the All-Russian public organisation of disabled people "All-Russian Order of

the Red Banner of Labour Society of the Blind" (Russian original: Донецкая республиканская общественная организация Общероссийской общественной организации инвалидов "Всероссийское ордена Трудового Красного Знамени общество слепых")

No. 1229300126593: Regional Public Organisation "Swimming Federation of the Donetsk People's Republic" (Russian original: Региональная Общественная Организация "Федерация Плавания Донецкой Народной Республики")

No. 1239300017164: Regional branch of the All-Russian public organisation "Russian Student Sports Union" of the Donetsk People's Republic (Russian original: Региональное отделение Общероссийской общественной организации "Российский студенческий спортивный союз" Донецкой Народной Республики)

No. 1239300015976: Regional public physical culture and sports organisation "Sambo Federation of the Donetsk People's Republic" (Russian original: Региональная общественная физкультурно-спортивная организация "Федерация самбо Донецкой Народной Республики")

No. 1239300011114: Regional public organisation "Wrestling Federation of the Donetsk People's Republic" (Russian original; Региональная общественная организация "Федерация спортивной борьбы Донецкой Народной Республики")

No. 1239300004899: Regional branch of the All-Russian public organisation "Union of Mechanical Engineers of Russia" in the Donetsk People's Republic (Russian original: Региональное отделение Общероссийской общественной организации "Союз машиностроителей России" в Донецкой Народной Республике)

No. 1239300005163: Donetsk regional public organisation — Creative association of lovers of original art "City of Artists and Craftsmen" (Russian original: Донецкая региональная общественная организация-Творческое объединение любителей самобытного искусства "Город художников и мастеров")

No. 1239300010960: Regional public organisation "RAS-SVET" (Russian original: Региональная общественная организация "РАССВЕТ")

No. 1239300010256: Regional public organisation of Greeks of the Azov region "ELLADA" (Russian original: Региональная общественная организация Греков Приазовья "ЭЛЛАДА")

No. 1239300005152: Regional public organisation "Center for Support of Combatants and Members of Their Families" (Russian original: Региональная общественная организация "Центр поддержки участников боевых действий и членов их семей")

No. 1239300009409: Mariupol local public organisation for the promotion of culture and sports "Sri Chinmoy Center" (Russian original: Мариупольская местная Общественная Организация содействия развитию культуры и спорта "Центр Шри Чинмоя")

No. 1239300010300: Regional public organisation "Donetsk Red Cross" (Russian original: Региональная общественная организация "Донецкий Красный Крест")

No. 1239300009640: Regional public physical culture and sports organisation "Federation of Power Extreme of the Donetsk People's Republic" (Региональная общественная физкультурно-спортивная организация "Федерация силового экстрима Донецкой Народной Республики")

No. 1239300008947: Regional public organisation "Women's Union of the Donetsk People's Republic" (Russian original: Региональная общественная организация "Союз женщин Донецкой Народной Республики")

No. 1239300010300: Regional public organisation "Donetsk Red Cross" (Russian original: Региональная общественная организация "Донецкий Красный Крест")

No. 1239300002721: Regional branch of the All-Russian public organisation "Association of Lawyers of Russia" in the Donetsk People's Republic (Russian original: Региональное отделение Общероссийской общественной организации

"Ассоциация юристов России" в Донецкой Народной Республике)

No. 1239300011015: Donetsk regional public organisation "DANCE UNION OF DONBAS" (Russian original: Донецкая региональная общественная организация "ТАНЦЕВАЛЬНЫЙ СОЮЗ ДОНБАССА")

No. 1239300013040: Regional Physical Culture and Sports Public Organisation "Taekwondo Federation of the Donetsk People's Republic" (Russian original: Региональная Физкультурно-Спортивная Общественная Организация "Федерация Тхэквондо Мфт Донецкой Народной Республики")

No. 1239300013050: Regional Physical Culture and Sports Public Organisation "Taekwondo Federation of the Donetsk People's Republic" (Russian original: Региональная Физкультурно-Спортивная Общественная Организация "Федерация Тхэквондо Донецкой Народной Республики")

No. 1229300124624: Regional Physical Culture and Sports Public Organisation "Koshiki Karate Federation of the Donetsk People's Republic" (Russian original: Региональная Физкультурно-Спортивная Общественная Организация "Федерация Косики Каратэ Донецкой Народной Республики")

No. 1239300016889: Regional sports public organisation "Federation of Backgammon of the Donetsk People's Republic" (Russian original: Региональная спортивная общественная организация "Федерация нард Донецкой Народной Республики")

No. 1239300011037: Donbas regional public organisation of special military operation veterans (Russian original: Донбасская региональная общественная организация ветеранов специальной военной операции)

No. 1239300011268: Regional Public Organisation "Donetsk Association of Animators and Composers (Russian original: Региональная Общественная Организация "Донецкое объединение Мультипликаторов и Композиторов")

Public-state association	No. 1239300015558: Local branch of the All-Russian public-state organisation "Voluntary Society for Assistance to the Army, Aviation and Navy of Russia" of the Novoazovsky Municipal District of the Donetsk People's Republic (Russian original: Местное отделение Общероссийской общественно-государственной организации "Добровольное общество содействия армии, авиации и флоту России" Новоазовского муниципального округа Донецкой Народной Республики)
	No. 1239300015569: Local branch of the All-Russian public-state organisation "Voluntary Society for Assistance to the Army, Aviation and Navy of Russia" in the urban district of Makeyevka, Donetsk People's Republic (Russian original: Местное отделение Общероссийской общественно-государственной организации "Добровольное общество содействия армии, авиации и флоту России" городского округа Макеевка Донецкой Народной Республики)
	No. 1239300010267: Regional branch of the All-Russian public-state organisation "Voluntary Society for Assistance to the Army, Aviation and Navy of Russia" of the Donetsk People's Republic" (Russian original: Региональное Отделение Общероссийской Общественно-Государственной Организации "Добровольное Общество Содействия Армии, Авиации И Флоту России" Донецкой Народной Республики")
	No. 1239300017868: Local branch of the All-Russian public-state organisation "Voluntary Society for Assistance to the Army, Aviation and Navy of Russia" of the Amvrosievsky Municipal District of the Donetsk People's Republic (Russian original: Местное отделение Общероссийской общественно-государственной организации "Добровольное общество содействия армии, авиации и флоту России" Амвросиевского муниципального округа Донецкой Народной Республики)
	No. 1239300015580: Local branch of the All-Russian public-state organisation "Voluntary Society for Assistance to the Army, Aviation and Navy of Russia" of the Donetsk urban district of the Donetsk People's Republic (Russian original: Местное отделение Общероссийской общественно-государственной организации "Добровольное

	общество содействия армии, авиации и флоту России" городского округа Донецк Донецкой Народной Республики) No. 1239300002039: Regional branch of the All-Russian public-state movement of children and youth "Movement of the First" of the Donetsk People's Republic (Russian original: Региональное отделение Общероссийского общественно-государственного движения детей и молодежи "Движение первых" Донецкой Народной Республики)
Social movement	No. 1239300008090: Regional branch of the All-Russian public movement in the field of environmental protection "Forest Volunteers" in the Donetsk People's Republic (Russian original: Региональное отделение Всероссийского общественного движения в сфере защиты окружающей среды "Волонтеры леса" по Донецкой Народной Республике) No. 1239300012522: Regional branch of the All-Russian public movement "PEOPLE'S FRONT "FOR RUSSIA" in the Donetsk People's Republic (Russian original: Региональное отделение Общероссийского общественного движения "НАРОДНЫЙ ФРОНТ "ЗА РОССИЮ" в Донецкой Народной Республике) Associations (union, association) of private persons No. 1239300017307: Association "Society of Donbas Builders Alliance Development" (Russian original: Ассоциация "Объединение строителей Донбасса Альянс Развитие") No. 1239300013897: Association (union) of manufacturers and entrepreneurs of Donbas (Russian original: Ассоциация (союз) производителей и предпринимателей Донбасса)

Is the Decolonisation of Eastern Europe Possible? The Cases of Ukraine and Belarus

Anton Saifullayeu

Since the outbreak of Russia's full-scale invasion in Ukraine, the terms "decolonisation of Ukraine" and "Russian influence in the post-Soviet space" have gained increased prominence in academic and expert discourse. The decolonisation of Western studies on Eastern Europe and Russia also became a more frequent discussion topic.[1] Given the critical moment that Ukrainian society is currently facing vis-à-vis the reactionary stance of Russian authorities and the nostalgic conservatism of the Russian society, the ontological choice of the Ukrainians to opt for the philosophy of liberation is entirely justified.

Methodologically speaking, decolonisation is a multifaceted process, entailing a qualitative shift that aims to deconstruct the established knowledge order and critically assess disciplinary frameworks. Crucially, it goes beyond explaining the consequences of colonialism or proposing solutions to them. This process encompasses active practices (cultural, political, and economic) and a gradual shift at the textual level, all while avoiding entanglement in the colonial matrix of knowledge-power. However, from a theoretical perspective, several factors currently hinder decolonisation of Eastern Europe. Decolonisation scholar, Nelson Maldonado-Torres, pointed out that "the problem emerges when liberation is translated as a claim for immediate political action, a kind of political immediatism that becomes antipathetic to theoretical reflection.

---

1   For in-depth materials on decolonisation in Ukraine, see: "Decolonization Selected articles published in the aftermath of Russia's invasion of Ukraine". https://ui.org.ua/sectors/decolonization-selected-articles/; Hundorova, T., "How Peripheries Talk Amongst Themselves—Or Ukraine, Eurocentrism and Decolonization", *Krytyka*. https://krytyka.com/en/articles/howperipheries-talk-amongst-themselves-or-ukraine-eurocentrism-and-decolonization.

When the two combine, that is, the worst aspects of the claim for identity and those of the search for liberation, then we have a form of what Lewis Gordon calls epistemological closure."[2]

The recent postcolonial challenges in Belarus and Ukraine also resemble an epistemological closure. While they exhibit signs of moving beyond postcolonialism (horizontal connections, emancipatory discourse, post-national identities), they also show elements of anticolonial nationalism, postcolonial mimicry, and the legitimation of an alternative centre (the "West" in Eastern Europe). This duality, marked by the simultaneous rejection of colonialism and the continued use of colonial aspects, raises questions about the feasibility and advisability of implementing decolonialism as a survival strategy in response to Russia's aggressive neo-imperialism.

Undoubtedly, Belarus and Ukraine, both before and after the culminating events of independence, represent different strategies of suppression or utilisation of colonial aspects. In general, the shared postcolonial experience in the post-Soviet era serves as the indicator within which various strategies for existing or coexisting with coloniality are implemented at different stages: acceptance of the experience, postcolonial mimicry (*rejection*),[3] anticolonial nationalism (*negation*), and models with an alternative centre (*overcoming*).

---

[2] Maldonado-Torres, N., 2011, "Thinking through the Decolonial Turn. Post-continental Interventions in Theory, Philosophy, and Critique – An Introduction", *Transmodernity. Journal of Peripheral Cultural Production of the Luso-Hispanic World*, 1 (2), p. 4.

[3] In this context, postcolonial rejection is synonymous with "postcolonial estrangement," as proposed by Sergey Alex Oushakine. Both terms recognise the colonial (or socialist) experience as an effort to distance from the past, yet it remains ingrained in the postcolonial subject's consciousness. "Estrangement" delves deeper, extending colonial heritage throughout past and present via imitation of colonial thinking in national or postcolonial realms, see: Oushakine, S. A., 2013, "Postcolonial Estrangements: Claiming a Space between Stalin and Hitler", in: Buckler J, Johnson, E. D. (eds.), *Rites of Place: Public Commemoration in Russia and Eastern Europe*, Evanston: Northwestern University Press, pp. 285–315.

Decolonise, yes. But what?

Within the context of the decolonial turn, the central concept is still the global coloniality of knowledge and power.[4] This is also of fundamental importance in Eastern Europe and in the political and cultural context in which coloniality have developed in Ukraine and Belarus since 1991. The post-Soviet paradigm in which Belarus and Ukraine have found themselves since then can be characterised as a state of glocal coloniality. This paradigm delineated the boundaries of discourse within the vertical power relations that persisted after the USSR's dissolution. The term "glocal coloniality" of knowledge reflects the epistemological ambivalence of Russian-Soviet colonialism embedded in its structures. On the one hand, it embodies the ambivalence of the socialist experience of Russian colonialism; on the other, it signifies its subordinate status in comparison to European (Western) modernity/coloniality.[5] The term essentially unifies the experiences of post-Soviet peripheries and the ambivalent understanding of Russian-Soviet colonialism as both subordinate and dominant. It encapsulates these elements into a single term, which may well become central to the decolonial turn, addressing what exactly needs to be decolonised.

That said, what exactly is the glocal coloniality of knowledge in Belarus and Ukraine? To answer this, we must turn to the ambivalent nature of the structures of subordination under Russian-Soviet colonialism and imperialism in the region. First, the specificity is the local legitimation of Eastern Europe's subordination to Russia. Russia's distinctive expansionism, particularly within the context of the Soviet and post-Soviet eras, has been marked by the

---

4 See: Escobar, A., 2004 "Beyond the Third World: imperial globality, global coloniality and anti-globalisation social movements", *Third World Quarterly*, 25 (1), pp. 207-230; Quijano, A., 2007, "Coloniality and Modernity/ Rationality", *Cultural Studies*, 21 (2-3), pp. 168-178.
5 Tlostanova, M., 2009, *Dekolonial'nye gendernye epistemologii*, Moscow: IPTs Maska; Tlostanova, M., 2017, *Postcolonialism and postsocialism in fiction and art: Resistance and re-existence*, New York: Palgrave McMillan; Kagarlitsky, B., 2008, *Empire of the Periphery: Russia and the World System*, Renfrey Clarke (trans.), London: Pluto Press; See also: Atanasoski N., Vora, K., 2018, "Introduction: Postsocialist Politics and the Ends of Revolution", *Social Identities*, 24 (2), pp. 139-154.

longstanding notion of a "return" to the original and exclusive civilisational core — the Russian Empire — which dates back to the late 18th century. This expansionism was not primarily justified by practical reasons, but rather grounded in a historical sense of rightfulness and inevitability. This idea remains relevant today, as articulated by Vladimir Putin on the anniversary of the Ukraine invasion.[6]

In the 19th and 20th centuries, local intelligentsia, educated in the metropolis, played a significant role in disseminating the coloniser's narrative, and developed a degree of autonomy within its framework; for example, the concepts of *Zapadnorussism* or *Malorussism*. The period of imperial reintegration from 1917 to 1922 saw a shift in terminology. The earlier concept of the "civilizing mission" for reuniting the lands gave way to a narrative emphasizing "fraternal peoples" and portraying Russia as the "elder brother."

The collapse of the empire in 1991 disrupted the hierarchised Soviet colonial system, suspending the intra-colonial hegemony of knowledge, which then shifted to the geopolitical level. This resulted in the decline of old ideologies and the emergence of new national forms of discourse that had previously been prohibited. The opening of the market and globalisation also triggered a moral revolution in the post-Soviet space, where the collective understanding of what was honourable and shameful evolved into a new capitalist code of ethics.[7]

At the level of identity, glocal coloniality represents an epistemological intertwining of the colonial, the national, and the global, giving rise to acute forms of postcolonial mimicry. On one hand, there is an acceptance of colonial baggage, including nostalgia and disappointment over the decline of empire. On the other, there is *rejection* and *negation*, manifesting as postcolonial and anticolonial nationalism. Furthermore, by the beginning of the 21st century,

---

6 RIA, 2023, "Putin: pryamo seychas idet boy na nashikh istoricheskikh rubezhakh za nashikh lyudey", https://ria.ru/20230222/putin-1853775704.html (Accessed:10 August 2023).

7 Gapova, E., 2016, *Klassy natsii. Feministskaia kritika natsiostroitel'stva*, Moscow: NLO, p. 120; Shparaga, O., 2018, *Soobshchestvo posle Kholokosta: na puti k obshchestvu inkliuzii*, Minsk: Medisont, p. 26.

globalism had introduced a new form of mimicry aimed at *overcoming* (democratisation of society).

The phenomenon of glocal coloniality characterises the entire postcolonial stage in Belarus and Ukraine: the coexistence of three discursive identity algorithms (colonial, national, global), with varying degrees of dominance of each, determines future decolonisation strategies. In both contexts, there coexisted two meta strategies of development (national and pro-Russian statehood) and models of nation-building (bilingual and monolingual). Furthermore, the primary effect of the increasing globalisation of the post-Soviet space was the symbiosis of national projects with the project of democratic transformation carried out in post-communist Central Europe. However, there were different degrees of consolidation of anti- and postcolonial elites, and different political conditions for colonial knowledge within each country. In Belarus, Lukashenka's opportunistic (post-)Soviet regime based its cultural and political capital on the proximity to Russia; Ukraine saw the oligarchic system gain strength and influence in the 1990s, translating the categories of glocal coloniality of knowledge into political capital, ultimately leading to the pluralisation of the political space.

Trying to escape from glocal coloniality of knowledge: The national idea and postcolonial revolution

The vertical and hierarchical relations of subordination between the centre and the colonies in the USSR are primarily the results of its continental type of empire, which implies a more intensive presence of the metropolis in the political and social structures of the subordinate entity. However, this type of empire also presupposes that the boundaries of colonies or peripheries will intersect with other empires or the so-called alternative centres or surrogate hegemons, which can act as competing colonialities.[8] Identifying an

---

8   Thompson, E., 2008, "Postkolonialne refleksje. Na marginesie pracy zbiorowej 'From Sovietology to Postcoloniality: Poland and Ukraine from a Postcolonial Perspective'", in: Korek, J. (ed.), *Porównania*, 5, pp. 115-128 and pp. 117-119.

alternative centre in the case of Eastern Europe does not seem to be a complex task. The surrogate hegemon (the Western world) is an element of constant resistance to the real hegemon (Russia) — which, however, also leads to the future peripheralisation of these countries in relation to the surrogate hegemon.[9] The surrogate hegemon acts as a counterbalance to the real hegemon, with whom the postcolonial subject seeks to nullify relations. Naturally, when the subordinate asserts belonging or expresses sympathy towards the surrogate hegemon, a new process of subordination occurs, often resembling a form of cooperation against the former real hegemon.

The surrogate hegemon, in addition to its political and economic dimensions, incorporates its own body of knowledge; that is, the cultural and discursive platform of Western coloniality becomes an alternative to glocal knowledge. This is evident, for example, in the general conceptualisation of the community and the categories inherent to the alternative centre. For Belarus and Ukraine, these concepts include nationhood and democracy, contrasting with the narrative of a singular nation and the total power of the metropolis. This also leads to the imitation of the structural mechanisms of nation-building and the foundations of the neoliberal interpretation of democratic society.[10] The East European space finds itself caught in a bipolar mimicry, grappling with the acceptance or rejection of *glocal* coloniality even while it engages in the imitation of *global* coloniality. This imitation can be seen as an attempt to overcome local forms of dependence by pursuing self-peripheralisation in relation to a surrogate hegemon, namely the West. The foundation of imitative mimicry in Eastern Europe lies in its adherence to the common principles of Western-centrism and nationalism. It is worth noting that neither Belarus nor Ukraine had any experience of anticolonial struggle, but ethnonational concepts within both states were developed from the beginning as anticolonial projects.

---

9   See: Zarycki, T., 2004, "Uses of Russia: The Role of Russia in the Modern Polish National Identity", *East European Politics & Societies*, 18 (4), pp. 595-627.
10 Vieira, M., 2019, "The decolonial subject and the problem of non-Western authenticity", *Postcolonial Studies*, 22 (2), pp. 150-167 and pp. 157-158.

Anticolonial nationalism, as the ideological foundation of the elites developed after an empire's collapse, can be understood as an attempt to break free from glocal coloniality by reversing one's own subordination to an alternative centre (Europe/the West). In post-Soviet states, nationalism was perceived by parts of the elite as a ticket to European modernity, which meant democratisation and economic prosperity. Therefore, in both countries the national projects became ideologically linked with the concept of liberation.

Another variety of state or egalitarian nationalism[11] was based on achieving autonomy from the former metropolis while using an anti-Western narrative of non-subordination to another centre.[12] A vivid example of this can be observed in Belarus, where the regime has built a patrimonial, Russian-speaking version of consolidation nationalism with a strong attachment to colonial and glocal knowledge, as occasionally voiced by Lukashenka himself.[13] This patrimonial nationalism can be seen as a version of "state patriotism," structurally based on the colonial baggage of knowledge, but in essence, politically separatist with respect to the metropolis. Such state projects in post-Soviet countries served to preserve and strengthen local power as a counterweight to Moscow's neocolonial ambitions.

In the 1990s, which was the first decade after the collapse of the USSR, anticolonial nationalism, based on the ethnocultural discourse about the past, culture, and language, acquired postcolonial properties thanks to its connection to the narrative of democratic transformation. That is, it became linked to the alternative centre.

---

11 Leshchenko, N., 2008, "The National Ideology and the Basis of the Lukashenka Regime in Belarus", *Europe-Asia Studies*, 60 (8), pp. 1419-1433.
12 An illustrative example of this may be the homophobic discourse in Belarus (or Russia) as an element opposing local traditional gender identities and "incorrect," "perverted" gender identities of the West: see, Frear, M., 2021, "'Better to be a Dictator than Gay': Homophobic Discourses in Belarusian Politics", *Europe-Asia Studies*, 73 (8), pp. 1467-1486.
13 See: 2022, "'Vse eto filosofski'. Lukashenko rasskazal, chto takoe 'denatsifikatsiya' i nazval Baraka Obamu 'kraynim natsionalistom'", *Zerkalo*. https://news.zerkalo.io/economics/21153.html. (Accessed: 15 August 2023)

After the so-called colour revolutions, anticolonial nationalism (*negation* of colonialism) coexisted with its postcolonial version (*rejection* of glocal coloniality through imitation of Western coloniality).

Vitaly Chernetsky highlights the disparity between anticolonialism and the postcolonial condition, emphasizing that anticolonialism remains bound by resistance ideologies. In contrast, he argues, postcolonialism has managed to free itself from the historical constraints and become a postmodern practice in the context of the former colony.[14] This is largely verified by the difference between the anticolonial and postcolonial versions of nationalism in Eastern Europe. However, there is one caveat: postmodernist practices represent a reverse mimicry, which fits into the general thesis of imitating European modernity, as well as the constant aspiration of the periphery to approach the centre.[15] This is why post-Soviet attempts to break free from the colonial past are based on both identification with Western civilisation and the nationalism of the elites, which is a sharp form of denying the Soviet-Russian background of dependence. This, in turn, strongly resonates with the emancipatory political paradigm of European neoliberalism. However, it also confirms Marco Vieira's thesis about the close connection between Western coloniality and its projects, such as nationalism or (neo)liberalism, and the attempt to build "purified" forms of non-colonial subjectivity for the subordinate.[16] Thus, in the case of the post-Soviet search for the authenticity of the precolonial, practices are recreated within Western coloniality and used as a counterweight to the glocal hegemon.

Initial indications of the fusion between anticolonial and postcolonial practices emerged during the colour revolutions. The revolutionary aesthetics in Ukraine (2004) and Belarus (2006), aimed at breaking free from Soviet-Russian influence, became intertwined with the expression of a European orientation. Concurrently, a narrative highlighting the distinctiveness of historical and cultural experiences was promoted for internal purposes. This process, dating

---

14 Chernetsky, V., 2003, "Postcolonialism, Russia and Ukraine", *Ulbandus Review*, 7, pp. 32–62 and p. 41.
15 Hundorova, T., *op.cit.*
16 See: Vieira, M., *op.cit.*, pp. 150-167.

back to the early 1990s, can be viewed as a "Europeanisation" or "Westernisation" of the elites' national identity, signifying their detachment from colonial or glocal affiliations with the coloniser. It laid the intellectual groundwork for political opposition to the authorities, particularly evident in the formats of national historiography in Belarus and Ukraine immediately after the USSR's dissolution.[17]

In both countries, since the mid-2000s, *negation* (nationalism) and *overcoming* (surrogate hegemon) have become central programme points for parts of the elites. The difference is that following the Orange Revolution, the postcolonial dualism of the national and colonial in Ukraine became part of the political discourse and was institutionalised within the government. The attempted Belarusian revolution of 2006 encountered a repressive strategy prepared in the context of previous successful uprisings (Georgia, Ukraine, Kyrgyzstan). The protests introduced a dichotomy into the Belarusian political scene. On the one side there were the old elites who accepted and exploited the colonial baggage; on the other was the national-pro-liberal format of postcolonial rejection and negation of the colonial narrative. The events of 2006 were extraordinary not only in terms of social processes[18] but also in establishing an asynchrony between ideological-political needs and the state of Belarusian society, and the political-cultural offerings of the elites (pro-government and oppositional). A further defining factor for the dichotomy within Belarusian society's sociopolitical discourse was the politicisation of two postcolonial modes of existence. An individual could not simultaneously embody ethnonational identity and vote for Lukashenka, nor could they support the opposition while identifying as a "Soviet person." The subsequent depoliticisation of society by the authorities, through repression and restrictions on civil liberties, and the stabilisation of the social component, led the national-democratic discourse to become

---

17 See: Saifullayeu, A., 2020, *Postkolonialne Historiografie. Casus jednego średniowiecza*, Warszawa: PAN.
18 Korosteleva, E., 2009, "Was There a Quiet Revolution? Belarus After the 2006 Presidential Election", *Journal of Communist Studies and Transition Politics*, 25 (2-3), pp. 324-346.

highly amorphous. In essence, political and civic engagement outside the ideological-political framework of the government was limited or suppressed as non-normative for public consciousness. However, the 2006 protests, doomed as they were from the start,[19] combined with the global development of the digital communication space to create the conditions for the functioning of a bipolar system of values (colonial and postcolonial) and the devaluation of state ideology in the public consciousness. In general, civil protest became an important element of the strategy of *negation* and *rejection* in Belarus, gaining circulation via the cycles of presidential elections. Protest accumulated during inter-election periods; during elections, it entered an active phase (protests in 2010 and limited protests in 2015), provoking a repressive response from the Lukashenka regime.[20]

The revolution as a means to break free from (neo)colonial dependency is particularly evident in Ukraine, where the period from the 2004 Orange Revolution to the 2014-2015 Revolution of Dignity marked the completion of the process of postcolonial disengagement from the empire. The full-scale war which started in 2022 confirms this thesis. Faced with the inevitable loss of political and economic control over its former colony, Russia initiated a process of direct, violent reintegration of the empire, similar to the period from 1917 to 1922. The Ukrainian case also demonstrates a break in the cyclical confrontation between glocal and postcolonial elite projects: 2004 was a crucial year for documenting these strategies in the political dimension, including the entry of anticolonial nationalism into the political discourse and its uniform integration at the political, intellectual, and educational levels with the negation of glocal knowledge. Essentially, what had developed in Belarus up to 2020

---

19 Marples, D., 2006, "Color revolutions: The Belarus case, Communist and Post-Communist Studies", *Communist and Post-Communist Studies*, 39 (3), pp. 351-364; Silitski, V., 2006, "Still Soviet? Why Dictatorship Persists in Belarus", *Harvard International Review*, 28 (1), pp. 46-53.

20 de Vogel, S., 2022, "Anti-opposition crackdowns and protest: the case of Belarus, 2000–2019", *Post-Soviet Affairs*, 38 (1-2), pp. 9-25; Ash, K., 2015, "The election trap: the cycle of post-electoral repression and opposition fragmentation in Lukashenko's Belarus", *Democratization*, 22 (6), pp. 1030-1053; Potocki, R., 2011, "Belarus: A Tale of Two Elections", *Journal of Democracy*, 22 (3), pp. 49-63.

as a cyclical form of binary confrontation between elites (and, to some extent, society) functioned in Ukraine in 2014 as an active political model of postcolonial statehood. Ilya Gerasimov formulated a thesis that in 2014 we should speak of a Ukrainian postcolonial revolution of subjectivity,[21] which largely explains the Ukrainian post-Soviet reality as a gradual liberation from the colonial matrix.

Symbolically, one of the reasons for the start of the Euromaidan protests in 2013 was the refusal of the Ukrainian authorities (President Viktor Yanukovych and Prime Minister Mykola Azarov) to sign the Association Agreement with the EU at the European Partnership Summit in Vilnius. The Euromaidan revolution which erupted as a result of this decision, in essence, exposed the confrontation between the glocal opportunism of the authorities and the national-surrogate (European) project of the opposition elite. The subsequent postcolonial revolution marked the completion of the phase in which multiple Ukrainian identities (national, European, anti-Soviet, Russian-speaking, etc.) converged into a single postcolonial existence (gradual *rejection*).

Unlike Belarus, Ukraine did not experience cycles (of elections or dependency on Russia). The acquisition of subjectivity within the framework of pluricultural identity projects was possibly due to the interplay of activism, new forms of mediation, and, most importantly, tangible social mobilisation.[22] Since 2004, anticolonial, postcolonial, and surrogate forms of dependency have been concurrently evolving in the sociopolitical landscape. Anticolonial nationalism, although it served as the political platform for certain post-revolutionary elites, essentially remained peripheral to the coloniality of the Eurocentric discourse of transformation. However, after 2014, anticolonial mechanisms of suppressing glocal knowledge became the wellspring of society's postcolonial identity. Simultaneously, in contrast to Belarus, the multiplicity inherent in the Ukrainian model of post-Soviet identity involves the gradual alignment of power (elites) and society.

---

21   Gerasimov, I., 2014, "Ukraine 2014: The First Postcolonial Revolution. Introduction to the Forum", *Ab Imperio*, 14 (3), pp. 22-44.
22   Onuch, O., Sasse, G., 2016, "The Maidan in Movement: Diversity and the Cycles of Protest", *Europe-Asia Studies*, 68 (4), pp. 556-587.

The election of Volodymyr Zelensky as Ukraine's president in 2019, therefore, marked the culmination of the multicultural project of the postcolonial nation. The inclusive political conjuncture presented by Zelensky (through the *Sluga Naroda* party) encompasses both an internal anticolonial narrative of breaking free from direct and hybrid forms of dependency on the coloniser, and an external affinity with a surrogate centre; that is, liberation through reverse peripheralisation. In this context, the strategy of the "new" elites encompasses a pluricultural interpretation of the nation's collective identity: it combines postcolonial mimicry of embracing glocal ethno-cultural imprints of colonial knowledge with their rejection and negation. Assessing the effectiveness of this project is challenging, as it remains incomplete. Russia's full-scale war against Ukraine presents a radical opportunity to break away from glocal coloniality through complete liberation, manifesting as an anticolonial struggle for the collective self's survival. On 24 February 2022, the Ukrainian postcolonial revolution of subjectivity, as delineated by Gerasimov, concluded, and the phase of decolonial transformation commenced.

Ukrainian breakthrough and Belarusian counterrevolution

"He [Putin — AS] only cured a substantial part of Ukrainian society from ambivalence — from infantile hopes to belong to both worlds, to embrace [the] European future and to praise the Soviet past, to combine incompatible values and geopolitical orientations."[23] These words of Mykola Riabchuk accurately describe the breakthrough of the postcolonial identity compromise in Ukraine after 2014, adjusted to the context of this article. If we consider the language factor[24] as an indicator of overcoming colonial conscious-

---

23 Riabchuk, M., "Russia's Agression Ended Ukrainian Ambivalence", Raamoprusland, https://www.raamoprusland.nl/dossiers/oekraine/2302-russia-s-agression-ended-ukrainian-ambivalence (Accessed: 14 August 2023).
24 In the post-Soviet space since 1991, the language issue is evident in the marginalisation of national languages compared to the dominant Russian, which can

ness, then this compromise is reflected in a multitude of sociological data. Even in 2015, after the annexation of Crimea and the beginning of the hybrid war in Donbas, more than half (52%) of the respondent in a survey by the Kyiv International Institute of Sociology were in favour of Russian being the second state language in the regions where it prevails.[25] In 2016, more than 54% of CISR-IRI survey respondents used Russian exclusively or equally with Ukrainian in everyday life.[26] However, research conducted by the Kyiv International Institute of Sociology in the last months of 2022 showed that by then, only 39% used the Russian language in everyday life.[27] The dynamics of the changes in attitudes towards the language in 2021-22 are also shown in the joint research conducted by the Ilko Kucheriv Democratic Initiatives Foundation and the Razumkov Center, which found that the number of people who used Russian in everyday life had fallen by almost 10%.[28]

In 2022, there was a significant increase in attention and attachment to Ukrainian and Ukrainian-language cultural content among the population. This can be interpreted as a breakthrough; an exit from the postcolonial compromise of coexistence of the national and colonial strategies within Ukraine. It was the war that ensured this breakthrough, but the concept itself is dynamic and

---

be seen as a colonial language. While usage of national languages has evolved differently in various countries, the language question remains unresolved in social, cultural, and political contexts across the former Soviet nations. Bilingualism is frequently leveraged by Russian authorities to exert external political and cultural influence.

25 Pirogova, D., "Attitude to the Status of the Russian language in Ukraine", KIIS, https://www.kiis.com.ua/?lang=eng&cat=reports&id=517&t=10&page=5 (Accessed: 14 August 2023).
26 "Public Opinion Survey Residents of Ukraine. November 19-30, 2015", https://www.iri.org/wp-content/uploads/legacy/iri.org/wysiwyg/2015_11_national_oversample_en_combined_natl_and_donbas_v3.pdf (Accessed: 14 August 2023).
27 Kulyk, V., 2022, "'Mova ta identychnist' v Ukraï'ni na kinec' 2022-go", https://zbruc.eu/node/114247 (Accessed: 14 August 2023).
28 "National Culture and Language in Ukraine: Changes in Public Opinion after a Year of the Full-Scale War", https://dif.org.ua/en/article/national-culture-and-language-in-ukraine-changes-in-public-opinion-after-a-year-of-the-full-scale-war (Accessed: 14 August 2023).

more of a response to Russian aggression.[29] In large part, it depends on the success of the resistance against the aggressor. At the same time, ethno-linguistic and cultural separation from the coloniser is not the dominant factor influencing the high level of social mobilisation and solidarity within Ukrainian society during the war. The connection between the strategy of negation (nationalism) and the process of social mobilisation in Ukraine is not deterministic, as was indeed observed during the Revolution of Dignity in 2014.[30] The "breakthrough" is a discursive strategy: it has a clear constructivist nature. Language as a component of collective identity illustrates this very well. After February 2022, all official discourse in Ukraine was conducted in Ukrainian; this was reflected, for example, in the blogosphere and popular culture. A multilayered narrative of decolonisation emerged. Within Ukraine, this signifies a complete departure from colonial heritage; externally, it positions itself as a change in the cognitive models for studying an entire region.

The specificity of Ukraine lies in the fact that postcolonial nationalism has evolved into anticolonialism without the social prerequisites. One reason for this is that the empire collapsed from above, not from the grassroots. The former colonies, therefore, gained independence despite internal processes and, importantly, without accepting the empire's disintegration within their social structures. The absence of an anticolonial phase led these societies to search for a "golden mean" between the development of national identity and colonial subalternity in the new economic realities of capitalism. The previous compromise, a synthesis of overcoming, *negation*, and *rejection*, is experiencing a breakthrough due also to several other factors: the radical narrative of Kremlin elites about the nonexistence of the Ukrainian nation, culture, and history; the amorphous narrative of liberal Russian elites appealing to "brotherhood" roots and a shared culture; and an amorphous anti-Putin

---

29   See: Busol, K., Koval, D., "Typy kolonializmu ta ukraï'ns'kyj kolonial'nyj dosvid", LB, https://lb.ua/culture/2023/03/26/549878_tipi_kolonializmu_u krainskiy.html.
30   Onuch, O., Sasse, G., *op.cit.*, pp. 556–587.

narrative.³¹ Russia's radical and militant departure from the prolongation of glocal coloniality—that is, the gradual conceptualisation of Eastern Europe as a space of shared (imperial and colonial) experience—disrupted the postcolonial paradigm in Ukraine. The war raised questions about the future existence of imperial nationalism in Russia, where Ukraine is a basic element of the concept of imperial identity, and the potential decolonisation of Russia itself.³²

The potential decolonisation has all the necessary elements to begin, but it is still very early to talk about a full-fledged decolonial turn in Ukraine. Undoubtedly, an important aspect is the ideological consolidation of the ruling populist elites, local authorities, and national intelligentsia, along with the blogosphere, media, and researchers both within and outside of Ukraine. Regrettable as it may be, it was the war and aggressive Russian imperialism that made the decisive contribution to this process. Also important are the entrenchment of decolonisation in the legal field0,³³ the rhetoric of official representatives,³⁴ and the understanding of the narrative structure of subjugation.³⁵ However, the dynamics and impulsiveness of the processes set in motion make decolonisation dependent on the war itself and its outcome. The Ukrainian society perceives decolonisation as a process of excluding colonial (Russian) heritage

---

31 For more see: Vynogradov, O., Korneichuk, L., "Russian Cultural Elites Want to Call This Putin's War. But They, Too, Bear Responsibility for the Atrocities in Ukraine", *Artnet*, https://news.artnet.com/opinion/russian-cultural-elites-putins-war-2079885.

32 Mälksoo, M., 2022, "The Postcolonial Moment in Russia's War Against Ukraine", *Journal of Genocide Research*, DOI: 10.1080/14623528.2022.2074947.

33 The processes were launched before the war of 2022; see: Oliinyk A., Kuzio, T., 2021, "The Euromaidan Revolution, Reforms and Decommunisation in Ukraine", *Europe-Asia Studies*, 73 (5), pp. 807-836; Enacted and supplemented laws, see: "Pro zasudzhennja ta zaboronu propagandy rosijs'koi' impers'koi' polityky v Ukrai'ni i dekolonizaciju toponimii'". https://zakon.rada.gov.ua/laws/show/3005-20#Text; "Pro Den' pam'jati ta peremogy nad nacyzmom u Drugij svitovij vijni 1939-1945 rokiv", https://zakon.rada.gov.ua/laws/show/3107-IX#Text; "Pro zabezpechennja funkcionuvannja ukrai'ns'koi' movy jak derzhavnoi'", https://zakon.rada.gov.ua/laws/show/2704-19#Text

34 Danilov, O., 2023, "The world must accept the irreversible event of Russia's internal decolonization", *Ukrainska Pravda*, https://www.pravda.com.ua/eng/columns/2023/02/11/7388917/.

35 See: Hundorova, T., *op.cit.*

and its influence, signifying the end of the postcolonial compromise. In the context of a liberation struggle, the Ukrainian society associates decolonisation narratives with military rhetoric, understanding the process as the construction of a strong national identity in opposition to the enemy's narrative of the "non-existence" of the Ukrainian nation. Moreover, given the rhetoric of Ukrainian political and military leaders about the complete liberation of Ukraine and a return to the borders of 1991, a strategy of anti-colonial nationalism will not be suitable for reintegrating Crimea and the occupied parts of the Donetsk and Luhansk regions. The impulsive nature of the logistics of Ukrainian decolonisation may have an impact on its outcomes, particularly in the most "sensitive" eastern and southern regions of the country. Cultural and historical cancelling – the primary tool of official decolonisation in Ukraine – may serve as a social irritant and a pretext for ideological manipulation by Russia.

In contrast, Belarus is still at the theoretical stage of potential decolonisation. The civil protests of 2020 concluded the electoral cycles and essentially affirmed the postcolonial state of society and the country as a whole. That year marked an important milestone in the acquisition of a civil collective self, albeit a declarative one, beyond the established binary elite division between the regime and its opposition. Afterwards, it became possible to discuss pluralistic and post-national formats of Belarusian identity.[36]

The protests were performative acts of inclusive solidarity without clear political content. They were embedded in the horizontal structure of social bonds within the protesting masses and characterised by multiple forms of identity (specifically, a combination of old ethnocultural forms and new pluralistic and civic forms). Postcolonial strategies of rejection and acceptance were deemphasised within the horizontal structure of relationships among protesters; the political and organisational layer of the movement was decentralised.

---

36 Gerasimov, I., 2020, "The Belarusian Postcolonial Revolution: Field Reports", *Ab Imperio*, 21 (3), pp. 259-272; Gabowitsch, M., 2021, "Belarusian Protest: Regimes of Engagement and Coordination", *Slavic Review*, 80 (1), pp. 27-37.

The old opposition elites' ethnocultural semiotics became part of the 2020 protest acts of disobedience, but not its main form. In the symbolic confrontation space during the protests' first months (August-September), the political regime became disoriented, ideologically unable to move beyond the colonial and postcolonial bipolar value system it had created. The protest movement managed to neutralise postcolonial patterns formed in electoral cycles until the authorities' counter-revolutionary actions. At the same time, isolating civic language from the protest's performative aspect led to its neutralisation through mass repression.

The active phase of civil protest in Belarus lasted until state structures began to employ mass and targeted repression, such as persecuting individuals for their activity on social media.[37] While the violence of the authorities during the active performative phase had previously been a mobilizing factor,[38] it typically had a spontaneous and reactive character. The abrupt totalitarian turn, with a complete lack of rights, worked together with the opposition political elites' misunderstanding of the process of postcolonial emergence of society beyond the existing binary cultural and political space in Belarus. In other words, the performative post-nationalism of the civil movement in 2020 began to be interpreted by opposition elites within the familiar categories of glocal postcoloniality: *negation* and *rejection* (nationalism or pro-European choice), and *mimicry*. This, in turn, led to a loss of electoral and, to some extent, symbolic capital for post-election elites.[39]

The Belarusian counterrevolution marked the end of the stage of postcolonial consensus and firmly established ideological boundaries within the country. In other words, neither nationalism[40] nor hybrid or global forms of identity can exist in an authori-

---

37 For example, see the analysis of the state of human rights in Belarus in 2022 "Human Rights Situation in Belarus in 2022", https://spring96.org/en/news/110509 (Accessed: 30 August 2023).
38 Stykow, P., 2020, "Der lange Abschied vom Bac'ka: Lukašenkas Popularität und ihr Niedergang", *Osteuropa*, 10-11, pp. 107–125 and p. 122.
39 "Belarusians' views on the political crisis (poll conducted 1-10 November 2021)", https://en.belaruspolls.org/wave-6 (Accessed: 30 August 2023).
40 Meaning nationalism based on ethno-cultural and linguistic foundations.

tarian state outside the established ideological framework. The regime has significantly heightened the polarisation of previous attitudes, not only in a political sense but also within the ideological sphere. Before 2020, the regime was closely tied to the glocal context, but used different postcolonial patterns (culture, history) to autonomise Belarus from its former metropolis. Afterwards, its maneuverability in this regard was limited due to the increasing geopolitical activity of Russian ruling elites in establishing a new colonial order in the region. The Kremlin's direct support for the Belarusian regime in resolving its internal political crisis should also be noted; this led to increased dependence on Moscow.[41]

Russia's involvement in the new colonial project is seen as a relationship between two separate states. However, since the early stages of the counterrevolution (October-December 2020), there has been an increased emphasis on "closeness to Russia" within the glocal discourse, evident in the information sphere, education, and political rhetoric opposing Western values. The 2021 migration crisis, orchestrated by Lukashenka's regime, clearly shows the Minsk authorities' active participation in this neocolonial reality, adopting a typical Russian geopolitical narrative of anti-Westernism that contrasts traditional values and social institutions with the neoliberal and emancipatory rhetoric of Western countries.

The Russian glocal discourse on the sociopolitical structure of the state involves a complex of alternatives to "Western" norms, centred on strong authoritarian power, which in ideological format is completely opposed to pluralism and the notion of political opposition.[42] More broadly, over the past two decades, the Belarusian

---

41 See more on the topic: Leukavets, A., 2021, "Russia's game in Belarus: 2020 presidential elections as a checkmate for Lukashenka?", *New Perspectives*, 29 (1), pp. 90-101; Samorukov, M., "Russia-Belarus Integration: Why Moscow Gained So Little", Carnegie Moscow. https://carnegiemoscow.org/commentary/85749; Leukavets, A., "Crisis in Belarus: Main Phases and the Role of Russia, the European Union, and the United States", Wilson Center, https://www.wilsoncenter.org/publication/kennan-cable-no-74-crisis-belarus-main-phases-and-role-russia-european-union-and-united; Rogoża, J., Chawryło, K., and Żochowski, P., 2020, "A friend in need. Russia on the protests in Belarus", OSW. https://www.osw.waw.pl/en/publikacje/osw-commentary/2020-08-20/a-friend-need-russia-protests-belarus.

42 Onuch O., Sasse, G., *op.cit.*, pp. 62-87 and p. 71.

regime has been constructing a comparable framework while simultaneously upholding the semblance of legitimate societal choice. This electoral-authoritarian model incorporates the notion that the legitimacy of power operates as a form of tacit acceptance of authoritarianism in exchange for a degree of social stability.[43] This conforms to a typical pattern in post-Soviet autocracies, which have sought to maintain legitimacy by relying on residual Soviet-era social capital: the principle of egalitarianism, and relatively unrestricted access to essential social services such as healthcare, education, or subsidies. The protests of 2020 disrupted the entrenched norms of elite political division and devalued the symbolic capital of authority; they penetrated far deeper into the social fabric of society, its values, and its projections onto the sociopolitical landscape than previous attempts in 2006, 2010, and 2015. Therefore, it appears that the term "postcolonial revolution," proposed by Ilya Gerasimov in reference to the protests, is justified. However, several years later, it is more appropriate to employ another term proposed by Gerasimov, namely "postcolonial counterrevolution," which is largely driven by the re-establishment of the binary opposition between acceptance and rejection of glocal coloniality.[44]

The Belarusian version of reverse mimicry has a limited empirical footprint. Since 2020, we can draw only on a handful of studies, which may not have been conducted to their full potential due to the closed and repressive attitude of the regime towards dissent and attempts to investigate it. For instance, research by Olga Onuch and Gwendolyn Sasse indicated that the geopolitical preferences of the 2020 protesters "align with normative values and meanings attributed to them (for the case of the EU and Belarusian protesters specifically, normative liberal democratic values)."[45] However, research by the Belarus Initiative project at Chatham House has revealed that the geopolitical preferences of Belarusian society are not unequivocal, even in the face of political and economic pressure from Moscow.

---

43   Stykow, P. *op.cit.*, pp. 107-108.
44   Gerasimov, I., 2020, *op.cit.*, p 271.
45   Onuch O., Sasse, G., *op.cit.*, p. 77.

Data for 2021 indicate that "of any foreign country, urban Belarusians still hold the most favourable attitude towards Russia: overall, 82% of respondents are at least somewhat positive, of which one in every three is very positive."[46] Even after the onset of the war in Ukraine, research indicates a consistent 33% to 38% expressing a highly positive disposition toward Russia. There has been an upward trend in the dynamics of European integration (support for EU association increased from 9% in September 2020 to 18% in June 2022), but this has been matched by an increase in support for a union with Russia (from 27% in September 2020 to 37% in June 2022), with approximately 40% of respondents expressing a preference for neutral status or a union with both the EU and Russia.[47] In 2023, the proportions of geopolitical sympathies remained largely consistent, although support for the EU association decreased to 14%. Notably, 56% of this support emanates from the audience of non-state media outlets.[48] Crucially, then, there is a clear inclination toward an alternative centre, serving as a support base for anti-authoritarian sentiments. This inclination is actively exploited by opposition elites. Meanwhile, despite heightened neocolonial ambitions from the former metropolis, sympathy toward Russia remains stable. Approximately every third respondent holds a positive view of Russia, while around 40% maintain a neutral stance or endorse the concept of a "third way" — a union with both sides. This stance reflects the foreign policy orientation of the Lukashenka regime in the 21st century. Essentially, these data underscore the extent to which Belarusian public opinion is glocal. A reverse mimicry within the framework of a potential post-authoritarian or decolonial project, based on a detachment from the old centre through self-peripherisation toward the West, are currently not as feasible in Belarus as in Ukraine.

---

46 "Belarusians' views on the political crisis (poll conducted 1-10 November 2021)", *op. cit.*
47 "How Russia's war against Ukraine has changed Belarusians' views on foreign affairs (poll conducted 6-17 June 2022)". https://en.belaruspolls.org/wave-10 (Accessed: 30 August 2023).
48 "Belarusians' views on the war and value orientations (poll conducted 15-27 March 2023)". https://en.belaruspolls.org/wave-15 (Accessed: 30 August 2023).

In the broader context of potential decolonisation within Eastern European paradigms, there exists another crucial element in the deconstruction of the viability of glocal knowledge or global colonial knowledge: how Belarus and Ukraine function within the realm of global academic discourse. Although the issue has been re-examined since the onset of the war in Ukraine, the focus has shifted from the accumulation or rebooting of specific academic fields (such as post-Soviet studies or Belarusian studies) to the decolonisation of Russian studies[49] or the search for an exit from Russophonism in knowledge about the region. However, this framing of the question, on the one hand, exhibits distorted epistemological characteristics; on the other, it clearly demonstrates the coloniality of Western knowledge concerning the post-Soviet region, a situation for which the term "Westsplaining" is aptly justified.[50]

The belated epiphany of the West

Decolonisation is a complex and intricate process that involves the simultaneous deconstruction of established knowledge systems. It can be argued that for successful decolonisation to occur, both internal and external forces are required to surmount the epistemological barriers ingrained within a society. The very act of challenging colonial knowledge poses a profound epistemological dilemma.

Post-Soviet decolonisation often leans towards internal positivism: a radical rejection of glocal colonial identity remnants. These nationalistic or imitative approaches do not inherently disrupt the epistemological coherence of global or colonial knowledge systems. Also, the knowledge system about the region is largely shaped by

---

49 See for example: Shaipov, A., Shaipova, Y., 2023, "It's High Time to Decolonize Western Russia Studies", *Foreign Policy,*: https://foreignpolicy.com/2023/02/11/russia-studies-war-ukraine-decolonize-imperialism-western-academics-soviet-empire-eurasia-eastern-europe-university.

50 For more on this term in the context of the war in Ukraine, see: Kazharski, A., "Explaining the 'Westsplainers': Can a Western scholar be an authority on Central and Eastern Europe?", https://ukrainian-studies.ca/2022/07/19/explaining-the-westsplainers-can-a-western-scholar-be-an-authority-on-central-and-eastern-europe/

the global epistemological exchange of knowledge from major centres and metropolises, which offer contextual knowledge about subalterns, often obscuring their subjectivity.[51]

There is no universal strategy for the decolonisation of Eastern Europe within the global knowledge system. For instance, the Ukrainian scenario of top-down decolonisation implies a reverse dependence in discursive terms on the West. This means that the epistemological challenge to the principles of modern knowledge, as Madina Tlostanova wrote,[52] serves as a political impetus to seek external legitimacy within the existing Western colonial framework. Ukrainian decolonisation is, therefore, an attempt to integrate local discursive subjectivity into Western epistemology.

One of the challenges of post-Soviet decolonisation is that, even in the initial stages of decolonial rethinking, the normative functions of epistemology, as discussed by Linda Martin Alcoff,[53] do not effectively apply to Eastern Europe. These functions, such as questions about the distribution and production of knowledge, often remain as rhetorical declarations about the need to decolonise Russian studies. However, as noted by Kateryna Ruban, there is a lack of construction of new principles of understanding or reorganisation of the knowledge institution structure in the West. There continues to be a predominance of programmes, institutions, or academic positions dedicated to the study of Russia, rather than Ukraine or the Eastern European region.[54]

---

51   See Adebisi, F., I., "Decolonisation of Knowledge Production and Knowledge Transmission in the Global South: Stalled, Stagnated or Full Steam Ahead?", *Afronomicslaw*, https://www.afronomicslaw.org/2020/10/20/decolonisation-of-knowledge-production-and-knowledge-transmission-inthe-global-south-stalled-stagnated-or-full-steam-ahead. (Accessed: 3 September 2023).
52   Tlostanova, M., 2015, "Between the Russian/Soviet dependencies, neoliberal delusions, dewesternizing options, and decolonial drives", *Cultural Dynamics*, 27 (2), p. 270.
53   Alcoff, L., M., 2011, "An Epistemology for the Next Revolution", *TRANSMODERNITY: Journal of Peripheral Cultural Production of the Luso-Hispanic World*, 1 (2), pp. 67-78, pp. 69-70.
54   "Interview: Kateryna Ruban on Decolonization in Slavic Studies", IWM, https://www.iwm.at/blog/interview-kateryna-ruban-on-decolonization-in-slavic-studies (Accessed: 3 September 2023).

The cognitive awakening in Western academia regarding the reconsideration of principles for studying Ukraine or the entire post-Soviet space has encountered a highly structured form of discourse that is inherently Russophone. Ewa Thompson explains this by noting that during the Cold War, a significant number of centres or departments for Slavic, Eurasian, or Eastern European studies were established, essentially serving as different names for Russian studies. Furthermore, after the Second World War Slavic studies in North American and Western European universities were heavily influenced by Russian anti-Soviet emigration, whose representatives were invited to academic positions.[55] This led to the transfer of a non-Soviet but pre-revolutionary narrative about the history and culture of Russia, consequently perceiving Soviet-Russian territories as essentially domestic territories.

Following the dissolution of the USSR, certain branches of Western Slavic studies began to evolve independently, such as the study of Ukraine.[56] However, these developments were generally overshadowed by entrenched Russo-centric paradigms.[57] The onset of a full-scale war triggered a re-evaluation within Western academia, challenging perceptions of concepts like "colonialism," "orientalism," or "decolonisation" in relation to Russia as mere theoretical tricks. The term "full-scale war" itself served as a euphemism, signifying the gravity of the situation and the imperative for change. However, at the outset of the conflict in 2014, academic circles primarily interpreted it as a political event rather than a procedural one. In other words, Crimea and the war in Donbas initially

---

55 Thompson, E., 2023, "On Decolonizing Slavic Studies in Europe and America", *Deliberatio*. https://deliberatio.eu/en/analyses/on-decolonizing-slavic-studies-in-europe-and-america (Accessed: 3 September 2023).
56 In turn, within Western academia, Belarusian studies were largely absent during the Cold War era.
57 Dudko, O., 2023, "Gate-crashing 'European' and 'Slavic' area studies: can Ukrainian studies transform the fields?", *Canadian Slavonic Papers*, 65 (2), pp. 174-189 and p. 176; Portnov, A., 2015, "Post-Maidan Europe and the New Ukrainian Studies", *Slavic Review*, 74 (4), pp. 723-731 and pp. 723-724.

became part of the discourse on Russia's geopolitical objectives, with their colonial nature not immediately recognised.[58]

In discussions surrounding the decolonisation of the region, even since 2022, the prevailing narrative focuses on decolonizing Western knowledge about Russia. This framing marginalises the phenomenon of Ukrainian decolonisation, not to mention Belarusian decolonisation. The postmodernist nature of Western colonial knowledge seeks to redefine the source of power (the centre), often overlooking the necessity of reconstructing the capacity for any collective "WE" among subalterns.[59] This is particularly evident for Belarus, where there is a noticeable absence of a discursive or even narrative component within Western knowledge. The pre-2020 external discourse largely expanded the existing area studies models, conforming to the conventional knowledge framework within the field, which centres on a core (Russia) and peripheral regions. Post-2020, the academic understanding of Belarus in the West continued to be comprehensive yet unorganised, exhibiting a significant reliance on Russocentric trends within Western Slavic studies in academic discussions.

The issue of decolonizing knowledge about Russia, its history, or culture occupies a relatively low priority within the global humanities. Besides the necessity of finding opportunities to restructure normative epistemological functions in Western academia, this is due to the global reach of knowledge coloniality. Current trends in the methodologies of critical humanities primarily focus on the Global South, which constitutes the mainstream of research in contemporary emancipatory areas within the humanities and social sciences, encompassing postcolonialism, the study of inequality, migration, racism, and decolonisation. Paradoxically, the much-needed postcolonial/decolonial framework for the post-Soviet

---

58 For different kinds of narration, see: Robinson, P., 2016, "Russia's role in the war in Donbass, and the threat to European security", *European Politics and Society*, 17 (4), pp. 506-521; Bukkvoll, T., 2016, "Why Putin went to war: ideology, interests and decision-making in the Russian use of force in Crimea and Donbas", *Contemporary Politics*, 22 (3), pp. 267-282; Clarke, R., 2016, "The Donbass in 2014: Ultra-Right Threats, Working-Class Revolt, and Russian Policy Responses", *International Critical Thought*, 6 (4), pp. 534-555.
59 Based on the theses from Alcoff, L. M., *op.cit.*, p. 77.

space is effectively omitted from the global discourse. This omission stems from the historical perception of Russia or the USSR as a liberating force on the world stage.[60] The narrative, exported since the 1950s to Africa, South America, and Asia, of the USSR's anti-colonial stance, its struggle against imperialism, and the promise of a communist utopia on Earth seamlessly aligned with the postmodern worldview of the left intellectual and academic community in the West and the emerging Global South.[61] Consequently, within the postcolonial world, which had experienced oppression under European empires, there emerged a simplified dichotomy of the West as the sole oppressor, while the colonialism perpetuated by Soviet Russia, as harsh as British or French colonialism, was largely passed over in silence.[62]

Discussions concerning decolonisation in Ukraine frequently encounter misunderstandings and assertions that the utilisation of this terminology lacks justification. Western support for Ukraine is sometimes perceived more as a form of colonisation by the United States and the EU in Eastern Europe, rather than as a neocolonial conflict orchestrated by Russia or as an anti-colonial endeavour by Ukrainians themselves.[63] The Putin regime, particularly since 2022, has actively employed the longstanding Soviet anti-colonial narrative in its foreign policy. It is evident that Russia's policy in Africa

---

60 See: Polman, M., "Ukraine must do more to counter Russian narratives in the Global South", Atlantic Council. https://www.atlanticcouncil.org/blogs/ukrainealert/ukraine-must-do-more-to-counter-russian-narratives-in-the-global-south/
61 Amarasinghe, A., "Reminiscence of Soviet soft power and the way it influenced the '"Global South"', *Modern Diplomacy*. https://moderndiplomacy.eu/2019/11/02/reminiscence-of-soviet-soft-power-and-the-way-it-influenced-the-global-south/
62 Thompson, E. *op. cit*.
63 See more on topic: Rodkiewicz, W., "An anti-colonial alliance with the Global South. The new 'Foreign Policy Concept of the Russian Federation'", OSW, https://www.osw.waw.pl/en/publikacje/osw-commentary/2023-04-07/anti-colonial-alliance-global-south-new-foreign-policy-concept; Mehta, K., 2023, "5 Reasons Why Much Of Global South Isn't Automatically Supporting The West In Ukraine—OpEd", *Eurasia Review*. https://www.eurasiareview.com/24022023-5-reasons-why-much-of-global-south-isnt-automatically-supporting-the-west-in-ukraine-oped/.

is primarily driven by economic interests. Nevertheless, the propagation of the containment narrative against the West and its perceived weakening through the war in Ukraine functions not solely as diplomatic propaganda from the Kremlin,[64] but also garners support within intellectual and expert circles in Africa, Asia, and South America. This support aligns with an anti-colonial and anti-Western narrative.

The attempt by Russian diplomacy to restore Soviet "soft power" in the Global South is undoubtedly losing to the dominance of China and India, which, over the 30 years since the collapse of the USSR, have taken on the role of new centres of the South. However, even in this context, Russian narratives continue to operate as a form of nostalgic residue from the era of Soviet "aid and solidarity policy."[65] Consequently, the conflict in Ukraine is not perceived by the Global South as a decolonial or liberating endeavour, but rather as an internal European conflict.[66] The endeavours of Ukrainian speakers, politicians, and researchers to construct a narrative of post/decolonial subjectivity for Ukraine encounter resistance from Kremlin elites, who actively promote the Soviet geopolitical anti-Wester discourse.

What's next?

I argue that in the cases analysed in this article, decolonisation occurs (Ukraine) or may occur (Belarus) in two dimensions: internal, as an attempt to detach or reject glocal coloniality and break free from direct dependence on Russia; and external, the decolonisation of knowledge through a reverse dependence aimed at legitimizing the internal process of liberation within Western academia. In both cases, the decolonial turn offers a potential opportunity to escape glocal coloniality, strongly contingent on the external (global) formulation, or on recognition of the existence of Russian colonialism alongside its Western counterpart.

---

64 See: "Russian Narratives in the Global South: Main Trends", *Spravdi*, https://spravdi.gov.ua/en/russian-narratives-in-the-global-south-main trends/
65 Amarasinghe, P., *op. cit.*
66 Mehta, K., *op. cit.*

The Ukrainian breakthrough prematurely concluded the postcolonial compromise, within which glocal colonial knowledge had a firm presence even after 2014. Meanwhile, the counterrevolution in Belarus marked the end of a prolonged phase of consensus during which the ethnonational paradigm coexisted, albeit in a strictly marginal and isolated state from the broader glocal identity in Belarus. However, in contrast to Ukraine, Belarusian decolonisation is currently a theoretical project. A relatively high level of societal sympathy toward Russia, ambivalence over the war in Ukraine, and the extreme amorphousness of alternative elites, which still lack a clear political identity, suggest that internal decolonisation is a hypothetical endeavour.

In both instances, a surrogate hegemon — the West — acts as a significant counterforce to the local authoritarian sociopolitical structure. In Ukraine, the concept of reverse mimicry is visibly evident through practical manifestations such as military and economic support, as well as a shared sense of solidarity with the West. The centralisation of the decolonisation process is grounded in a narrative and symbolic Europeanisation of Ukraine's colonial past. The self-peripheralisation in relation to the Western centre should, however, be viewed alongside a vehement form of anti-colonial nationalism, contradicting the values of European/Western neoliberalism. This mirrors a common post-Soviet pattern of postcolonial detachment from the colonial past and the sphere of memory. Nonetheless, this process has been launched in Ukraine.

Knowledge about Ukraine and Belarus varies in discourse dynamics, interest within the West, and institutionalisation levels. Belarus lacks distinct historical and cultural subjectivity, with discourse mainly event-driven; for example, by the 2020 protests. The lack of systematic research, Belarusian dependence on the Russian context in Western academia, and a sometimes stereotypical approach will hinder critical rethinking of Belarus in the near future. Unlike Ukrainian studies, Belarusian studies are non-institutionalised in Western academia. However, within the framework of the narrative concerning the decolonisation of Russian and Slavic studies, it is crucial to recognise that the ontology of East European decolonisation cannot rely solely on one case. Without Belarus and the broader post-Soviet space, it would be impossible to discuss the decolonisation of knowledge about Ukraine on a global scale. The new regional geography should not only chart a fresh course for the epistemological research process but also establish the groundwork for an alternative, decentralised (geo)political comprehension of the post-Soviet region.[67] Consequently, all regions and countries hold significance.

From the perspective of knowledge decolonisation, the key question is the distribution of knowledge: the decentralisation of the global process of cognition. For Ukraine, the goal is to reconfigure knowledge: to strengthen its presence in the postmodern coloniality/present of the West. This runs counter to the philosophy of decoloniality, but simultaneously creates a unique precedent for decolonisation through the construction of reverse dependence. The reconfiguration of Western knowledge about Ukraine confronts not only strong, structured Russophone discourse, but also a lack of institutional recognition of the Ukrainian language and culture within Western Slavic studies or Eastern European research.

Although Western institutions understand the importance of Ukrainian liberation, they are strongly motivated by (geo)political factors. Recognizing the process of liberation (anticolonial struggle) alongside the reconfiguration of knowledge could therefore significantly accelerate the decolonisation of Eastern European studies, Slavic studies, and knowledge about the region as a whole. However, because liberation implies nativism as a tool for internal identity politics, Western epistemology is currently unable to disrupt the existing normativity of knowledge about the region.

---

67 Dudko, O., *op. cit.*, p. 182.

Afterword

Richard Butterwick

Taken together, the essays in this volume demonstrate how much has changed in Ukraine, and how much less has changed in Belarus, in the two decades since the Orange Revolution. They also show that the death-agony of the post-Soviet world has been protracted, with little immediate prospect of it ending in most of the former USSR. Concerted efforts by political and economic actors to revive characteristic Soviet modes of operation, using new, and not-so-new technologies, have brought some significant successes. As this book goes to press, following elections subjected to far-reaching Russian interference, Georgia and Moldova seem headed in opposite directions, but the future of both countries remains in the balance. While this volume concludes the 3R: Three Ukrainian Revolutions project, conducted within the European Civilization Chair at the College of Europe in Natolin since 2015, it cannot offer a conclusive answer to the question of when the post-Soviet world will finally be consigned to the past.

Future scholars, including students of the College of Europe, will have at their disposal the three previous volumes generated by the first phase of the project, containing conceptual frameworks and a wealth of oral testimony and documentary sources.[1] The intellectual coherence of the project was assured by its leaders—Professors Georges Mink and Paweł Kowal—and researchers, including Iwona and Adam Reichardt, Kateryna Pryshchepa, and Mariusz Marszałkowski. The team was generously and sagely advised

---

[1] Kowal, P., Mink, G., Reichardt, I. (eds.), 2019, *Three Revolutions: Mobilization and Change in Contemporary Ukraine, Vol. 1: Theoretical Aspects and Analyses on Religion, Memory, and Identity*, Hanover: ibidem; Kowal, P. Mink, G., Reichardt, I., Reichardt, A., (eds.), 2019, *Three Revolutions: Mobilization and Change in Contemporary Ukraine, Vol. 2: An Oral History of the Revolution on Granite, Orange Revolution, and Revolution of Dignity*, Hanover: ibidem; Kowal, P., Pryshchepa, K., Reichardt, I. (eds.), 2022, *Three Revolutions: Mobilization and Change in Contemporary Ukraine, Vol. 3: Archival Records and Historical Sources on the 1990 Revolution on Granite*, Hanover: ibidem.

by some of the world's foremost experts from a variety of disciplines. The project's webpages have now been reconfigured into a record and resource maintained by the College of Europe in Natolin. Together with the four published volumes, the webpages are the tangible legacy of the project. The site gives researchers unique access to transcripts and translations of interviews with key participants and first-hand observers of the three revolutions, to scans and transcripts of crucial documents, and to recordings and images of the symposia and seminars.

The lists of the participants in these events read like a roll-call of the politicians, diplomats, journalists, and academics most closely involved in the events of 1990, 2004-2005, and 2013-2014, as well as those since 2022. Students and scholars conversed freely with former presidents and prime ministers, ambassadors and advisors, and even generals and gurus. The staging of these encounters was a marvel of logistics and convivial hospitality, in which the seasonal beauties of the Natolin Campus and the unflagging dedication of the campus staff played their parts. The success of the entire project required significant investment, risking time, money, and reputation, in scholarly inquiry (called *historia* in ancient Greek) whose outcomes—unlike so much of today's grant-funded research on modish subjects—were not, and could not be safely determined in advance. The success of the 3R project was no foregone conclusion. For this courageous taking of responsibility, scholars of revolutionary Ukraine and the wider post-Soviet world owe the Vice-Rector of the College of Europe, Mrs Ewa Ośniecka-Tamecka, an exceptional debt.

When voyagers reach their destination, before pressing on to new places, they do well to pause and reflect on whence they have come, taking in a longer and wider view of their journey. If only because Vladimir Putin simply cannot stop himself from indulging in millennial monologues on why, in his view, Ukrainians should be Russians, it seems legitimate to suggest a longer-term perspective to colleagues who practise political science, sociology, international relations, and cultural anthropology. I take my cue from Georges Mink's distinguished contribution to this volume, focused on the Russian regime's manipulation of memory.

Catherine II, empress of all the Russias since 1762, had a commemorative medal struck thirty-one years later. The obverse conventionally depicts her imperial head and title. The reverse shows a double-headed eagle clutching maps of the lands, with the names of towns and rivers, annexed in the first partition of the Polish-Lithuanian Commonwealth in 1772, and the second partition in 1793. The words *"Отторженная Возвратихъ"* (*Ottorzhennaia vozvratikh"*) — "the lost have returned"' — makes the mendacious claim, repeated by generations of official Russian and Soviet historians and propagandists, that the tsaritsa was merely recovering the territories that by right belonged to her as the inheritor of Moscow's holy mission to "gather the lands of Rus'". The implication for the Commonwealth's remaining territories coveted by the empress was unambiguous. The message was duly repeated in the inscription on the pedestal of the statue of Catherine II unveiled next to Vilnius Cathedral in 1904. On that occasion imperial hubris was overtaken by Nemesis just eleven years later, when the retreating Russian authorities dismantled, packed up, and removed the statue before the German army entered the city. Three years after that, Lithuania and Poland regained their independence, and in 1920 the Polish army threw back the Red Army from the banks of the River Vistula. Whether imperial, Soviet, or neo-imperial, Russia is not invincible.

The ruler of the Russian empire could not tolerate any endeavours of her south-western neighbour to haul itself out of the mire of corruption, oligarchy, and anarchy that so suited Russian strategic and economic interests. This "enlightened despot" responded to her republican neighbour's initiatives for enlightened reform by manipulating its religious and political scene, applying the tried and tested methods of *divide et impera*, by defaming it to enlightened Europe's opinion-formers, and by carving off limbs of its territory. When despite this treatment this neighbouring nation, composed of citizens, rather than subjects, persisted in striving for liberty and independence, when it moved towards other alliances, when its reforms testified to its vitality and potential, then the empress, whose rule was threatened geopolitically, demographically, and ideologically, mustered all the force at her disposal, and destroyed the

Polish-Lithuanian Commonwealth. She, her servants, and her fellow-travellers all the while proclaimed that she was merely reclaiming her own. The analogies with the attempts of Russia's current ruler to snuff out by any means the existential threat posed to his dictatorship by the growing success — with every revolution — of Ukraine's vibrant civic society in combating the imperial and Soviet legacy of ingrained corruption and dependency are all too obvious.

On the other hand, there are, as usual in history, discontinuities as well as continuities. The late 18th-century Russian Empire was not a decaying, shrinking post-Muscovite world, whose ruler and military establishment struck out viciously in an attempt to restore lost greatness. Catherine II's Russia was an ascending great power, despite underlying structural weaknesses, which the Crimean War of 1853-1856 and the Russo-Japanese war of 1904-1905 would embarrassingly reveal. The Russian imperial zenith was Alexander I's triumphant entry into Paris in 1814. Putin, in contrast, despite expensively purchased assistance from North Korea, Iran, and China, and willing saboteurs in the persons of Viktor Orbán and Robert Fico, cannot count on partners in the destruction of Ukraine comparable to the Prussian and Austrian monarchs who joined with Catherine II in twice amputating and finally annihilating the friendless Polish-Lithuanian Commonwealth.

Ukraine has — at least until the time of writing in November 2024 — received enormous military, logistical, financial, and humanitarian support from the United States, Poland, and in varying degrees from other North Atlantic and European countries. The neutrality of Turkey, now a rising rather than a declining power, has in practice tended to favour Ukraine over Russia. Russian aggression has resuscitated NATO, now much strengthened by the accession of Finland and Sweden, to the point where it may even survive the presidency of Donald Trump. The EU, having obstructed Ukraine's aspirations for two decades, opened a path to membership within four months of the full-scale Russian invasion of 2022. Neither is yet a certain, or even a completely secure destination for Ukraine, but the gates are not locked. Although the timing, and conditions of Western assistance have not sufficed for Ukraine to achieve the decisive military breakthrough that might have forced Russia to make peace on Ukrainian terms, it has enabled Ukraine to defend most of its territory, and to inflict colossal losses on the invaders. Without it, the ongoing resistance to the Russian army and its collaborators would by now be conducted by partisans, and the scale of the appalling crimes against humanity daily committed by the occupants would be much greater.

A further advantage enjoyed by today's Ukraine *vis-à-vis* the Commonwealth of old is the skill of so many Ukrainian citizens in satirizing and exposing the enemy to vast international audiences via electronic social media. They however do face an army of trolls. Poles and their sympathisers scored some successes in the propaganda wars of the later 18th century, which later helped to keep the "Polish Question" alive for much of the 19th. However, when it came to the crunch in 1791, a well-financed campaign of lobbying and agitation orchestrated from the Russian Embassy in London scuppered the international coalition that British Prime Minister William Pitt the Younger tried to assemble against Russian expansionism. Graffiti proclaiming "no war with Russia!" appeared on public buildings. *Déjà vu*? While Putin's hand of cards is in almost every respect weaker than that played by Catherine II, he does have one ace that she did not: nuclear weapons. Fears he might use them appear to have braked American aid at a crucial juncture in the late summer and autumn of 2022, when Ukraine seemed on the verge of a breakthrough. Hindsight tells us that Ukraine's understandable decision in 1994 to relinquish its nuclear arsenal, in exchange for economic rescue and international guarantees of its security and integrity, has cost it dearly.

Three Ukrainian revolutions have not by themselves ended the post-Soviet world. They, have, however, achieved something of more long-term significance. Ukrainians' repeated rejections of attempts to subject them to the Kremlin's proxies have so far prevented the re-emergence of the Russian empire. Zbigniew Brzeziński's famous insight that "Without Ukraine, Russia ceases to be an empire, but with Ukraine suborned and then subordinated, Russia automatically becomes an empire" is as accurate now as it was thirty years ago.[2]

---

[2] Brzeziński, Z, 1994, "The Premature Partnership", *Foreign Affairs*, 73 (2).

Author Biographies

Butterwick, Richard—Chairholder of the European Civilization Chair at the College of Europe in Natolin, where the Three Ukrainian Revolutions (3R) project was carried out. He is also Professor of Polish-Lithuanian History at University College London and Principal Historian of the Polish History Museum in Warsaw. His research and publications concentrate on the Polish-Lithuanian Commonwealth in the Age of Enlightenment. Awards include the Polish Historical Society's Pro historia Polonorum Prize for the book *The Polish-Lithuanian Commonwealth 1733-1795: Light and Flame* (2020).

Cichocki, Marek—Professor at the College of Europe in Natolin and Professor of International Relations at the Collegium Civitas in Warsaw. He specialises in international relations, German European politics, intellectual and political history of Europe. He lectured at the Institute of Applied Social Sciences of the Warsaw University (1995-2015), Postgraduate School for Social Research at the Polish Academy of Sciences (2001-2003) and at the Pontifical University of Saint Thomas Aquinas in Rome (2021-2022). He is also editor-in-chief of the *Teologia Polityczna* yearly. He has authored books, essays, articles and dissertations on international relations and history.

Gajda, Kinga Anna—Associate Professor and Director of the Institute of European Studies at the Jagiellonian University. She is a professor of cultural studies, and holds a doctorate in literary studies. Her research interests include memory and heritage, with a particular focus on Central and Eastern Europe in the post-communist era. She is an author and editor of numerous publications as well as a member of the editorial teams of *The International Journal of Interdisciplinary Civic and Political Studies; The International Journal of Interdisciplinary Cultural Studies; The International Journal of Interdisciplinary Educational Studies and The International Journal of Interdisciplinary Social and Community Studies*.

Kasparov, Gary — Former world chess champion. His famous matches against the IBM super-computer Deep Blue in 1996-97 were key to bringing artificial intelligence, and chess, into the mainstream. He has been a contributing editor to *The Wall Street Journal* since 1991 and is a frequent commentator on politics and human rights. In 2013 he was named a Senior Visiting Fellow at the Oxford-Martin School. Kasparov's book *How Life Imitates Chess* on decision-making is available in over 20 languages. He is the author of two acclaimed series of chess books: *My Great Predecessors* and *Modern Chess*.

Lachowicz, Magdalena — Assistant Professor at the Department of Eastern Studies at Adam Mickiewicz University in Poznań, Poland. Her research interests include: ethnic relations and regional movements in the former Soviet republics, the history of the Soviet Union, and civil society movements in contemporary Russia, Belarus and Ukraine.

Michnik, Wojciech — Assistant Professor of International Relations and Security Studies at the Jagiellonian University and the Transatlantic Project Coordinator for the Central and South-East Europe Programme at London School of Economics IDEAS at the Jagiellonian University and contributing editor for *New Eastern Europe*. He was a 2023-24 Fulbright-NATO Security Studies Fellow at the University of Arizona. In 2019 he was the Eisenhower Defense Fellow at NATO Defense College in Rome. Previously he served as a Fulbright visiting scholar at Columbia University's Harriman Institute (in 2015-2016) and as a foreign and security policy analyst at the Department of Americas, Ministry of Foreign Affairs of the Republic of Poland (2014). He holds a PhD in International Relations from the Jagiellonian University. His main research interests include Transatlantic security, particularly NATO-Russia relations, and Great Power competition in the Middle East.

Mink, Georges — Permanent Professor at the College of Europe in Natolin. From 2019 to 2023 he was the Chairholder of the Chair of European History and Civilization. He is a sociologist and political scientist, specialising in Central and Eastern Europe. He has been one of the main two leaders of the Three Ukrainian Revolutions (3R) research project which was carried out by the College of Europe in Natolin from 2016 to 2024. He is Director Emeritus of Research at the Institut des Sciences Sociales et du Politique (CNRS - France), Université de Paris X, Nanterre and former President of the International Council for Central and East European Studies (ICCEES), 2015-2021. His research and publications — more than 250 — include books, chapters in the collective publications, articles and expert papers, and are dedicated to political systems, the sociopolitical evolution of these regimes, the conversion of ex-communist elites in Central and Eastern Europe and the Europeanisation of national political systems. He was also a co-editor of the first two volumes of the Three Ukrainian Revolutions publication prepared in the framework of the 3R research project and published by Ibidem. Among his recent books is also *La Pologne au coeur de l'Europe, de 1914 à aujourd'hui, histoire politique et conflits de mémoire*, published by Buchet-Chastel in 2015 (French version) and in 2017 (Polish version).

Olędzka, Justyna — Lecturer at the Faculty of History of the University of Białystok, Poland, and coordinator of the Interdisciplinary Eastern Studies Team. She is an expert at the Academic Center for Strategic Analysis and a member of the international analytical group "Belarus-Ukraine-Region" operating at the Center for Eastern Europe at the University of Warsaw. Her research interests focus on the issues of legitimisation and de-legitimisation of leadership in the post-Soviet area, the role of propaganda and disinformation in non-democracies, and the theory and practice of social engineering.

Reichardt, Iwona — Deputy Editor-in-Chief of the *New Eastern Europe* journal at the Jan Nowak-Jeziorański College of Eastern Europe in Wrocław. She holds a PhD in political science from the Jagiellonian University where she now teaches courses on Ukraine, Belarus and Moldova since the collapse of the Soviet Union. Since 2015 she has been a member of the Three Ukrainian Revolutions (3R) research team at the College of Europe in Natolin. She co-edited the three volume publication titled *Three Revolutions. Mobilisation and Change in Contemporary Ukraine* (2019-2022).

Saifullayeu, Anton — Adjunct Professor at the University of Warsaw. He holds a PhD in humanities from the University of Warsaw. His area of academic interests include postcolonial theory, cultural anthropology of post-Soviet Eastern Europe, theory of historiography, and Belarusian history of ideas. He is an author of numerous academic articles and a book on post-colonial historiographies titled *Postkolonialne historiografie* which was published in Poland in 2020.

Wańczyk, Kacper — Analyst focusing on Belarus, Russia and Ukraine and a PhD student at Koźmiński University in Warsaw. His doctoral research focuses on the idea of property in Belarus and Estonia and its influence on contemporary macroeconomic policies. He works at the Academic Centre of Strategic Analysis of the War Studies University and is a member of the analytical group "Belarus-Ukraine-Region" operating at the Center for Eastern Europe at the University of Warsaw. He is a former diplomat who has served in Belarus and Afghanistan, among other places.

Wolczuk, Kataryna — Professor of East European Politics at the Centre for Russian, European and Eurasian Studies (CREES) at the University of Birmingham, United Kingdom. She holds a PhD in Russian and East European Studies from the University of Birmingham. Her research focuses on politics in Eastern Europe, the EU's relations with post-Soviet states as well as on Russia and Eurasian integration. Her publications include: *Eurasian Economic Integration: Law, Policy, and Politics*, Edward Elgar: 2013, *Ukraine between the EU and Russia: the Integration Challenge*, Palgrave Macmillan, 2015 (with R. Dragneva) and *The Ukraine Conflict: Security, Identity and Politics in the Wider Europe*, Routledge: London and New York, 2017 (co-edited with D. Averre). She is an Associate Fellow at the Russia and Eurasia Programme at Chatham House and a Senior Professorial

Fellow at the European Neighbourhood Chair at the College of Europe in Natolin.

Wilson, Andrew — Professor of Ukrainian Studies at University College London. He is an author of numerous books on Ukraine, Belarus and post-Soviet states. His most recent books are *Political Technology: The Globalisation of Political Manipulation* (CUP, 2024) and *The Ukrainians* (Yale UP, 2022). His materials are also available at www.politicaltechnology.blog. He is forthcoming book is titled *How Russia Created the Propaganda that Helped Create the War against Ukraine*.

SOVIET AND POST-SOVIET POLITICS AND SOCIETY
Edited by Dr. Andreas Umland | ISSN 1614-3515

1   Андреас Умланд (ред.) | Воплощение Европейской конвенции по правам человека в России. Философские, юридические и эмпирические исследования | ISBN 3-89821-387-0

2   *Christian Wipperfürth* | Russland – ein vertrauenswürdiger Partner? Grundlagen, Hintergründe und Praxis gegenwärtiger russischer Außenpolitik | Mit einem Vorwort von Heinz Timmermann | ISBN 3-89821-401-X

3   *Manja Hussner* | Die Übernahme internationalen Rechts in die russische und deutsche Rechtsordnung. Eine vergleichende Analyse zur Völkerrechtsfreundlichkeit der Verfassungen der Russländischen Föderation und der Bundesrepublik Deutschland | Mit einem Vorwort von Rainer Arnold | ISBN 3-89821-438-9

4   *Matthew Tejada* | Bulgaria's Democratic Consolidation and the Kozloduy Nuclear Power Plant (KNPP). The Unattainability of Closure | With a foreword by Richard J. Crampton | ISBN 3-89821-439-7

5   Марк Григорьевич Меерович | Квадратные метры, определяющие сознание. Государственная жилищная политика в СССР. 1921 – 1941 гг | ISBN 3-89821-474-5

6   *Andrei P. Tsygankov, Pavel A.Tsygankov (Eds.)* | New Directions in Russian International Studies | ISBN 3-89821-422-2

7   Марк Григорьевич Меерович | Как власть народ к труду приучала. Жилище в СССР – средство управления людьми. 1917 – 1941 гг. | С предисловием Елены Осокиной | ISBN 3-89821-495-8

8   *David J. Galbreath* | Nation-Building and Minority Politics in Post-Socialist States. Interests, Influence and Identities in Estonia and Latvia | With a foreword by David J. Smith | ISBN 3-89821-467-2

9   Алексей Юрьевич Безугольный | Народы Кавказа в Вооруженных силах СССР в годы Великой Отечественной войны 1941-1945 гг. | С предисловием Николая Бугая | ISBN 3-89821-475-3

10 Вячеслав Лихачев и Владимир Прибыловский (ред.) | Русское Национальное Единство, 1990-2000. В 2-х томах | ISBN 3-89821-523-7

11 Николай Бугай (ред.) | Народы стран Балтии в условиях сталинизма (1940-е – 1950-е годы). Документированная история | ISBN 3-89821-525-3

12 *Ingmar Bredies (Hrsg.)* | Zur Anatomie der Orange Revolution in der Ukraine. Wechsel des Elitenregimes oder Triumph des Parlamentarismus? | ISBN 3-89821-524-5

13 *Anastasia V. Mitrofanova* | The Politicization of Russian Orthodoxy. *Actors and Ideas* | With a foreword by William C. Gay | ISBN 3-89821-481-8

14 *Nathan D. Larson* | Alexander Solzhenitsyn and the Russo-Jewish Question | ISBN 3-89821-483-4

15 *Guido Houben* | Kulturpolitik und Ethnizität. Staatliche Kunstförderung im Russland der neunziger Jahre | Mit einem Vorwort von Gert Weisskirchen | ISBN 3-89821-542-3

16 *Leonid Luks* | Der russische „Sonderweg"? Aufsätze zur neuesten Geschichte Russlands im europäischen Kontext | ISBN 3-89821-496-6

17 Евгений Мороз | История «Мёртвой воды» – от страшной сказки к большой политике. Политическое неоязычество в постсоветской России | ISBN 3-89821-551-2

18 Александр Верховский и Галина Кожевникова (ред.) | Этническая и религиозная интолерантность в российских СМИ. Результаты мониторинга 2001-2004 гг. | ISBN 3-89821-569-5

19 *Christian Ganzer* | Sowjetisches Erbe und ukrainische Nation. Das Museum der Geschichte des Zaporoger Kosakentums auf der Insel Chortycja | Mit einem Vorwort von Frank Golczewski | ISBN 3-89821-504-0

20 Эльза-Баир Гучинова | Помнить нельзя забыть. Антропология депортационной травмы калмыков | С предисловием Кэролайн Хамфри | ISBN 3-89821-506-7

21 Юлия Лидерман | Мотивы «проверки» и «испытания» в постсоветской культуре. Советское прошлое в российском кинематографе 1990-х годов | С предисловием Евгения Марголита | ISBN 3-89821-511-3

22 *Tanya Lokshina, Ray Thomas, Mary Mayer (Eds.)* | The Imposition of a Fake Political Settlement in the Northern Caucasus. The 2003 Chechen Presidential Election | ISBN 3-89821-436-2

23 *Timothy McCajor Hall, Rosie Read (Eds.)* | Changes in the Heart of Europe. Recent Ethnographies of Czechs, Slovaks, Roma, and Sorbs | With an afterword by Zdeněk Salzmann | ISBN 3-89821-606-5

24 Christian Autengruber | Die politischen Parteien in Bulgarien und Rumänien. Eine vergleichende Analyse seit Beginn der 90er Jahre | Mit einem Vorwort von Dorothée de Nève | ISBN 3-89821-476-1

25 Annette Freyberg-Inan with Radu Cristescu | The Ghosts in Our Classrooms, or: John Dewey Meets Ceauşescu. The Promise and the Failures of Civic Education in Romania | ISBN 3-89821-416-8

26 John B. Dunlop | The 2002 Dubrovka and 2004 Beslan Hostage Crises. A Critique of Russian Counter-Terrorism | With a foreword by Donald N. Jensen | ISBN 3-89821-608-X

27 Peter Koller | Das touristische Potenzial von Kam"janec'–Podil's'kyj. Eine fremdenverkehrsgeographische Untersuchung der Zukunftsperspektiven und Maßnahmenplanung zur Destinationsentwicklung des „ukrainischen Rothenburg" | Mit einem Vorwort von Kristiane Klemm | ISBN 3-89821-640-3

28 Françoise Daucé, Elisabeth Sieca-Kozlowski (Eds.) | Dedovshchina in the Post-Soviet Military. Hazing of Russian Army Conscripts in a Comparative Perspective | With a foreword by Dale Herspring | ISBN 3-89821-616-0

29 Florian Strasser | Zivilgesellschaftliche Einflüsse auf die Orange Revolution. Die gewaltlose Massenbewegung und die ukrainische Wahlkrise 2004 | Mit einem Vorwort von Egbert Jahn | ISBN 3-89821-648-9

30 Rebecca S. Katz | The Georgian Regime Crisis of 2003-2004. A Case Study in Post-Soviet Media Representation of Politics, Crime and Corruption | ISBN 3-89821-413-3

31 Vladimir Kantor | Willkür oder Freiheit. Beiträge zur russischen Geschichtsphilosophie | Ediert von Dagmar Herrmann sowie mit einem Vorwort versehen von Leonid Luks | ISBN 3-89821-589-X

32 Laura A. Victoir | The Russian Land Estate Today. A Case Study of Cultural Politics in Post-Soviet Russia | With a foreword by Priscilla Roosevelt | ISBN 3-89821-426-5

33 Ivan Katchanovski | Cleft Countries. Regional Political Divisions and Cultures in Post-Soviet Ukraine and Moldova | With a foreword by Francis Fukuyama | ISBN 3-89821-558-X

34 Florian Mühlfried | Postsowjetische Feiern. Das Georgische Bankett im Wandel | Mit einem Vorwort von Kevin Tuite | ISBN 3-89821-601-2

35 Roger Griffin, Werner Loh, Andreas Umland (Eds.) | Fascism Past and Present, West and East. An International Debate on Concepts and Cases in the Comparative Study of the Extreme Right | With an afterword by Walter Laqueur | ISBN 3-89821-674-8

36 Sebastian Schlegel | Der „Weiße Archipel". Sowjetische Atomstädte 1945-1991 | Mit einem Geleitwort von Thomas Bohn | ISBN 3-89821-679-9

37 Vyacheslav Likhachev | Political Anti-Semitism in Post-Soviet Russia. Actors and Ideas in 1991-2003 | Edited and translated from Russian by Eugene Veklerov | ISBN 3-89821-529-6

38 Josette Baer (Ed.) | Preparing Liberty in Central Europe. Political Texts from the Spring of Nations 1848 to the Spring of Prague 1968 | With a foreword by Zdeněk V. David | ISBN 3-89821-546-6

39 Михаил Лукьянов | Российский консерватизм и реформа, 1907-1914 | С предисловием Марка Д. Стейнберга | ISBN 3-89821-503-2

40 Nicola Melloni | Market Without Economy. The 1998 Russian Financial Crisis | With a foreword by Eiji Furukawa | ISBN 3-89821-407-9

41 Dmitrij Chmelnizki | Die Architektur Stalins | Bd. 1: Studien zu Ideologie und Stil | Bd. 2: Bilddokumentation | Mit einem Vorwort von Bruno Flierl | ISBN 3-89821-515-6

42 Katja Yafimava | Post-Soviet Russian-Belarussian Relationships. The Role of Gas Transit Pipelines | With a foreword by Jonathan P. Stern | ISBN 3-89821-655-1

43 Boris Chavkin | Verflechtungen der deutschen und russischen Zeitgeschichte. Aufsätze und Archivfunde zu den Beziehungen Deutschlands und der Sowjetunion von 1917 bis 1991 | Ediert von Markus Edlinger sowie mit einem Vorwort versehen von Leonid Luks | ISBN 3-89821-756-6

44 Anastasija Grynenko in Zusammenarbeit mit Claudia Dathe | Die Terminologie des Gerichtswesens der Ukraine und Deutschlands im Vergleich. Eine übersetzungswissenschaftliche Analyse juristischer Fachbegriffe im Deutschen, Ukrainischen und Russischen | Mit einem Vorwort von Ulrich Hartmann | ISBN 3-89821-691-8

45 Anton Burkov | The Impact of the European Convention on Human Rights on Russian Law. Legislation and Application in 1996-2006 | With a foreword by Françoise Hampson | ISBN 978-3-89821-639-5

46 Stina Torjesen, Indra Overland (Eds.) | International Election Observers in Post-Soviet Azerbaijan. Geopolitical Pawns or Agents of Change? | ISBN 978-3-89821-743-9

47 Taras Kuzio | Ukraine – Crimea – Russia. Triangle of Conflict | ISBN 978-3-89821-761-3

48 Claudia Šabić | „Ich erinnere mich nicht, aber L'viv!" Zur Funktion kultureller Faktoren für die Institutionalisierung und Entwicklung einer ukrainischen Region | Mit einem Vorwort von Melanie Tatur | ISBN 978-3-89821-752-1

49 *Marlies Bilz* | Tatarstan in der Transformation. Nationaler Diskurs und Politische Praxis 1988-1994 | Mit einem Vorwort von Frank Golczewski | ISBN 978-3-89821-722-4

50 *Марлен Ларюэль (ред.)* | Современные интерпретации русского национализма | ISBN 978-3-89821-795-8

51 *Sonja Schüler* | Die ethnische Dimension der Armut. Roma im postsozialistischen Rumänien | Mit einem Vorwort von Anton Sterbling | ISBN 978-3-89821-776-7

52 *Галина Кожевникова* | Радикальный национализм в России и противодействие ему. Сборник докладов Центра «Сова» за 2004-2007 гг. | С предисловием Александра Верховского | ISBN 978-3-89821-721-7

53 *Галина Кожевникова и Владимир Прибыловский* | Российская власть в биографиях I. Высшие должностные лица РФ в 2004 г. | ISBN 978-3-89821-796-5

54 *Галина Кожевникова и Владимир Прибыловский* | Российская власть в биографиях II. Члены Правительства РФ в 2004 г. | ISBN 978-3-89821-797-2

55 *Галина Кожевникова и Владимир Прибыловский* | Российская власть в биографиях III. Руководители федеральных служб и агентств РФ в 2004 г.| ISBN 978-3-89821-798-9

56 *Ileana Petroniu* | Privatisierung in Transformationsökonomien. Determinanten der Restrukturierungs-Bereitschaft am Beispiel Polens, Rumäniens und der Ukraine | Mit einem Vorwort von Rainer W. Schäfer | ISBN 978-3-89821-790-3

57 *Christian Wipperfürth* | Russland und seine GUS-Nachbarn. Hintergründe, aktuelle Entwicklungen und Konflikte in einer ressourcenreichen Region| ISBN 978-3-89821-801-6

58 *Togzhan Kassenova* | From Antagonism to Partnership. The Uneasy Path of the U.S.-Russian Cooperative Threat Reduction | With a foreword by Christoph Bluth | ISBN 978-3-89821-707-1

59 *Alexander Höllwerth* | Das sakrale eurasische Imperium des Aleksandr Dugin. Eine Diskursanalyse zum postsowjetischen russischen Rechtsextremismus | Mit einem Vorwort von Dirk Uffelmann | ISBN 978-3-89821-813-9

60 *Олег Рябов* | «Россия-Матушка». Национализм, гендер и война в России XX века | С предисловием Елены Гощило | ISBN 978-3-89821-487-2

61 *Ivan Maistrenko* | Borot'bism. A Chapter in the History of the Ukrainian Revolution | With a new Introduction by Chris Ford | Translated by George S. N. Luckyj with the assistance of Ivan L. Rudnytsky | Second, Revised and Expanded Edition ISBN 978-3-8382-1107-7

62 *Maryna Romanets* | Anamorphosic Texts and Reconfigured Visions. Improvised Traditions in Contemporary Ukrainian and Irish Literature | ISBN 978-3-89821-576-3

63 *Paul D'Anieri and Taras Kuzio (Eds.)* | Aspects of the Orange Revolution I. Democratization and Elections in Post-Communist Ukraine | ISBN 978-3-89821-698-2

64 *Bohdan Harasymiw in collaboration with Oleh S. Ilnytzkyj (Eds.)* | Aspects of the Orange Revolution II. Information and Manipulation Strategies in the 2004 Ukrainian Presidential Elections | ISBN 978-3-89821-699-9

65 *Ingmar Bredies, Andreas Umland and Valentin Yakushik (Eds.)* | Aspects of the Orange Revolution III. The Context and Dynamics of the 2004 Ukrainian Presidential Elections | ISBN 978-3-89821-803-0

66 *Ingmar Bredies, Andreas Umland and Valentin Yakushik (Eds.)* | Aspects of the Orange Revolution IV. Foreign Assistance and Civic Action in the 2004 Ukrainian Presidential Elections | ISBN 978-3-89821-808-5

67 *Ingmar Bredies, Andreas Umland and Valentin Yakushik (Eds.)* | Aspects of the Orange Revolution V. Institutional Observation Reports on the 2004 Ukrainian Presidential Elections | ISBN 978-3-89821-809-2

68 *Taras Kuzio (Ed.)* | Aspects of the Orange Revolution VI. Post-Communist Democratic Revolutions in Comparative Perspective | ISBN 978-3-89821-820-7

69 *Tim Bohse* | Autoritarismus statt Selbstverwaltung. Die Transformation der kommunalen Politik in der Stadt Kaliningrad 1990-2005 | Mit einem Geleitwort von Stefan Troebst | ISBN 978-3-89821-782-8

70 *David Rupp* | Die Rußländische Föderation und die russischsprachige Minderheit in Lettland. Eine Fallstudie zur Anwaltspolitik Moskaus gegenüber den russophonen Minderheiten im „Nahen Ausland" von 1991 bis 2002 | Mit einem Vorwort von Helmut Wagner | ISBN 978-3-89821-778-1

71 *Taras Kuzio* | Theoretical and Comparative Perspectives on Nationalism. New Directions in Cross-Cultural and Post-Communist Studies | With a foreword by Paul Robert Magocsi | ISBN 978-3-89821-815-3

72 *Christine Teichmann* | Die Hochschultransformation im heutigen Osteuropa. Kontinuität und Wandel bei der Entwicklung des postkommunistischen Universitätswesens | Mit einem Vorwort von Oskar Anweiler | ISBN 978-3-89821-842-8

73 Julia Kusznir | Der politische Einfluss von Wirtschaftseliten in russischen Regionen. Eine Analyse am Beispiel der Erdöl- und Erdgasindustrie, 1992-2005 | Mit einem Vorwort von Wolfgang Eichwede | ISBN 978-3-89821-821-4

74 Alena Vysotskaya | Russland, Belarus und die EU-Osterweiterung. Zur Minderheitenfrage und zum Problem der Freizügigkeit des Personenverkehrs | Mit einem Vorwort von Katlijn Malfliet | ISBN 978-3-89821-822-1

75 Heiko Pleines (Hrsg.) | Corporate Governance in post-sozialistischen Volkswirtschaften | ISBN 978-3-89821-766-8

76 Stefan Ihrig | Wer sind die Moldawier? Rumänismus versus Moldowanismus in Historiographie und Schulbüchern der Republik Moldova, 1991-2006 | Mit einem Vorwort von Holm Sundhaussen | ISBN 978-3-89821-466-7

77 Galina Kozhevnikova in collaboration with Alexander Verkhovsky and Eugene Veklerov | Ultra-Nationalism and Hate Crimes in Contemporary Russia. The 2004-2006 Annual Reports of Moscow's SOVA Center | With a foreword by Stephen D. Shenfield | ISBN 978-3-89821-868-9

78 Florian Küchler | The Role of the European Union in Moldova's Transnistria Conflict | With a foreword by Christopher Hill | ISBN 978-3-89821-850-4

79 Bernd Rechel | The Long Way Back to Europe. Minority Protection in Bulgaria | With a foreword by Richard Crampton | ISBN 978-3-89821-863-4

80 Peter W. Rodgers | Nation, Region and History in Post-Communist Transitions. Identity Politics in Ukraine, 1991-2006 | With a foreword by Vera Tolz | ISBN 978-3-89821-903-7

81 Stephanie Solywoda | The Life and Work of Semen L. Frank. A Study of Russian Religious Philosophy | With a foreword by Philip Walters | ISBN 978-3-89821-457-5

82 Vera Sokolova | Cultural Politics of Ethnicity. Discourses on Roma in Communist Czechoslovakia | ISBN 978-3-89821-864-1

83 Natalya Shevchik Ketenci | Kazakhstani Enterprises in Transition. The Role of Historical Regional Development in Kazakhstan's Post-Soviet Economic Transformation | ISBN 978-3-89821-831-3

84 Martin Malek, Anna Schor-Tschudnowskaja (Hgg.) | Europa im Tschetschenienkrieg. Zwischen politischer Ohnmacht und Gleichgültigkeit | Mit einem Vorwort von Lipchan Basajewa | ISBN 978-3-89821-676-0

85 Stefan Meister | Das postsowjetische Universitätswesen zwischen nationalem und internationalem Wandel. Die Entwicklung der regionalen Hochschule in Russland als Gradmesser der Systemtransformation | Mit einem Vorwort von Joan DeBardeleben | ISBN 978-3-89821-891-7

86 Konstantin Sheiko in collaboration with Stephen Brown | Nationalist Imaginings of the Russian Past. Anatolii Fomenko and the Rise of Alternative History in Post-Communist Russia | With a foreword by Donald Ostrowski | ISBN 978-3-89821-915-0

87 Sabine Jenni | Wie stark ist das „Einige Russland"? Zur Parteibindung der Eliten und zum Wahlerfolg der Machtpartei im Dezember 2007 | Mit einem Vorwort von Klaus Armingeon | ISBN 978-3-89821-961-7

88 Thomas Borén | Meeting-Places of Transformation. Urban Identity, Spatial Representations and Local Politics in Post-Soviet St Petersburg | ISBN 978-3-89821-739-2

89 Aygul Ashirova | Stalinismus und Stalin-Kult in Zentralasien. Turkmenistan 1924-1953 | Mit einem Vorwort von Leonid Luks | ISBN 978-3-89821-987-7

90 Leonid Luks | Freiheit oder imperiale Größe? Essays zu einem russischen Dilemma | ISBN 978-3-8382-0011-8

91 Christopher Gilley | The 'Change of Signposts' in the Ukrainian Emigration. A Contribution to the History of Sovietophilism in the 1920s | With a foreword by Frank Golczewski | ISBN 978-3-89821-965-5

92 Philipp Casula, Jeronim Perovic (Eds.) | Identities and Politics During the Putin Presidency. The Discursive Foundations of Russia's Stability | With a foreword by Heiko Haumann | ISBN 978-3-8382-0015-6

93 Marcel Viëtor | Europa und die Frage nach seinen Grenzen im Osten. Zur Konstruktion ‚europäischer Identität' in Geschichte und Gegenwart | Mit einem Vorwort von Albrecht Lehmann | ISBN 978-3-8382-0045-3

94 Ben Hellman, Andrei Rogachevskii | Filming the Unfilmable. Casper Wrede's 'One Day in the Life of Ivan Denisovich' | Second, Revised and Expanded Edition | ISBN 978-3-8382-0044-6

95 Eva Fuchslocher | Vaterland, Sprache, Glaube. Orthodoxie und Nationenbildung am Beispiel Georgiens | Mit einem Vorwort von Christina von Braun | ISBN 978-3-89821-884-9

96 Vladimir Kantor | Das Westlertum und der Weg Russlands. Zur Entwicklung der russischen Literatur und Philosophie | Ediert von Dagmar Herrmann | Mit einem Beitrag von Nikolaus Lobkowicz | ISBN 978-3-8382-0102-3

97 Kamran Musayev | Die postsowjetische Transformation im Baltikum und Südkaukasus. Eine vergleichende Untersuchung der politischen Entwicklung Lettlands und Aserbaidschans 1985-2009 | Mit einem Vorwort von Leonid Luks | Ediert von Sandro Henschel | ISBN 978-3-8382-0103-0

98 *Tatiana Zhurzhenko* | Borderlands into Bordered Lands. Geopolitics of Identity in Post-Soviet Ukraine | With a foreword by Dieter Segert | ISBN 978-3-8382-0042-2

99 *Кирилл Галушко, Лидия Смола (ред.)* | Пределы падения – варианты украинского будущего. Аналитико-прогностические исследования | ISBN 978-3-8382-0148-1

100 *Michael Minkenberg (Ed.)* | Historical Legacies and the Radical Right in Post-Cold War Central and Eastern Europe | With an afterword by Sabrina P. Ramet | ISBN 978-3-8382-0124-5

101 *David-Emil Wickström* | Rocking St. Petersburg. Transcultural Flows and Identity Politics in the St. Petersburg Popular Music Scene | With a foreword by Yngvar B. Steinholt | Second, Revised and Expanded Edition | ISBN 978-3-8382-0100-9

102 *Eva Zabka* | Eine neue „Zeit der Wirren"? Der spät- und postsowjetische Systemwandel 1985-2000 im Spiegel russischer gesellschaftspolitischer Diskurse | Mit einem Vorwort von Margareta Mommsen | ISBN 978-3-8382-0161-0

103 *Ulrike Ziemer* | Ethnic Belonging, Gender and Cultural Practices. Youth Identitites in Contemporary Russia | With a foreword by Anoop Nayak | ISBN 978-3-8382-0152-8

104 *Ksenia Chepikova* | ‚Einiges Russland' - eine zweite KPdSU? Aspekte der Identitätskonstruktion einer postsowjetischen „Partei der Macht" | Mit einem Vorwort von Torsten Oppelland | ISBN 978-3-8382-0311-9

105 *Леонид Люкс* | Западничество или евразийство? Демократия или идеократия? Сборник статей об исторических дилеммах России | С предисловием Владимира Кантора | ISBN 978-3-8382-0211-2

106 *Anna Dost* | Das russische Verfassungsrecht auf dem Weg zum Föderalismus und zurück. Zum Konflikt von Rechtsnormen und -wirklichkeit in der Russländischen Föderation von 1991 bis 2009 | Mit einem Vorwort von Alexander Blankenagel | ISBN 978-3-8382-0292-1

107 *Philipp Herzog* | Sozialistische Völkerfreundschaft, nationaler Widerstand oder harmloser Zeitvertreib? Zur politischen Funktion der Volkskunst im sowjetischen Estland | Mit einem Vorwort von Andreas Kappeler | ISBN 978-3-8382-0216-7

108 *Marlène Laruelle (Ed.)* | Russian Nationalism, Foreign Policy, and Identity Debates in Putin's Russia. New Ideological Patterns after the Orange Revolution | ISBN 978-3-8382-0325-6

109 *Michail Logvinov* | Russlands Kampf gegen den internationalen Terrorismus. Eine kritische Bestandsaufnahme des Bekämpfungsansatzes | Mit einem Geleitwort von Hans-Henning Schröder und einem Vorwort von Eckhard Jesse | ISBN 978-3-8382-0329-4

110 *John B. Dunlop* | The Moscow Bombings of September 1999. Examinations of Russian Terrorist Attacks at the Onset of Vladimir Putin's Rule | Second, Revised and Expanded Edition | ISBN 978-3-8382-0388-1

111 *Андрей А. Ковалёв* | Свидетельство из-за кулис российской политики I. Можно ли делать добро из зла? (Воспоминания и размышления о последних советских и первых послесоветских годах) | With a foreword by Peter Reddaway | ISBN 978-3-8382-0302-7

112 *Андрей А. Ковалёв* | Свидетельство из-за кулис российской политики II. Угроза для себя и окружающих (Наблюдения и предостережения относительно происходящего после 2000 г.) | ISBN 978-3-8382-0303-4

113 *Bernd Kappenberg* | Zeichen setzen für Europa. Der Gebrauch europäischer lateinischer Sonderzeichen in der deutschen Öffentlichkeit | Mit einem Vorwort von Peter Schlobinski | ISBN 978-3-89821-749-1

114 *Ivo Mijnssen* | The Quest for an Ideal Youth in Putin's Russia I. Back to Our Future! History, Modernity, and Patriotism according to Nashi, 2005-2013 | With a foreword by Jeronim Perović | Second, Revised and Expanded Edition | ISBN 978-3-8382-0368-3

115 *Jussi Lassila* | The Quest for an Ideal Youth in Putin's Russia II. The Search for Distinctive Conformism in the Political Communication of Nashi, 2005-2009 | With a foreword by Kirill Postoutenko | Second, Revised and Expanded Edition | ISBN 978-3-8382-0415-4

116 *Valerio Trabandt* | Neue Nachbarn, gute Nachbarschaft? Die EU als internationaler Akteur am Beispiel ihrer Demokratieförderung in Belarus und der Ukraine 2004-2009 | Mit einem Vorwort von Jutta Joachim | ISBN 978-3-8382-0437-6

117 *Fabian Pfeiffer* | Estlands Außen- und Sicherheitspolitik I. Der estnische Atlantizismus nach der wiedererlangten Unabhängigkeit 1991-2004 | Mit einem Vorwort von Helmut Hubel | ISBN 978-3-8382-0127-6

118 *Jana Podßuweit* | Estlands Außen- und Sicherheitspolitik II. Handlungsoptionen eines Kleinstaates im Rahmen seiner EU-Mitgliedschaft (2004-2008) | Mit einem Vorwort von Helmut Hubel | ISBN 978-3-8382-0440-6

119 *Karin Pointner* | Estlands Außen- und Sicherheitspolitik III. Eine gedächtnispolitische Analyse estnischer Entwicklungskooperation 2006-2010 | Mit einem Vorwort von Karin Liebhart | ISBN 978-3-8382-0435-2

120 *Ruslana Vovk* | Die Offenheit der ukrainischen Verfassung für das Völkerrecht und die europäische Integration | Mit einem Vorwort von Alexander Blankenagel | ISBN 978-3-8382-0481-9

121 *Mykhaylo Banakh* | Die Relevanz der Zivilgesellschaft bei den postkommunistischen Transformationsprozessen in mittel- und osteuropäischen Ländern. Das Beispiel der spät- und postsowjetischen Ukraine 1986-2009 | Mit einem Vorwort von Gerhard Simon | ISBN 978-3-8382-0499-4

122 *Michael Moser* | Language Policy and the Discourse on Languages in Ukraine under President Viktor Yanukovych (25 February 2010–28 October 2012) | ISBN 978-3-8382-0497-0 (Paperback edition) | ISBN 978-3-8382-0507-6 (Hardcover edition)

123 *Nicole Krome* | Russischer Netzwerkkapitalismus Restrukturierungsprozesse in der Russischen Föderation am Beispiel des Luftfahrtunternehmens „Aviastar" | Mit einem Vorwort von Petra Stykow | ISBN 978-3-8382-0534-2

124 *David R. Marples* | 'Our Glorious Past'. Lukashenka's Belarus and the Great Patriotic War | ISBN 978-3-8382-0574-8 (Paperback edition) | ISBN 978-3-8382-0675-2 (Hardcover edition)

125 *Ulf Walther* | Russlands „neuer Adel". Die Macht des Geheimdienstes von Gorbatschow bis Putin | Mit einem Vorwort von Hans-Georg Wieck | ISBN 978-3-8382-0584-7

126 *Simon Geissbühler (Hrsg.)* | Kiew – Revolution 3.0. Der Euromaidan 2013/14 und die Zukunftsperspektiven der Ukraine | ISBN 978-3-8382-0581-6 (Paperback edition) | ISBN 978-3-8382-0681-3 (Hardcover edition)

127 *Andrey Makarychev* | Russia and the EU in a Multipolar World. Discourses, Identities, Norms | With a foreword by Klaus Segbers | ISBN 978-3-8382-0629-5

128 *Roland Scharff* | Kasachstan als postsowjetischer Wohlfahrtsstaat. Die Transformation des sozialen Schutzsystems | Mit einem Vorwort von Joachim Ahrens | ISBN 978-3-8382-0622-6

129 *Katja Grupp* | Bild Lücke Deutschland. Kaliningrader Studierende sprechen über Deutschland | Mit einem Vorwort von Martin Schulz | ISBN 978-3-8382-0552-6

130 *Konstantin Sheiko, Stephen Brown* | History as Therapy. Alternative History and Nationalist Imaginings in Russia, 1991-2014 | ISBN 978-3-8382-0665-3

131 *Elisa Kriza* | Alexander Solzhenitsyn: Cold War Icon, Gulag Author, Russian Nationalist? A Study of the Western Reception of his Literary Writings, Historical Interpretations, and Political Ideas | With a foreword by Andrei Rogatchevski | ISBN 978-3-8382-0589-2 (Paperback edition) | ISBN 978-3-8382-0690-5 (Hardcover edition)

132 *Serghei Golunov* | The Elephant in the Room. Corruption and Cheating in Russian Universities | ISBN 978-3-8382-0570-0

133 *Manja Hussner, Rainer Arnold (Hgg.)* | Verfassungsgerichtsbarkeit in Zentralasien I. Sammlung von Verfassungstexten | ISBN 978-3-8382-0595-3

134 *Nikolay Mitrokhin* | Die „Russische Partei". Die Bewegung der russischen Nationalisten in der UdSSR 1953-1985 | Aus dem Russischen übertragen von einem Übersetzerteam unter der Leitung von Larisa Schippel | ISBN 978-3-8382-0024-8

135 *Manja Hussner, Rainer Arnold (Hgg.)* | Verfassungsgerichtsbarkeit in Zentralasien II. Sammlung von Verfassungstexten | ISBN 978-3-8382-0597-7

136 *Manfred Zeller* | Das sowjetische Fieber. Fußballfans im poststalinistischen Vielvölkerreich | Mit einem Vorwort von Nikolaus Katzer | ISBN 978-3-8382-0757-5

137 *Kristin Schreiter* | Stellung und Entwicklungspotential zivilgesellschaftlicher Gruppen in Russland. Menschenrechtsorganisationen im Vergleich | ISBN 978-3-8382-0673-8

138 *David R. Marples, Frederick V. Mills (Eds.)* | Ukraine's Euromaidan. Analyses of a Civil Revolution | ISBN 978-3-8382-0660-8

139 *Bernd Kappenberg* | Setting Signs for Europe. Why Diacritics Matter for European Integration | With a foreword by Peter Schlobinski | ISBN 978-3-8382-0663-9

140 *René Lenz* | Internationalisierung, Kooperation und Transfer. Externe bildungspolitische Akteure in der Russischen Föderation | Mit einem Vorwort von Frank Ettrich | ISBN 978-3-8382-0751-3

141 *Juri Plusnin, Yana Zausaeva, Natalia Zhidkevich, Artemy Pozanenko* | Wandering Workers. Mores, Behavior, Way of Life, and Political Status of Domestic Russian Labor Migrants | Translated by Julia Kazantseva | ISBN 978-3-8382-0653-0

142 *David J. Smith (Eds.)* | Latvia – A Work in Progress? 100 Years of State- and Nation-Building | ISBN 978-3-8382-0648-6

143 *Инна Чувычкина (ред.)* | Экспортные нефте- и газопроводы на постсоветском пространстве. Анализ трубопроводной политики в свете теории международных отношений | ISBN 978-3-8382-0822-0

144 *Johann Zajaczkowski* | Russland – eine pragmatische Großmacht? Eine rollentheoretische Untersuchung russischer Außenpolitik am Beispiel der Zusammenarbeit mit den USA nach 9/11 und des Georgienkrieges von 2008 | Mit einem Vorwort von Siegfried Schieder | ISBN 978-3-8382-0837-4

145 *Boris Popivanov* | Changing Images of the Left in Bulgaria. The Challenge of Post-Communism in the Early 21st Century | ISBN 978-3-8382-0667-7

146 *Lenka Krátká* | A History of the Czechoslovak Ocean Shipping Company 1948-1989. How a Small, Landlocked Country Ran Maritime Business During the Cold War | ISBN 978-3-8382-0666-0

147 *Alexander Sergunin* | Explaining Russian Foreign Policy Behavior. Theory and Practice | ISBN 978-3-8382-0752-0

148 *Darya Malyutina* | Migrant Friendships in a Super-Diverse City. Russian-Speakers and their Social Relationships in London in the 21st Century | With a foreword by Claire Dwyer | ISBN 978-3-8382-0652-3

149 *Alexander Sergunin, Valery Konyshev* | Russia in the Arctic. Hard or Soft Power? | ISBN 978-3-8382-0753-7

150 *John J. Maresca* | Helsinki Revisited. A Key U.S. Negotiator's Memoirs on the Development of the CSCE into the OSCE | With a foreword by Hafiz Pashayev | ISBN 978-3-8382-0852-7

151 *Jardar Østbø* | The New Third Rome. Readings of a Russian Nationalist Myth | With a foreword by Pål Kolstø | ISBN 978-3-8382-0870-1

152 *Simon Kordonsky* | Socio-Economic Foundations of the Russian Post-Soviet Regime. The Resource-Based Economy and Estate-Based Social Structure of Contemporary Russia | With a foreword by Svetlana Barsukova | ISBN 978-3-8382-0775-9

153 *Duncan Leitch* | Assisting Reform in Post-Communist Ukraine 2000–2012. The Illusions of Donors and the Disillusion of Beneficiaries | With a foreword by Kataryna Wolczuk | ISBN 978-3-8382-0844-2

154 *Abel Polese* | Limits of a Post-Soviet State. How Informality Replaces, Renegotiates, and Reshapes Governance in Contemporary Ukraine | With a foreword by Colin Williams | ISBN 978-3-8382-0845-9

155 *Mikhail Suslov (Ed.)* | Digital Orthodoxy in the Post-Soviet World. The Russian Orthodox Church and Web 2.0 | With a foreword by Father Cyril Hovorun | ISBN 978-3-8382-0871-8

156 *Leonid Luks* | Zwei „Sonderwege"? Russisch-deutsche Parallelen und Kontraste (1917-2014). Vergleichende Essays | ISBN 978-3-8382-0823-7

157 *Vladimir V. Karacharovskiy, Ovsey I. Shkaratan, Gordey A. Yastrebov* | Towards a New Russian Work Culture. Can Western Companies and Expatriates Change Russian Society? | With a foreword by Elena N. Danilova | Translated by Julia Kazantseva | ISBN 978-3-8382-0902-9

158 *Edmund Griffiths* | Aleksandr Prokhanov and Post-Soviet Esotericism | ISBN 978-3-8382-0963-0

159 *Timm Beichelt, Susann Worschech (Eds.)* | Transnational Ukraine? Networks and Ties that Influence(d) Contemporary Ukraine | ISBN 978-3-8382-0944-9

160 *Mieste Hotopp-Riecke* | Die Tataren der Krim zwischen Assimilation und Selbstbehauptung. Der Aufbau des krimtatarischen Bildungswesens nach Deportation und Heimkehr (1990-2005) | Mit einem Vorwort von Swetlana Czerwonnaja | ISBN 978-3-89821-940-2

161 *Olga Bertelsen (Ed.)* | Revolution and War in Contemporary Ukraine. The Challenge of Change | ISBN 978-3-8382-1016-2

162 *Natalya Ryabinska* | Ukraine's Post-Communist Mass Media. Between Capture and Commercialization | With a foreword by Marta Dyczok | ISBN 978-3-8382-1011-7

163 *Alexandra Cotofana, James M. Nyce (Eds.)* | Religion and Magic in Socialist and Post-Socialist Contexts. Historic and Ethnographic Case Studies of Orthodoxy, Heterodoxy, and Alternative Spirituality | With a foreword by Patrick L. Michelson | ISBN 978-3-8382-0989-0

164 *Nozima Akhrarkhodjaeva* | The Instrumentalisation of Mass Media in Electoral Authoritarian Regimes. Evidence from Russia's Presidential Election Campaigns of 2000 and 2008 | ISBN 978-3-8382-1013-1

165 *Yulia Krasheninnikova* | Informal Healthcare in Contemporary Russia. Sociographic Essays on the Post-Soviet Infrastructure for Alternative Healing Practices | ISBN 978-3-8382-0970-8

166 *Peter Kaiser* | Das Schachbrett der Macht. Die Handlungsspielräume eines sowjetischen Funktionärs unter Stalin am Beispiel des Generalsekretärs des Komsomol Aleksandr Kosarev (1929-1938) | Mit einem Vorwort von Dietmar Neutatz | ISBN 978-3-8382-1052-0

167 *Oksana Kim* | The Effects and Implications of Kazakhstan's Adoption of International Financial Reporting Standards. A Resource Dependence Perspective | With a foreword by Svetlana Vlady | ISBN 978-3-8382-0987-6

168 *Anna Sanina* | Patriotic Education in Contemporary Russia. Sociological Studies in the Making of the Post-Soviet Citizen | With a foreword by Anna Oldfield | ISBN 978-3-8382-0993-7

169 *Rudolf Wolters* | Spezialist in Sibirien Faksimile der 1933 erschienenen ersten Ausgabe | Mit einem Vorwort von Dmitrij Chmelnizki | ISBN 978-3-8382-0515-1

170 *Michal Vít, Magdalena M. Baran (Eds.)* | Transregional versus National Perspectives on Contemporary Central European History. Studies on the Building of Nation-States and Their Cooperation in the 20th and 21st Century | With a foreword by Petr Vágner | ISBN 978-3-8382-1015-5

171 *Philip Gamaghelyan* | Conflict Resolution Beyond the International Relations Paradigm. Evolving Designs as a Transformative Practice in Nagorno-Karabakh and Syria | With a foreword by Susan Allen | ISBN 978-3-8382-1057-5

172 *Maria Shagina* | Joining a Prestigious Club. Cooperation with Europarties and Its Impact on Party Development in Georgia, Moldova, and Ukraine 2004–2015 | With a foreword by Kataryna Wolczuk | ISBN 978-3-8382-1084-1

173 *Alexandra Cotofana, James M. Nyce (Eds.)* | Religion and Magic in Socialist and Post-Socialist Contexts II. Baltic, Eastern European, and Post-USSR Case Studies | With a foreword by Anita Stasulane | ISBN 978-3-8382-0990-6

174 *Barbara Kunz* | Kind Words, Cruise Missiles, and Everything in Between. The Use of Power Resources in U.S. Policies towards Poland, Ukraine, and Belarus 1989–2008 | With a foreword by William Hill | ISBN 978-3-8382-1065-0

175 *Eduard Klein* | Bildungskorruption in Russland und der Ukraine. Eine komparative Analyse der Performanz staatlicher Antikorruptionsmaßnahmen im Hochschulsektor am Beispiel universitärer Aufnahmeprüfungen | Mit einem Vorwort von Heiko Pleines | ISBN 978-3-8382-0995-1

176 *Markus Soldner* | Politischer Kapitalismus im postsowjetischen Russland. Die politische, wirtschaftliche und mediale Transformation in den 1990er Jahren | Mit einem Vorwort von Wolfgang Ismayr | ISBN 978-3-8382-1222-7

177 *Anton Oleinik* | Building Ukraine from Within. A Sociological, Institutional, and Economic Analysis of a Nation-State in the Making | ISBN 978-3-8382-1150-3

178 *Peter Rollberg, Marlene Laruelle (Eds.)* | Mass Media in the Post-Soviet World. Market Forces, State Actors, and Political Manipulation in the Informational Environment after Communism | ISBN 978-3-8382-1116-9

179 *Mikhail Minakov* | Development and Dystopia. Studies in Post-Soviet Ukraine and Eastern Europe | With a foreword by Alexander Etkind | ISBN 978-3-8382-1112-1

180 *Aijan Sharshenova* | The European Union's Democracy Promotion in Central Asia. A Study of Political Interests, Influence, and Development in Kazakhstan and Kyrgyzstan in 2007–2013 | With a foreword by Gordon Crawford | ISBN 978-3-8382-1151-0

181 *Andrey Makarychev, Alexandra Yatsyk (Eds.)* | Boris Nemtsov and Russian Politics. Power and Resistance | With a foreword by Zhanna Nemtsova | ISBN 978-3-8382-1122-0

182 *Sophie Falsini* | The Euromaidan's Effect on Civil Society. Why and How Ukrainian Social Capital Increased after the Revolution of Dignity | With a foreword by Susann Worschech | ISBN 978-3-8382-1131-2

183 *Valentyna Romanova, Andreas Umland (Eds.)* | Ukraine's Decentralization. Challenges and Implications of the Local Governance Reform after the Euromaidan Revolution | ISBN 978-3-8382-1162-6

184 *Leonid Luks* | A Fateful Triangle. Essays on Contemporary Russian, German and Polish History | ISBN 978-3-8382-1143-5

185 *John B. Dunlop* | The February 2015 Assassination of Boris Nemtsov and the Flawed Trial of his Alleged Killers. An Exploration of Russia's "Crime of the 21st Century" | ISBN 978-3-8382-1188-6

186 *Vasile Rotaru* | Russia, the EU, and the Eastern Partnership. Building Bridges or Digging Trenches? | ISBN 978-3-8382-1134-3

187 *Marina Lebedeva* | Russian Studies of International Relations. From the Soviet Past to the Post-Cold-War Present | With a foreword by Andrei P. Tsygankov | ISBN 978-3-8382-0851-0

188 *Tomasz Stępniewski, George Soroka (Eds.)* | Ukraine after Maidan. Revisiting Domestic and Regional Security | ISBN 978-3-8382-1075-9

189 *Petar Cholakov* | Ethnic Entrepreneurs Unmasked. Political Institutions and Ethnic Conflicts in Contemporary Bulgaria | ISBN 978-3-8382-1189-3

190 *A. Salem, G. Hazeldine, D. Morgan (Eds.)* | Higher Education in Post-Communist States. Comparative and Sociological Perspectives | ISBN 978-3-8382-1183-1

191 *Igor Torbakov* | After Empire. Nationalist Imagination and Symbolic Politics in Russia and Eurasia in the Twentieth and Twenty-First Century | With a foreword by Serhii Plokhy | ISBN 978-3-8382-1217-3

192 *Aleksandr Burakovskiy* | Jewish-Ukrainian Relations in Late and Post-Soviet Ukraine. Articles, Lectures and Essays from 1986 to 2016 | ISBN 978-3-8382-1210-4

193 *Natalia Shapovalova, Olga Burlyuk (Eds.)* | Civil Society in Post-Euromaidan Ukraine. From Revolution to Consolidation | With a foreword by Richard Youngs | ISBN 978-3-8382-1216-6

194 *Franz Preissler* | Positionsverteidigung, Imperialismus oder Irredentismus? Russland und die „Russischsprachigen", 1991–2015 | ISBN 978-3-8382-1262-3

195 *Marian Madeła* | Der Reformprozess in der Ukraine 2014-2017. Eine Fallstudie zur Reform der öffentlichen Verwaltung | Mit einem Vorwort von Martin Malek | ISBN 978-3-8382-1266-1

196 *Anke Giesen* | „Wie kann denn der Sieger ein Verbrecher sein?" Eine diskursanalytische Untersuchung der russlandweiten Debatte über Konzept und Verstaatlichungsprozess der Lagergedenkstätte „Perm'-36" im Ural | ISBN 978-3-8382-1284-5

197 *Victoria Leukavets* | The Integration Policies of Belarus and Ukraine vis-à-vis the EU and Russia. A Comparative Analysis Through the Prism of a Two-Level Game Approach | ISBN 978-3-8382-1247-0

198 *Oksana Kim* | The Development and Challenges of Russian Corporate Governance I. The Roles and Functions of Boards of Directors | With a foreword by Sheila M. Puffer | ISBN 978-3-8382-1287-6

199 *Thomas D. Grant* | International Law and the Post-Soviet Space I. Essays on Chechnya and the Baltic States | With a foreword by Stephen M. Schwebel | ISBN 978-3-8382-1279-1

200 *Thomas D. Grant* | International Law and the Post-Soviet Space II. Essays on Ukraine, Intervention, and Non-Proliferation | ISBN 978-3-8382-1280-7

201 *Slavomír Michálek, Michal Štefansky* | The Age of Fear. The Cold War and Its Influence on Czechoslovakia 1945–1968 | ISBN 978-3-8382-1285-2

202 *Iulia-Sabina Joja* | Romania's Strategic Culture 1990–2014. Continuity and Change in a Post-Communist Country's Evolution of National Interests and Security Policies | With a foreword by Heiko Biehl | ISBN 978-3-8382-1286-9

203 *Andrei Rogatchevski, Yngvar B. Steinholt, Arve Hansen, David-Emil Wickström* | War of Songs. Popular Music and Recent Russia-Ukraine Relations | With a foreword by Artemy Troitsky | ISBN 978-3-8382-1173-2

204 *Maria Lipman (Ed.)* | Russian Voices on Post-Crimea Russia. An Almanac of Counterpoint Essays from 2015–2018 | ISBN 978-3-8382-1251-7

205 *Ksenia Maksimovtsova* | Language Conflicts in Contemporary Estonia, Latvia, and Ukraine. A Comparative Exploration of Discourses in Post-Soviet Russian-Language Digital Media | With a foreword by Ammon Cheskin | ISBN 978-3-8382-1282-1

206 *Michal Vít* | The EU's Impact on Identity Formation in East-Central Europe between 2004 and 2013. Perceptions of the Nation and Europe in Political Parties of the Czech Republic, Poland, and Slovakia | With a foreword by Andrea Pető | ISBN 978-3-8382-1275-3

207 *Per A. Rudling* | Tarnished Heroes. The Organization of Ukrainian Nationalists in the Memory Politics of Post-Soviet Ukraine | ISBN 978-3-8382-0999-9

208 *Kaja Gadowska, Peter Solomon (Eds.)* | Legal Change in Post-Communist States. Progress, Reversions, Explanations | ISBN 978-3-8382-1312-5

209 *Pawel Kowal, Georges Mink, Iwona Reichardt (Eds.)* | Three Revolutions: Mobilization and Change in Contemporary Ukraine I. Theoretical Aspects and Analyses on Religion, Memory, and Identity | ISBN 978-3-8382-1321-7

210 *Pawel Kowal, Georges Mink, Adam Reichardt, Iwona Reichardt (Eds.)* | Three Revolutions: Mobilization and Change in Contemporary Ukraine II. An Oral History of the Revolution on Granite, Orange Revolution, and Revolution of Dignity | ISBN 978-3-8382-1323-1

211 *Li Bennich-Björkman, Sergiy Kurbatov (Eds.)* | When the Future Came. The Collapse of the USSR and the Emergence of National Memory in Post-Soviet History Textbooks | ISBN 978-3-8382-1335-4

212 *Olga R. Gulina* | Migration as a (Geo-)Political Challenge in the Post-Soviet Space. Border Regimes, Policy Choices, Visa Agendas | With a foreword by Nils Muižnieks | ISBN 978-3-8382-1338-5

213 *Sanna Turoma, Kaarina Aitamurto, Slobodanka Vladiv-Glover (Eds.)* | Religion, Expression, and Patriotism in Russia. Essays on Post-Soviet Society and the State. ISBN 978-3-8382-1346-0

214 *Vasif Huseynov* | Geopolitical Rivalries in the "Common Neighborhood". Russia's Conflict with the West, Soft Power, and Neoclassical Realism | With a foreword by Nicholas Ross Smith | ISBN 978-3-8382-1277-7

215 *Mikhail Suslov* | Geopolitical Imagination. Ideology and Utopia in Post-Soviet Russia | With a foreword by Mark Bassin | ISBN 978-3-8382-1361-3

216 *Alexander Etkind, Mikhail Minakov (Eds.)* | Ideology after Union. Political Doctrines, Discourses, and Debates in Post-Soviet Societies | ISBN 978-3-8382-1388-0

217 *Jakob Mischke, Oleksandr Zabirko (Hgg.)* | Protestbewegungen im langen Schatten des Kreml. Aufbruch und Resignation in Russland und der Ukraine | ISBN 978-3-8382-0926-5

218 *Oksana Huss* | How Corruption and Anti-Corruption Policies Sustain Hybrid Regimes. Strategies of Political Domination under Ukraine's Presidents in 1994-2014 | With a foreword by Tobias Debiel and Andrea Gawrich | ISBN 978-3-8382-1430-6

219 *Dmitry Travin, Vladimir Gel'man, Otar Marganiya* | The Russian Path. Ideas, Interests, Institutions, Illusions | With a foreword by Vladimir Ryzhkov | ISBN 978-3-8382-1421-4

220 *Gergana Dimova* | Political Uncertainty. A Comparative Exploration | With a foreword by Todor Yalamov and Rumena Filipova | ISBN 978-3-8382-1385-9

221 *Torben Waschke* | Russland in Transition. Geopolitik zwischen Raum, Identität und Machtinteressen | Mit einem Vorwort von Andreas Dittmann | ISBN 978-3-8382-1480-1

222 *Steven Jobbitt, Zsolt Bottlik, Marton Berki (Eds.)* | Power and Identity in the Post-Soviet Realm. Geographies of Ethnicity and Nationality after 1991 | ISBN 978-3-8382-1399-6

223 *Daria Buteiko* | Erinnerungsort. Ort des Gedenkens, der Erholung oder der Einkehr? Kommunismus-Erinnerung am Beispiel der Gedenkstätte Berliner Mauer sowie des Soloveckij-Klosters und -Museumsparks | ISBN 978-3-8382-1367-5

224 *Olga Bertelsen (Ed.)* | Russian Active Measures. Yesterday, Today, Tomorrow | With a foreword by Jan Goldman | ISBN 978-3-8382-1529-7

225 *David Mandel* | "Optimizing" Higher Education in Russia. University Teachers and their Union "Universitetskaya solidarnost'" | ISBN 978-3-8382-1519-8

226 *Mikhail Minakov, Gwendolyn Sasse, Daria Isachenko (Eds.)* | Post-Soviet Secessionism. Nation-Building and State-Failure after Communism | ISBN 978-3-8382-1385-9

227 *Jakob Hauter (Ed.)* | Civil War? Interstate War? Hybrid War? Dimensions and Interpretations of the Donbas Conflict in 2014–2020 | With a foreword by Andrew Wilson | ISBN 978-3-8382-1383-5

228 *Tima T. Moldogaziev, Gene A. Brewer, J. Edward Kellough (Eds.)* | Public Policy and Politics in Georgia. Lessons from Post-Soviet Transition | With a foreword by Dan Durning | ISBN 978-3-8382-1535-8

229 *Oxana Schmies (Ed.)* | NATO's Enlargement and Russia. A Strategic Challenge in the Past and Future | With a foreword by Vladimir Kara-Murza | ISBN 978-3-8382-1478-8

230 *Christopher Ford* | Ukapisme – Une Gauche perdue. Le marxisme anti-colonial dans la révolution ukrainienne 1917-1925 | Avec une préface de Vincent Présumey | ISBN 978-3-8382-0899-2

231 *Anna Kutkina* | Between Lenin and Bandera. Decommunization and Multivocality in Post-Euromaidan Ukraine | With a foreword by Juri Mykkänen | ISBN 978-3-8382-1506-8

232 *Lincoln E. Flake* | Defending the Faith. The Russian Orthodox Church and the Demise of Religious Pluralism | With a foreword by Peter Martland | ISBN 978-3-8382-1378-1

233 *Nikoloz Samkharadze* | Russia's Recognition of the Independence of Abkhazia and South Ossetia. Analysis of a Deviant Case in Moscow's Foreign Policy | With a foreword by Neil MacFarlane | ISBN 978-3-8382-1414-6

234 *Arve Hansen* | Urban Protest. A Spatial Perspective on Kyiv, Minsk, and Moscow | With a foreword by Julie Wilhelmsen | ISBN 978-3-8382-1495-5

235 *Eleonora Narvselius, Julie Fedor (Eds.)* | Diversity in the East-Central European Borderlands. Memories, Cityscapes, People | ISBN 978-3-8382-1523-5

236 *Regina Elsner* | The Russian Orthodox Church and Modernity. A Historical and Theological Investigation into Eastern Christianity between Unity and Plurality | With a foreword by Mikhail Suslov | ISBN 978-3-8382-1568-6

237 *Bo Petersson* | The Putin Predicament. Problems of Legitimacy and Succession in Russia | With a foreword by J. Paul Goode | ISBN 978-3-8382-1050-6

238 *Jonathan Otto Pohl* | The Years of Great Silence. The Deportation, Special Settlement, and Mobilization into the Labor Army of Ethnic Germans in the USSR, 1941–1955 | ISBN 978-3-8382-1630-0

239 *Mikhail Minakov (Ed.)* | Inventing Majorities. Ideological Creativity in Post-Soviet Societies | ISBN 978-3-8382-1641-6

240 *Robert M. Cutler* | Soviet and Post-Soviet Foreign Policies I. East-South Relations and the Political Economy of the Communist Bloc, 1971–1991 | With a foreword by Roger E. Kanet | ISBN 978-3-8382-1654-6

241 *Izabella Agardi* | On the Verge of History. Life Stories of Rural Women from Serbia, Romania, and Hungary, 1920–2020 | With a foreword by Andrea Pető | ISBN 978-3-8382-1602-7

242 *Sebastian Schäffer (Ed.)* | Ukraine in Central and Eastern Europe. Kyiv's Foreign Affairs and the International Relations of the Post-Communist Region | With a foreword by Pavlo Klimkin and Andreas Umland| ISBN 978-3-8382-1615-7

243 *Volodymyr Dubrovskyi, Kalman Mizsei, Mychailo Wynnyckyj (Eds.)* | Eight Years after the Revolution of Dignity. What Has Changed in Ukraine during 2013–2021? | With a foreword by Yaroslav Hrytsak | ISBN 978-3-8382-1560-0

244 *Rumena Filipova* | Constructing the Limits of Europe Identity and Foreign Policy in Poland, Bulgaria, and Russia since 1989 | With forewords by Harald Wydra and Gergana Yankova-Dimova | ISBN 978-3-8382-1649-2

245 *Oleksandra Keudel* | How Patronal Networks Shape Opportunities for Local Citizen Participation in a Hybrid Regime A Comparative Analysis of Five Cities in Ukraine | With a foreword by Sabine Kropp | ISBN 978-3-8382-1671-3

246 *Jan Claas Behrends, Thomas Lindenberger, Pavel Kolar (Eds.)* | Violence after Stalin Institutions, Practices, and Everyday Life in the Soviet Bloc 1953–1989 | ISBN 978-3-8382-1637-9

247 *Leonid Luks* | Macht und Ohnmacht der Utopien Essays zur Geschichte Russlands im 20. und 21. Jahrhundert | ISBN 978-3-8382-1677-5

248 *Iuliia Barshadska* | Brüssel zwischen Kyjiw und Moskau Das auswärtige Handeln der Europäischen Union im ukrainisch-russischen Konflikt 2014-2019 | Mit einem Vorwort von Olaf Leiße | ISBN 978-3-8382-1667-6

249 *Valentyna Romanova* | Decentralisation and Multilevel Elections in Ukraine Reform Dynamics and Party Politics in 2010–2021 | With a foreword by Kimitaka Matsuzato | ISBN 978-3-8382-1700-0

250 *Alexander Motyl* | National Questions. Theoretical Reflections on Nations and Nationalism in Eastern Europe | ISBN 978-3-8382-1675-1

251 *Marc Dietrich* | A Cosmopolitan Model for Peacebuilding. The Ukrainian Cases of Crimea and the Donbas | With a foreword by Rémi Baudouï | ISBN 978-3-8382-1687-4

252 *Eduard Baidaus* | An Unsettled Nation. Moldova in the Geopolitics of Russia, Romania, and Ukraine | With forewords by John-Paul Himka and David R. Marples | ISBN 978-3-8382-1582-2

253 *Igor Okunev, Petr Oskolkov (Eds.)* | Transforming the Administrative Matryoshka. The Reform of Autonomous Okrugs in the Russian Federation, 2003–2008 | With a foreword by Vladimir Zorin | ISBN 978-3-8382-1721-5

254 *Winfried Schneider-Deters* | Ukraine's Fateful Years 2013–2019. Vol. I: The Popular Uprising in Winter 2013/2014 | ISBN 978-3-8382-1725-3

255 *Winfried Schneider-Deters* | Ukraine's Fateful Years 2013–2019. Vol. II: The Annexation of Crimea and the War in Donbas | ISBN 978-3-8382-1726-0

256 *Robert M. Cutler* | Soviet and Post-Soviet Russian Foreign Policies II. East-West Relations in Europe and the Political Economy of the Communist Bloc, 1971–1991 | With a foreword by Roger E. Kanet | ISBN 978-3-8382-1727-7

257 *Robert M. Cutler* | Soviet and Post-Soviet Russian Foreign Policies III. East-West Relations in Europe and Eurasia in the Post-Cold War Transition, 1991–2001 | With a foreword by Roger E. Kanet | ISBN 978-3-8382-1728-4

258 *Paweł Kowal, Iwona Reichardt, Kateryna Pryshchepa (Eds.)* | Three Revolutions: Mobilization and Change in Contemporary Ukraine III. Archival Records and Historical Sources on the 1990 Revolution on Granite | ISBN 978-3-8382-1376-7

259 *Mikhail Minakov (Ed.)* | Philosophy Unchained. Developments in Post-Soviet Philosophical Thought. | With a foreword by Christopher Donohue | ISBN 978-3-8382-1768-0

260 *David Dalton* | The Ukrainian Oligarchy After the Euromaidan. How Ukraine's Political Economy Regime Survived the Crisis | With a foreword by Andrew Wilson | ISBN 978-3-8382-1740-6

261 *Andreas Heinemann-Grüder (Ed.)* | Who Are the Fighters? Irregular Armed Groups in the Russian-Ukrainian War since 2014 | ISBN 978-3-8382-1777-2

262 *Taras Kuzio (Ed.)* | Russian Disinformation and Western Scholarship. Bias and Prejudice in Journalistic, Expert, and Academic Analyses of East European, Russian and Eurasian Affairs | ISBN 978-3-8382-1685-0

263 *Darius Furmonavicius* | LithuaniaTransforms the West. Lithuania's Liberation from Soviet Occupation and the Enlargement of NATO (1988–2022) | With a foreword by Vytautas Landsbergis | ISBN 978-3-8382-1779-6

264 *Dirk Dalberg* | Politisches Denken im tschechoslowakischen Dissens. Egon Bondy, Miroslav Kusý, Milan Šimečka und Petr Uhl (1968-1989) | ISBN 978-3-8382-1318-7

265 *Леонид Люкс* | К столетию «философского парохода». Мыслители «первой» русской эмиграции о русской революции и о тоталитарных соблазнах XX века | ISBN 978-3-8382-1775-8

266 *Daviti Mtchedlishvili* | The EU and the South Caucasus. European Neighborhood Policies between Eclecticism and Pragmatism, 1991-2021 | With a foreword by Nicholas Ross Smith | ISBN 978-3-8382-1735-2

267 *Bohdan Harasymiw* | Post-Euromaidan Ukraine. Domestic Power Struggles and War of National Survival in 2014–2022 | ISBN 978-3-8382-1798-7

268 *Nadiia Koval, Denys Tereshchenko (Eds.)* | Russian Cultural Diplomacy under Putin. Rossotrudnichestvo, the "Russkiy Mir" Foundation, and the Gorchakov Fund in 2007–2022 | ISBN 978-3-8382-1801-4

269 *Izabela Kazejak* | Jews in Post-War Wrocław and L'viv. Official Policies and Local Responses in Comparative Perspective, 1945-1970s | ISBN 978-3-8382-1802-1

270 *Jakob Hauter* | Russia's Overlooked Invasion. The Causes of the 2014 Outbreak of War in Ukraine's Donbas | With a foreword by Hiroaki Kuromiya | ISBN 978-3-8382-1803-8

271 *Anton Shekhovtsov* | Russian Political Warfare. Essays on Kremlin Propaganda in Europe and the Neighbourhood, 2020-2023 | With a foreword by Nathalie Loiseau | ISBN 978-3-8382-1821-2

272 *Андреа Пето* | Насилие и Молчание. Красная армия в Венгрии во Второй Мировой войне | ISBN 978-3-8382-1636-2

273 *Winfried Schneider-Deters* | Russia's War in Ukraine. Debates on Peace, Fascism, and War Crimes, 2022–2023 | With a foreword by Klaus Gestwa | ISBN 978-3-8382-1876-2

274 *Rasmus Nilsson* | Uncanny Allies. Russia and Belarus on the Edge, 2012-2024 | ISBN 978-3-8382-1288-3

275 *Anton Grushetskyi, Volodymyr Paniotto* | War and the Transformation of Ukrainian Society (2022–23). Empirical Evidence | ISBN 978-3-8382-1944-8

276 *Christian Kaunert, Alex MacKenzie, Adrien Nonjon (Eds.)* | In the Eye of the Storm. Origins, Ideology, and Controversies of the Azov Brigade, 2014–23 | ISBN 978-3-8382-1750-5

277 *Gian Marco Moisé* | The House Always Wins. The Corrupt Strategies that Shaped Kazakh Oil Politics and Business in the Nazarbayev Era | With a foreword by Alena Ledeneva | ISBN 978-3-8382-1917-2

278 *Mikhail Minakov* | The Post-Soviet Human | Philosophical Reflections on Social History after the End of Communism | ISBN 978-3-8382-1943-1

279 *Natalia Kudriavtseva, Debra A. Friedman (Eds.)* | Language and Power in Ukraine and Kazakhstan. Essays on Education, Ideology, Literature, Practice, and the Media | With a foreword by Laada Bilaniuk | ISBN 978-3-8382-1949-3

280 *Georges Mink, Iwona Reichardt (Eds.)* | The End of the Soviet World? Essays on Post-Communist Political and Social Change | With an afterword by Richardt Butterwick | ISBN 978-3-8382-1961-5

281 *Kateryna Zarembo, Michèle Knodt, Maksym Yakovlyev (Eds.)* | Teaching IR in Wartime. Experiences of University Lecturers during Russia's Full-Scale Invasion of Ukraine | ISBN 978-3-8382-1954-7

282 *Oleksiy V. Kresin* | The United Nations General Assembly Resolutions. Their Nature and Significance in the Context of the Russian War Against Ukraine | Edited by William E. Butler | ISBN 978-3-8382-1967-7

283 *Jakob Hauter* | Russlands unbemerkte Invasion. Die Ursachen des Kriegsausbruchs im ukrainischen Donbas im Jahr 2014 | Mit einem Vorwort von Hiroaki Kuromiya | ISBN 978-3-8382-2003-1

284 *"Alles kann sich ändern".* Letzte Worte politisch Angeklagter vor Gericht in Russland | Herausgegeben von Memorial Deutschland e.V. | ISBN 978-3-8382-1994-3

285 *Nadiya Kiss, Monika Wingender (Eds.)* | Contested Language Diversity in Contemporary Ukraine. National Minorities, Language Biographies, and Linguistic Landscape | ISBN 978-3-8382-1966-0

286 *Richard Ottinger (Ed.)* | Religious Elements in the Russian War of Aggression Against Ukraine. Propaganda, Religious Politics and Pastoral Care, 2014–2024 | ISBN 978-3-8382-1981-3

287 *Yuri Radchenko* | Helping in Mass Murders. Auxiliary Police, Indigenous Administration, SD, and the Shoa in the Ukrainian-Russian-Belorussian Borderlands, 1941–43 | With forewords by John-Paul Himka and Kai Struve | ISBN 978-3-8382-1878-6

288 *Zsofia Maria Schmidt* | Hungary's System of National Cooperation. Strategies of Framing in Pro-Governmental Media and Public Discourse, 2010–18 | With a foreword by Andreas Schmidt-Schweizer | ISBN 978-3-8382-1983-7

289 *Richard Ottinger (Hrsg.)* | Religiöse Elemente im russischen Angriffskrieg gegen die Ukraine. Propaganda, Religionspolitik und Seelsorge, 2014–2024 | ISBN 978-3-8382-1980-6

ibidem.eu